Unrequited Love

UNREQUITED LOVE

Diary of an Accidental Activist

Dennis Altman

Unrequited Love: Diary of an Accidental Activist
© Copyright 2019 Dennis Altman

All rights reserved. Apart from any uses permitted by Australia's Copyright Act 1968, no part of this book may be reproduced by any process without prior written permission from the copyright owners. Inquiries should be directed to the publisher.

Monash University Publishing
Matheson Library Annexe
40 Exhibition Walk
Monash University
Clayton, Victoria 3800, Australia
www.publishing.monash.edu

Monash University Publishing brings to the world publications which advance the best traditions of humane and enlightened thought.

Monash University Publishing titles pass through a rigorous process of independent peer review.

ISBN: 9781925835120 (paperback)
ISBN: 9781925835137 (pdf)
ISBN: 9781925835144 (epub)

www.publishing.monash.edu/books/ul-9781925835120.html

Series: Biography

Design: Les Thomas

Cover image: Dennis Altman in Rome, 1975. Courtesy of the author.

A catalogue record for this book is available from the National Library of Australia.

Printed in Australia by Griffin Press an Accredited ISO AS/NZS 14001:2004 Environmental Management System printer.

The paper this book is printed on is certified against the Forest Stewardship Council ® Standards. Griffin Press holds FSC chain of custody certification SGS-COC-005088. FSC promotes environmentally responsible, socially beneficial and economically viable management of the world's forests.

Contents

Dedication vi
Acknowledgements vii
Introduction ix

2016 1
2017 11
2018 127
2019 215
Postscript 219

Index 221
About the Author 231

Dedication

For my sister, Vivien

Acknowledgements

Many of the people mentioned in this book also contributed to its writing, but there are some whose role in my life is far greater than is apparent, in particular my extended family: Vivien, Rafael, Raul, Bojana, Mila, Archer, Dani, Scott and all the Rugg and King clan. Vivien was an invaluable support in retrieving lost memories.

Thanks to my agent, Fiona Inglis, who encouraged me to preserve when I was unsure if there was a book developing, and to Peter Christoff and Ian See, who read some of the early drafts, and provided tough guidance. I've come to know and respect Nathan Hollier at Monash over the past few years, so I was delighted to take the project to him, and for the support of the team at Monash UP. Thanks too to the editors at *ABR*, the *Griffith Review*, *Inside Story*, *Meanjin*, *Overland* and the *Gay and Lesbian Review* who worked with me on stories from which I've drawn in writing this book.

Can a writer have a better friend than a fellow writer who is prepared to read through a draft manuscript and give honest feedback? Andrea Goldsmith did just that for me. Nick Henderson at the Australian Lesbian and Gay Archives helped chase down the cover image. Any book bears the marks of people whose conversations and hospitality sparked off ideas which they may not recognise, so apologies if you're not mentioned.

A special thanks for the support of John Dewar, Vice Chancellor at La Trobe University, and to Rosemary Nanev and Katie Phillis in his office, whose support was crucial for much of my travel. Although I am officially retired, I've benefitted enormously from ongoing links with the La Trobe community, in particular many coffee conversations with Nicholas Barry, Gavin Height, Marian Pitts, Bec Strating and Jasmine Kim-Westendorf, as I have from the organisers of the conferences I've attended, the remarkable crew at the Wheeler Centre and the guys at Bookshop Darlinghurst and Hares and Hyenas.

Introduction

This book started to take shape the week following Donald Trump's election. I was wandering around San Francisco, which had voted overwhelmingly against him, aware that the more time I spend in the United States the more it seems like a foreign country.

Like most Australians of my generation I dreamt of Europe, specifically of studying further in Britain. I was an undergraduate at the University of Tasmania in the early 1960s, where one of my lecturers, Peter Boyce, persuaded me to apply for scholarships to several American Universities. On my twenty-first birthday I left home, several months before Lyndon Johnson's election, to become a graduate student at Cornell University in upstate New York. My first glimpse of New York City was as startling as the moment in *The Wizard of Oz* when black and white images burst into Technicolor: the glass and concrete of the newly renamed Kennedy Airport, the noise of the subways, the delis open into late evening, the people streaming across night streets. Since then I have spent eight years of my life in the United States, mainly in New York and California, and a large part of my academic career back in Australia has revolved around teaching and commenting on American politics.

The year after Johnson's election Australia committed troops to fight alongside the US in Vietnam, and our relations with the United States stoked bitter political debate about Australian foreign policy. The following year decimal currency was introduced, and Robert Menzies, the Anglophone PM who had wanted to name the dollar 'the royal', retired. When his successor, Harold Holt, proclaimed "all the way with LBJ" he marked both a political and a cultural shift. President Johnson, the first sitting American President to visit Australia, returned for Holt's funeral in 1967.

Australia's love affair with the United States over the past half century mirrors in some ways my own. Frank Knopfelmacher, the influential right-wing philosopher, once referred to me as "an agent of American cultural imperialism", pointing to the dilemma for Australian conservatives in the period of the Vietnam War. For them supporting the United States was a political imperative, but they deeply distrusted the new radical politics that came from the United States and threatened to upend the conventional norms of a small, smug and still largely Anglo-Celtic society.

When I flew home a week after Trump's election it felt as if I were still in the US, so strong were the emotional reactions here. They were not just realistic fears of what a narcissistic and unpredictable President might do, there was also a sense of betrayal: America had let us down. Australians struggle to regard the United States as a purely foreign power. Some years ago I enraged several right-wing Labor frontbenchers when I suggested we should view the American alliance solely through the prism of national interest. "You can't say that" expostulated one of them, though why not was never clear. Rather as older monarchists referred to Britain as the 'mother country', many Australians today draw on American culture to define ourselves, even as we protest our national uniqueness.

In his novel *Amnesia* Peter Carey gnaws at our dependence on the United States like a broken tooth, drawing parallels between a rape by a World War II serviceman in Brisbane and the overthrow of Whitlam in 1975. We are all haunted by the United States, even though our love goes largely unrequited; at best we are the dependable smaller brother, who gets forgotten when the real guys show up. In the American science fiction film *Arrival* the links to Australia are cut by the US military with the same ruthlessness with which they dispatch the Sudan. In Ben Rhodes' account of his eight years as a foreign policy adviser to Barack Obama, *The World As It Is*, there is one fleeting reference to Australia, no mention of any of the three Prime Ministers in office during his Presidency.

In his 2016 Quarterly Essay *Enemy Within*, which foresees the rise of Trump, Don Watson desperately wants to believe in America: it is, he tells us: "a miracle of an ever-evolving pluralist democracy and

Introduction

... the last great hope of humankind. It is a wonderland of invention, a marvel of freedom and tolerance, and, by most measures, the greatest country on earth." I doubt that Don would write that sentence today.

Some of my earliest writings were born of the counter-culture that developed in the States in the mid-1960s, and I flirted with the excitement of new ways of seeing the world, even if, metaphorically, I smoked but never fully inhaled. I spent the last few months of 1970 in New York City and fell into the emerging gay liberation movement, the subject of my first book. Writing about the early gay liberation movement made me an accidental activist, and most of my writings since have touched in various ways upon the shifting terrain of sexual politics.

Over the past few years I have spent considerable time with people far younger than me who are fascinated by the history of the gay and AIDS movements and are engaged in archival projects to recover the memories of the past several decades. This is not an impulse confined to the queer world, but it seems stronger there for two interconnected reasons: there is no biological family to pass on these stories, and the deaths from AIDS in the 1980s and 1990s have hollowed out the generation who should now be reaching retirement. I have always believed that analysis divorced from personal experience is one dimensional but experience unmediated by analysis is equally one-sided. "The personal is political" is a useful slogan, but it provides limited guidance for full understanding.

The increasing emphasis on oral history, and the pressure for 'authenticity', means that as we age there are greater demands on us to tell our stories. Personal reminiscences merge into a larger narrative about recapturing the past, more attractive as the pace of change speeds up and nostalgia for past certainties emerges out of present doubts. For those of us without children writing becomes a tangible way of passing on our legacy, and the urge to correct contemporary misreadings—sometimes events in which we have known the central characters—becomes more urgent. The queer world, a term I prefer to the now obligatory LGBTI acronym, is perhaps the only imagined community which does not pass on its stories through the biological family.

Memoir, as distinct from autobiography, is a way of capturing the terrain of both past and present in ways that differ from either a novel or a more analytic book. All lives are endlessly fascinating, at least to those who live them. But memoir can also become self-indulgence: an excuse to name-drop shamelessly or to boast of exploits—in work or in the bedroom. Moreover, our memories are very imperfect guides to the past: as Penelope Lively wrote: "A diary is an ambivalent reflection of memory. Much that is in mine I no longer remember; the diary is testimony, but memory has wiped."[1] Like Lively I find my old diaries are full of names now forgotten, while transitory meetings with famous faces remain clear. But even scrawled names that are hard to decipher and fade from memory are valuable for fixing dates and places, which in turn conjure up the past, even if memories are always imperfect and constantly re-invented.

There are other props for memory: photos (irritatingly undated); films seen and books read; old passports, which give dates the stern mark of authority. I am a stamp collector, of which more later, and they too can evoke time and place. So, too, an old box of matchbooks, souvenirs from the time when every café and bar produced its own, which recall road stops and lost evenings long forgotten.

Unrequited Love is both an account of experiences that have shaped my life, and of how they, in turn, reflect our antipodean ambivalence towards America over the past half century. I have often written in the first person, a largely unacceptable style within academia, and twenty years ago I wrote a rather self-indulgent memoir, *Defying Gravity*, which I began after seeing the film *Priscilla: Queen of the Desert* in a run-down Vancouver cinema. Unlike *Defying Gravity* this book centres on the strange love affair Australians have with the United States, and the very different ways in which sexual politics are understood several decades later, after same-sex marriage, the MeToo movement, a revolution in our understanding of trans* and huge advances in controlling HIV.

---

1   Penelope Lively, *Dancing Fish & Ammonites*, Viking, 2013, p.104.

Introduction

I lived in the United States during the early stages of both gay liberation and the AIDS epidemic, and my enthusiasm for the US sometimes blinded me to what was happening at home, as it continues to blind others. AIDS exemplifies this paradox: we took its symbols from the US—the T-shirts; the Quilt; even ACT UP—while we developed policy responses far ahead of those in the US. But while we are fascinated by the American story of the epidemic, they show almost zero interest in ours, a constant reminder that Australia is a small country with very different interests. The idea that what really matters happens in the North Atlantic world continues to frame a great deal of political and cultural debate in Australia, despite consistent rhetoric about the need to develop more contacts with Asia.

The election of Donald Trump seemed to harbinger a global collapse of mainstream politics, and the rise of national and ethnic hatreds. In Australia the Turnbull government lurched through a series of mishaps until the Prime Minister was overthrown in August 2018. Across the world—Syria, the Congo, Chechnya, the Philippines, Venezuela—we have seen a return to the worst sorts of oppressive governments. When I wrote *Defying Gravity* twenty years ago I dedicated it to Burmese leader Aung San Suu Kyi, "a symbol of the fight against oppression, violence and inequality everywhere". After the massacres of the Rohingya under her premiership that dedication seems hollow, a reminder of the brute realities of realpolitik.

2016

November: California

The weekend before the election of Donald Trump, one of my cats died. I was in Los Angeles, and friends back in Melbourne had the stressful task of taking Thomas to emergency vet services and making the crucial decision to euthanase him. On the Monday after his death, the day before the election, I drove across the city to give a lecture at Occidental College, Barack Obama's former school, in the northeast suburbs of Los Angeles. On the way I drove up into the hills of Griffith Park to shed a few tears for the cat who'd lived with us for ten years. His dying meant another link with my life with Anthony was gone. I'd met Anthony Smith in 1990 at a national community AIDS meeting when he was President of the Northern Territory AIDS Council. I visited him in Darwin; we met again in Canberra. By the end of the year he was living with me in Melbourne, where he died just as Obama's second election win was confirmed. After his death I wrote a piece in which I described him as my familiar, a concept taken from Philip Pullman's *His Dark Materials* trilogy.

At Occidental I spoke to a largely undergraduate audience about global queer politics and was struck by the absence of references to the elections; most of us assumed Hillary Clinton was sure to win. On Election Day I walked past one of the larger polling places in West Hollywood, but there was no sense of the community that Australians associate with elections, no enthusiasts handing out election materials, no sausage sizzle or school fetes. That night I drove down to Venice Beach for a celebratory dinner with friends, performance artist Tim Miller and his Australian husband, novelist Alistair McCartney. Instead it became a long and increasingly depressing evening as numbers started coming in from states we had counted on—Pennsylvania,

Michigan, Wisconsin—and the expected surge of Clinton votes from cities such as Miami and Detroit failed to balance rural and suburban votes.

Driving back to West Hollywood that evening the streets were unnaturally quiet. The bar on Santa Monica Boulevard that had promised "high fives for Hillary" was gloomy. The following weekend in San Francisco I saw several protests, small and unsure of their objectives. The anti-Donald Trump marches were largely expressions of collective grief, with occasional flashes of anger at a system that gave the presidency to the candidate with fewer votes than his opponent.

The following weekend I was in the Castro, perhaps the best known of all the 'gay ghettoes' that developed since the 1970s in most Western cities. San Francisco is changing rapidly as real estate prices force older tenants from their homes and new apartment blocks replace Victorian homes, but the Castro remains remarkably similar to the area where Harvey Milk mobilised support forty years ago to become one of the first openly gay elected politicians in the United States. In 1978 Milk was shot, along with Mayor George Moscone, by an angry former City Supervisor, who was controversially found guilty of manslaughter rather than murder after the first so-called 'twinkie defense'. Where Milk's camera shop stood there is now a manicure salon, next to the storefront of the Human Rights Campaign Fund, so that if one skews one's view it becomes possible to read their adjoining signs as: "Hand Jobs are a Human Right", as indeed they are. Some of the bars and restaurants which date back to the early 1970s are still there, though the menus have changed, and the street remains dominated by the splendid Castro Theater, built in the 1920s as a mixture of deco and baroque influences.

I spent Sunday with my friend and colleague Carolyn D'Cruz, who teaches gender and sexuality at La Trobe University in the department where I spent over twenty years. We ate in the Norse Cove, a favourite gay haunt since the mid-1970s, and crossed the street to watch Elia Kazan's 1957 film *A Face in the Crowd*. The story of an apparently artless hillbilly from Arkansas who becomes a national television celebrity, and then seeks political fortune, seemed an eerily accurate harbinger of the rise of Trump, even though it came from a world without mobiles and computers, in which television was still a novelty and long-distance phone calls required the assistance of an operator. Like the Castro itself the film reminded me that we experience the past and the future together, that the present is composed of what Raymond Williams termed residual and emergent cultures. The drag queen going into the new Q bar on Castro might look like someone I first saw on the same strip forty years ago.

November 1: Los Angeles

I'd arrived in Los Angeles two weeks earlier, over fifty years after my first glimpse of the United States in 1964, when I'd left Hobart, a shy and naïve graduate student, to study at Cornell University. This was only a few years into the jet age, and the Boeing 707 from Sydney seemed huge and powerful, even if it had to make a re-fuelling stop at Fiji: now there are up to a dozen non-stops from Australia to Los Angeles every day. All I remember of a short stop-over in Honolulu is that I stayed in a YMCA near Waikiki Beach, unaware of the sexual possibilities that the Village People would announce to the world fifteen years later, and wondered why the beach was so famous, when the strip of sand seemed meanly narrow and the sea, while blissfully warm, was full of rocks.

I would discover Los Angeles some years later, when I went back to the United States just before taking up a position at Sydney University, and over four decades it has become strangely familiar. My guide to Los Angeles had been John Rechy's first novel *City of Night*, from which I learnt about the many cruising spots within the city, especially the hills and gullies of Griffith Park, which stretches above the city towards the mountains that ring Los Angeles. Here men followed each other along trails beneath the tourists at the Observatory, a view made famous in *Rebel Without A Cause*, and the moment when James Dean embraces Sal Mineo in a remarkably homoerotic scene. The Observatory is revisited, in a set piece dance sequence, in *La La Land*.

During my early visits to Los Angeles I met some of the pioneers of the gay movement and saw its transition from a small group of brave leftist activists, for whom going public could destroy their lives, to an established community whose leaders were important figures in city, sometimes national, public life. By the time Gore Vidal contested the Democratic Senate nomination in 1982—which he lost to Jerry Brown, who in turn lost the election to Republican Pete Wilson—I sat at a fundraiser breakfast in a smart Beverley Hills hotel, surrounded by hundreds of gay and lesbian supporters who seemed to belong to a different world to the one I knew from New York Gay Liberation: real estate brokers, lawyers, accountants, small business owners, women and men willing to pledge real money to change laws and attitudes.

I am staying at a somewhat decaying small motel-like guest house just off the main strip, which used to be famous for its naked swimming pool. Now the 'Inn' is going through a clumsy evolution into an upscale boutique resort, but it's still furnished much as it was twenty years ago, as if a collection of hand-me-downs from better hotels had been thrown at random into the rooms. But there is a courtyard, fringed by semi-tropical plants, and small verandas set around a small pool, and it's surprisingly quiet, set back only a few hundred metres from the main drag. Last time I was in Los Angeles I read most of Hilary Mantel's *Wolf Hall* sitting in this courtyard, moving chairs to follow the sun which sets surprisingly fast in California winter.

The motel sits in the centre of West Hollywood, the city which was carved out of Los Angeles County as a separate city in 1984, based on an alliance of queers and elderly renters, many of them now Russian emigres. Santa Monica Boulevard is the central spine of West Hollywood, lined by spacious bars, coffee shops, menswear stores, health food outlets touting pills for sexual potency and lusher hair, and massive glass-fronted gyms, testament to the Californian faith in remaking oneself. Sixty years ago street-cars ran along the Boulevard; now the median strip flies rainbow flags, and the sidewalks have discreet paving stones with the names of those who died from AIDS. Here one sees three generations of queer life, from an elegant lesbian couple walking their matching dogs, to young guys, half-cruising for money and opportunity, caught up in the excitement of a rainbow space. Gay bars used to be closed and dark; now they spill out onto the street, so passers-by can see the muscled young go-go dancers gyrate slowly on the counters, arching forward for the dollar bills that are stuffed into their briefs.

The Boulevard offers a time capsule of gay life, with bars shared by drag queens and guys in leather playing pool alongside the modernist City Hall. Here are antique and second-hand clothing stores, gay medical clinics, the long-established Circus of Books, with its collection of old body building magazines where I once sought, unsuccessfully, to find a magazine for a cycling fetishist. Cross Fairfax Avenue and the strip becomes shabbier and more Russian; I take a picture of a shopfront full of posters in both Russian and English, advertising concert performances alongside speed dating.

November 3: Los Angeles

The drive to the University of Southern California cuts across layers of the class and racial divisions that make Los Angeles a metaphor for the United States. I head east along Santa Monica Boulevard, leaving behind the glitter of West Hollywood to pass long flat lines of warehouses, drive-in shopping centres, small restaurants and diners, skirting the southern end of Hollywood and the cemetery now used in summer for open air film screenings. The largely deserted blocks along this strip were once the home of street hustlers, boys from across the country who shivered in their vests and short shorts, hoping to score; they are largely gone now, whether because of the police or because of the internet, I'm not sure.

Then a long slow drive down through Koreatown, across streets which stretch endlessly into the dusky haze of the mountains and the sea. The campus sprawls across a number of blocks south of downtown, manicured lawns and an eclectic range of buildings, monuments to the ambitions of Romanesque revival and art deco (thirteen of them have been named by the City as historic cultural monuments). I am here to lecture on global sexual politics, at the invitation of Sofia Gruskin, currently professor in both the law and medical schools. Sofia has been a friend since the early days of the AIDS epidemic, when we were brought together by Jeff O'Malley, then working with Jonathan Mann, founding director of the World Health Organisation's Global Program on AIDS in 1986. Jeff has been a friend since he was an undergraduate in Winnipeg and we met at the offices of the *Body Politic* in Toronto. He is one of a handful of Canadians who helped shape the international AIDS world; he was the founding director of the International AIDS Alliance, the largest NGO working directly on HIV, then worked in India for PATH and New York for UNDP, later UNICEF.

I was able to spend time with Sofia in 2005 when A and I lived for five months at Harvard where I had been awarded the Chair of Australian Studies for that year. The Chair, which was Australia's gift to the United States for their Bicentennial, sums up the imbalance of our relationship. The sense of importance on winning the Chair evaporates when one discovers it is virtually unnoticed at Harvard, where visiting professors struggle to persuade a handful of students to find Australia interesting enough to enrol in a subject. I was located in the School of Sociology, where every junior professor seemed to be in therapy to cope with the stress of seeking tenure, even as they knew how rarely Harvard tenures its own.

Sofia was an almost tenured professor in the School of Public Health, one of the founders of the study of health and human rights and someone with extraordinary energy and passion, a good friend in the frigid atmosphere of Cambridge. She and her husband, Anthony Chase, an international relations scholar, were among a group of friends in Los Angles who looked after me when I fled Melbourne a couple of months after Anthony's death, not wanting to be at home over New Year's Eve.

Four years ago I was visiting Sofia in her house on Mount Washington, a small enclave which rises above Eagle Rock, with sudden views over the Los Angeles basin. As usual we took her two dogs for a walk, letting them run free in the lanes and gullies that dot the neighbourhood, and talked about the growing international debates around 'LGBT' or queer rights. Out of that conversation developed a workshop on sexual rights which was held at USC in 2014, co-sponsored by the City of West Hollywood, which hosted a dinner for us in a ridiculously lavish hotel on Sunset Boulevard. The meeting took place after both President Obama and Secretary of State Clinton had pledged their support for LGBT rights globally, and the discussion at that workshop echoed a new stage in American acceptance of homosexuality, alongside growing international debate and, in many countries, resistance to what is portrayed as the imposition of Western decadence.

It was a great workshop, though not without strange tensions and undercurrents. Slightly less than half those present came from outside the United States, and we shared an ambivalent resentment at American dominance while wanting American leadership globally. At one point, I commented on President Obama's visit to Senegal, where he called for the removal of anti-sodomy laws, and reflected on my reaction were an American President to land in Canberra and call for the repeal of restrictions on gun ownership. My objections to the United States ignoring local pride in the eagerness of the Obama Administration to defend queer rights led to my being branded as 'anti-American', despite my long love affair with the United States. Workshops demand a polite attention span that I lack: at one point I lounged on a row of chairs behind the main table, flirting with H- from Zambia, a young lawyer and activist, who is also something of a fabulist. That he had faced persecution and danger back home as a gay man was undoubted; but in telling his stories H- embroidered to the point where one never quite knew what to believe. H- fascinated my Australian colleague, Jonathan Symons; one evening Jon was hunched over his laptop working on a grant application for H-, while H- held court at the other end of his hotel room, recounting stories of his clashes with the local police.

The lecture over, I go for dinner with Sofia and her colleagues, Laura Ferguson and Alice Echols. Someone mentions the Barnard Conference on Sexuality, where Alice, now the Barbara Streisand

Professor of Gender Studies, but then a Michigan graduate student, had been a keynote speaker. That Conference, held in April 1982, saw bitter reactions to the deliberate intervention by feminists, led by Carole Vance, to respond to what seemed growing hostility towards sexual pleasure and adventure that was associated with the feminist anti-pornography movement. I was one of about ten men who were present—"There were *men* there?" exclaimed Alice, bearing out my memory that we were largely invisible.

Pressure was put on Barnard to cancel the conference; it went ahead but there were attempts to confiscate copies of the *Diary*, notes prepared for participants, and the conference was picketed by members of the Women Against Pornography group, wearing t-shirts that had "Against S/M" printed on their backs. They were particularly incensed by a small group of attendees, led by Gayle Rubin and Pat (now Patrick) Califia, who were dressed in full leather attire, looking uncomfortably hot in the New York spring. It was at that Conference that Gayle gave the paper which resulted in her seminal paper 'Thinking Sex', and Carole later pulled together much of the strands of the Conference in her book *Pleasure and Danger*, taking off from her own notes in the *Diary* where she wrote of the need to "envision a world which makes possible women's sexual autonomy and sexual choice".

In part inspired by that Conference I wrote a piece for *Socialist Review*, a small leftist journal based in the Bay Area, called 'Sex: The New Front Line for Gay Politics', in which I argued for an assertion of gay sexual adventure rather than assuming homosexuals only wanted safe and monogamous coupling. Both the Barnard Conference and my article came against a backdrop of what then seemed increasing violence directed at the gay community, which led me to write of "a major outbreak of homophobia", now largely forgotten in the desire to reimagine a pre-AIDS world. (I referred to increasing reports of street violence and the growing influence of the Moral Majority, which had seized upon homosexuals as a target for their campaigns.) I cringe a little at some of what I wrote then, influenced as I was by both a utopian reading of Freud and a desire to not reveal my own personal discomfort at some of the sexual mores of urban gay life. But perhaps there is still relevance to the closing optimism that: "the gay movement is ultimately about a freer view of sexuality, one in which kids will not find it necessary to resolve their ambivalence about sexuality by beating us up in the streets, and the Rev. Jerry Falwell will be seen for the pathetic charlatan he really is".

November 5: Los Angeles

I am driving to meet Paul Amar, who's trained in both politics and anthropology, and has written about masculinity and power in Egypt and Brazil. Paul teaches in Santa Barbara but lives in the old deco neighbourhood of Silverlake, where I stayed several times in the late 1970s. Memories disinter themselves as if half buried time capsules: close to the intersection where Santa Monica merges with Sunset Boulevard, a few kilometres from downtown, stood A Different Light Bookstore, whose owners became my friends and occasionally allowed me to man the counter. Gene London, who I met at the store, and with whom I was slightly besotted, took me to a fairy circle gathering at the home of Mattachine founder, Harry Hay, then in his eighties, craggy and forbidding. The Mattachine Society was one of the first American homophile organisations, influenced by Hay's links to the Communist Party; now, forty years later, Hay was one of the moving spirits behind the Radical Faeries, a loosely connected network of gay men who sought a spiritual alternative to the increasing respectability of the mainstream gay movement. I relished the sheer anarchy of the Fairies even as my rational sense held back from their spiritualism. In a small bungalow in the Hollywood flatlands Hay led us in circle dancing, which I found vaguely embarrassing.

At that time Silverlake was the centre of gay life in Los Angeles, but it was already being challenged by demographic change; in 1990 A Different Light moved fifty blocks down the Boulevard to West Hollywood. Within twenty years it became one of a string of gay bookstores to close, victim of on-line bookselling and a declining interest in the sorts of readings and cultural events such bookstores once offered. The rise and fall of A Different Light, which spawned shops in both San Francisco and New York, encapsulates a larger trajectory from silence to self-affirmation and then mainstreaming. While queer writing continues to thrive it no longer is so reliant on the physical structures of the ghetto.

Paul takes me and a film director friend to dinner at the Casita del Campo, a fixture now for fifty years, since it was founded by a cast member from the film of *West Side Story*. Posters from that movie hang everywhere, the restaurant a maze of booths and hidden enclaves, rainbow flags and kitsch Mexicana, as is the menu, whose four food groups, wrote one reviewer, are tortillas, sour cream, guacamole and cheese. We gossip about films and sex, Paul, as ever, a font of information on sexual politics in the Middle East. His friend is an established film director in the Middle East, wary of saying too much. We move on, briefly, to one of the few remaining gay bars in Silverlake, although this is clearly 'queer' rather than 'gay', plush lounges behind a grim steel exterior. Again, the forthcoming election is barely mentioned.

November 16: back to Australia

I slept through the day: the flight left Los Angeles late on the 14th and arrived early on the morning of the 16th in Melbourne. Somewhere in mid-air, during my fitful napping, we crossed the International Date Line. Back in Australia there seemed incessant coverage of the reality that Donald Trump was now President-elect of the United States. I will find myself increasingly stressing that he is NOT our President.

Over the following summer I sensed the need to write something that might reflect the tectonic shifts that seemed unleashed by Trump's election but avoid the instant polemic that characterises so much of political commentary. I made a couple of stabs at writing a book proposal but struggled to find a structure that would allow for more than the conventional journalistic approach to current affairs. At the same time I was increasingly drawn to using the present to reflect on the past, recognising that as one ages our memories are the raw materials for the next generation's history.

2017

(Five months later)

April 27: Melbourne

I am perched on a bar stool in an overly trendy restaurant waiting for my friend Edward Hunter while reading P.D. James. I have long been a fan of her detective stories, but today I am reading a diary she kept for a year in her late seventies as a way of writing a non-continuous memoir. She explains that writing her memoir in the form of a diary was ultimately due to "the need to capture time, to have some small mastery over that which so masters us ... I write, therefore I am."[2]

"I could do that" I say to Ed, who arrives, wet and apologetic. "Start today" he says. "See where it takes you."

Ed is a yoga teacher who has studied law and German; we met shortly after Anthony's death, and have become close friends and confidantes. Tonight we are going to see *The Book of Mormon*, the musical that has been a Broadway hit for the past six years and looks set to break box office records in Australia. When it appeared, it was hailed as one of the catchiest and funniest musicals ever. In a review of the Melbourne production Stephanie van Schilt called it "an exceptional, visionary and all-round musical masterpiece" (*Guardian* Feb 6 2017). There was some disquiet about the casting of Americans in the main roles, an argument that goes back decades.

I couldn't fully share the enthusiasm; despite the clear irony I was discomforted by the depiction of Ugandans, which reinforced the worst stereotypes: corrupt war lords; men raping babies to protect against AIDS etc. It's one thing for smart white boys to mock their own culture, another when they mock a culture of which they have

---

[2] PD James, *Time to be in Earnest*, Faber, 1999, p.xii.

only superficial knowledge. But the audience loved it and lapped up the American references.

At least since the major hits of Rogers and Hammerstein, American musicals have been central in bringing us into the American cultural sphere, and certain musicals—*South Pacific*, *West Side Story*, *Hair*, most recently *Hamilton*—all explore aspects of American life in ways that shook up the received wisdom of the day. (Perhaps the most overtly political musical, *Les Miserables*, is French, though some of Stephen Sondheim's works—*Assassins*, *Pacific Overtures*—take politics as a central theme). Of them all *Hair* remains the most important for me: I first saw it in New York in 1969 and was captivated by the sheer excitement of a theatrical piece that captured the mood of change swept in by the anti-war, feminist and black movements. *Hair* arrived in Sydney in the summer of 1969, and great excitement surrounded the (brief) nude scene and the risky language; even today mention of 'fucking' and a 'clitoris' at *Mormon* was still capable of raising uneasy titters. It was through *Hair* that I met Jim Sharman, already known as a theatrical and operatic director; he visited me in my Paddington flat, made straight for the pile of LPs, and picked up one by Phil Ochs (*Pleasures of the Harbour*). "After *Hair*" he said "No one will be able to dismiss hippies as scum." Perhaps; thirty years later I showed some clips from Milos Forman's film *Hair* to a politics class—a very different, and stronger version—and was surprised at the lack of empathy my students felt for the counter cultural figures of the late 1960s.

I know Jim said this, not because I have an eidetic memory but because I wrote up my interview with him, and because for almost half a century I have kept a very sketchy diary of my life. I owe this habit to Christopher Isherwood, whose novel *A Single Man* was probably the most self-accepting gay novel yet published when it first appeared in 1964. For my generation novels were enormously important in discovering and justifying our sexual longings, and Isherwood, along with Gore Vidal and James Baldwin, were major influences on me in ways I doubt novelists are any longer.

I must have written craving fan letters to Isherwood—typed on the flimsy aerograms of the period—and I first risked driving a car in Los Angeles because of my determination to meet him on a visit in 1969. Out of some generosity Christopher invited me to meet him and his partner, Don Bachardy, in their house above the Pacific Palisades; they were the first gay couple I had ever met, and their relationship, which lasted from their meeting in 1953 until Christopher's death in 1986, is an important reminder of the reality that many homosexual relationships flourished long before the idea of gay marriage reached mainstream acceptance. I learnt a lot from Christopher: most important was his comment that you know you are homosexual when you fall in love with a man. The most lasting impact of that visit was that ever since I have kept a record of my daily life in a series of diaries that are the raw material for much of this book.

Christopher himself kept copious diaries and noted that I came to supper that winter: "Dennis has been seeing a lot of Negroes while here. Two of his impressions; that those who talk loudest about Black Power are the ones who are most apt to have non-Negro lovers, they 'talk black and fuck white'; that black homosexuals are queers first and blacks second ... He also remarked on the growing hostility between blacks and Jews."[3]

Reading this makes me cringe—I am not sure which 'Negroes' Christopher is referring to, nor how I might have made such pronouncements. It may have referred to an extraordinary few days I had spent in Washington as the guest of a professor at Howard University, whose husband was one of those rare people, a black Republican. Howard had been founded in 1867 for black students and remains a leading African-American University. I had met Letitia Brown when she was visiting Australia as a visiting professor of history, and although she was almost thirty years older than me, there was a rapport, which looking back must have come from a mutual recognition of being outsiders. Perhaps not surprising in the Australia of that era Letitia

---

3   Christopher Isherwood, 'Feb 26 1969', *Diaries Vol. II*, Vintage, 2012.

later wrote of her visit that: "Never before in my life had I been so conscious I was female."

The Browns took me to the *Ebony* Inauguration Day party after Nixon's 1968 victory, joining Washington's establishment African-Americans—not a term we would have used back then—and I felt conspicuous in a room of people all more elegantly dressed than me. Through Laetitia's contacts I went on to Atlanta with introductions to a group of young black politicians. Looking back I suspect Christopher reversed what I said; there was at least one homosexual amongst the politicians in Atlanta, and he was clear that his primary identity was African American. He drove me back to where I was staying that evening, and we had quick, urgent sex in his car, clearly not to be repeated or discussed.

April 28: Melbourne

Dinner with old friends, survivors from the awful days of the AIDS crisis of the 1980s. Andrew Foster's lover, Peter Charlton, was one of the first men to die of AIDS in Melbourne, and his was a slow and difficult death in a period when there were no effective treatments. David Stephens has been HIV-positive for over thirty years, and is one of the few people who survived long enough to benefit from anti-retroviral treatments; both he and his wife, Julienne Carey, worked in the Victorian AIDS Council when it was just beginning, a small community organisation staffed largely by dedicated volunteers, who might segue in one day from caring for young men on their death beds to lobbying governments for resources to produce 'safe sex' pamphlets.

For those of us who lived through the terrible years in the gay world of the late 1980s and early 1990s, when hospitals and funerals became all too familiar parts of everyday life, memory becomes particularly important. When I was at school several of our teachers were much older spinsters, of whom it was said that they had lost fiancés during the war. I only understood the lifelong grief and longing this phrase conjured up when Anthony died. I no longer feel the need to cry, as I did every day for many months, but I feel pangs of sadness when I drive through certain parts of the city, knowing that it is changing in ways he would no longer know, and that each day the dead are further lost to us.

Death changes how one sees the people we think we know; one learns, precipitously, on whom one can rely. One such was Michael Williams, a smart young lawyer with whom I became friendly when he became President of the local AIDS Council and shook up the entrenched management structures. When Anthony died Mikey came with me to the funeral home; the woman who greeted us seemed rather bemused why I had turned up with a good-looking young man to bury my partner. "I'm his lawyer" said Mikey, and with his help we rejected all the unnecessary extras that funeral directors like to flog when one is most vulnerable. Why, we asked, would we pay for a mahogany casket when it would be consumed by fire at the end of the service?

I was in the United States when AIDS first emerged, having left my lectureship at Sydney University to live for four years in and out of New York before I returned to the attractions of a permanent academic job in Australia. I was slow to acknowledge what was happening—the first cases of a virulent pneumonia in young homosexual men were reported in June 1981—but by the following year men who read the gay press and moved in gay circles were beginning to glimpse the extent to which AIDS would remake our world. The following year I went to see a doctor, terrified by what seemed to be swollen lymph glands, which turned out to be benign. My New York doctor was Joseph Sonnabend, a gloomy South African, whom I first consulted for recurrent sinusitis: "It's the humidity in your apartment", he said glumly, and I conjure up vivid images of old radiators hissing steam, a feature of old apartments in Manhattan. Sonnabend was one of the first doctors to see AIDS patients and had to fight a threat of eviction from his offices in the West Village. He was also a mentor for Michael Callen, whom I knew through my then boyfriend, Joshua Sippen, and who would become one of the founders of the People with AIDS movement. (David France has chronicled this period in moving detail in his book *How to Survive a Plague*.)

Unrequited Love

I'd met Joshua at a black-tie Human Rights Campaign Fund dinner at the Waldorf Astoria, an event addressed by Vice President Mondale, who carefully avoided any direct references to the gay and lesbian community through his entire speech. I still have the menu for the evening, which featured the Waldorf's walnut pâté, roast of veal and chocolate charlotte russe, a meal we might today regard as politically flawed. I was there because I was writing an article for *The Nation*; Joshua was there because he was singing with the Gay Men's Chorus. He was wearing a dinner suit too large for him; I asked him to take me swimming to the pool at New York University where he was studying social work. We were together on and off for the next three years, until I returned permanently to Australia in mid-1985.

That dinner encapsulated the state of the gay movement in the early Reagan years: in a decade it had moved from protest to inclusion. In my article I lamented "the movement's new rhetoric, which downplays assertiveness and participation in favour of anonymous fund-raising and voting for straight candidates".[4] One survey of gay leaders by the *Advocate*, the leading gay publication of the time, asked how much have you contributed, not how often have you been arrested.

But there were other, less mainstream expressions of gay assertion in those years, and I plunged into them. I'm not sure how I had met Tom Waddell, the remarkable ex-Olympian decathlete medico who founded the Gay Games, first held in San Francisco in 1982. I remember sitting with him in a café on Castro Street, sharing a fascination with bel canto opera, then staying as a guest in his home on the eve of a flight to Sydney, raiding the fridge and in my innocence eating three hash cookies, which proved remarkably effective in muting the effects of the flight. Tom died in 1987, but his legacy was to strengthen a community that could so easily have been destroyed.

---

4   Martin Duberman makes a similar criticism of the dinner: "Racism in the Gay Male World" (1982). See *Left Out: The Politics of Exclusion: Essays 1964–2002*, South End Press, 2002.

I was at those first Games, writing a story which never found a publisher. I still have notes from a magical evening in the Castro Theater when an Australian, Peter Todd, won the Physique Contest:

> The line formed outside the Castro Theater an hour before it began; apart from the Opening and Closing ceremonies this was clearly the highlight. Maybe the real Olympics don't have 'physique' as a recognised sport. But as MC Dick Ferris, himself a winner in the diving, said: 'We don't care what they do.'
>
> The evening opened with a presentation of colours and the unfurling of the flag, as the audience rose and joined in singing the anthem—followed by two tap dancers doing a number from the musical *A Day in Hollywood, A Night in the Ukraine*. Mutual congratulations and awards for Tom Waddell and state senator Milton Marks, and the competition was ready to begin.

How quickly things changed from the period when we saw liberation as meaning unlimited sexual possibilities to the fear of infection by what was as yet an unknown agent. Gradually gay men began to censor their behaviour, to limit what became known as the transmission of bodily fluids, even before it was clear that HIV was unlikely to be spread other than through direct contact with the blood stream. In their pamphlet *How to Have Sex in an Epidemic* (May 1983) Michael Callen and Richard Berkowitz warned against a wide range of sexual practices, some of them actually low-risk, and helped invent 'safe sex', involving non-penetrative sex and the widespread use of condoms. By the time the pamphlet appeared I had discovered 'jerk off' parties, organised to allow men to engage in mutual touching and stroking without danger. The New York Jacks already existed as an informal group of men who gathered at the infamous Mineshaft bar for mutual masturbation; within a couple of years, terrified by the prospect of contracting AIDS, there were groups across the country, and there were moves to close gay bathhouses. We gathered in dark basements in New York and San Francisco to play with other men, usually wearing nothing but sneakers and white socks, men forming ever reshaping groups and couples, sometimes with a monitor, bearing a flashlight, patrolling to make sure the limits on physical contact—even kissing was at times discouraged—were maintained. As I wrote at the time: "Oddly the lights are fully on, and men stand or sit around, sometimes stroking themselves or others while they talk. There is a lot of good humour here, a lot of long hugs and chaste kisses (for who is sufficiently sure about saliva…?) The men are all in differing states of erection… white jism shoots from one man's erect cock, leading those around him to sigh in empathy, and several to start beating off very vigorously."

Like many gay men, Michael Callen struggled to reconcile his belief in sexual adventure with the new dangers of HIV transmission. When the city of San Francisco closed its gay bathhouses in the fall of 1984 Michael was opposed, but he also knew that few bathhouses were willing to acknowledge the need to provide information and resources (i.e. condoms and lube) for safe sex. At one point, Michael dragged me with him on an inspection tour of one of New York's grottier bathhouses, the Everard, known as a homosexual rendezvous since its opening in the 1880s (it burnt down in 1986). He was shocked by what he found: "Can *you* see a lesion at arm's length?" he demanded, complaining to the management about the level of lighting. Michael ultimately supported closing the baths, which New York did several years later. A rather different approach was taken in Australia. Sex venues were kept open on the pragmatic grounds that they were among the easiest places to target men with information about safe sex.

Back at dinner in Melbourne Andrew speaks of a visit to a gay sex club and his unease with the assumption that condoms were no longer needed. It's true that in rich countries more and more gay men are either on anti-retroviral drugs, if HIV positive, or on pre-exposure prophylaxis (PrEP), if not. Currently the drugs can only be obtained through clinical trials or a complex import scheme from Botswana. (A year later the government agreed to list PrEP on the pharmaceutical benefits scheme.) And we shared gossip about some of the figures from that time, especially one very Orthodox Jewish woman, who threw herself into early support activities while maintaining a large family in the strangely suburban streets of Hasidic East St. Kilda. We wondered what drove her, but we wondered less when she reappeared in full leather, an attractive young woman on her arm, and became one of the 'dykes on bikes' who lead off the Sydney Mardi Gras Parade each summer.

I remember her when I return to my Freudian insistence that sexuality is never totally fixed. One of the oddities of today's movement rhetoric is the tension between fluidity, expressed in the idea that someone can transform their gender, and the essentialism about sexuality that echoes Lady Gaga's "born that way". I've been watching the Mexican film *Four Moons* (*Cuatro Lunas*), which is yet another variant of the standard gay coming out film, interesting because it brings together contemporary and former versions of gay life. An ageing poet seeks paid sex from a hustler in a sauna; a younger wealthy Mexican looks for his boyfriend in a sex party in a richer part of the city. A pubescent boy is branded *maricon* because of his interest in his cousin's dick, and I wonder why no one tells him it's a normal curiosity rather than assuming this determines his life identity.

But at least the film subverts the idea that our sexuality is innate, unchanging, impervious to unexpected flashes of lust or opportunity. One of the reasons I hate the ubiquitous LGBTI acronym is that it positions us as a confined minority rather than an expression of unexplored potential.

May 5: Bendigo

At six o'clock the main streets of Bendigo are empty. Only a couple of desultory pedestrians hurry past the now closed cafes and antique shops that climb up the slow Victorian hill towards the Art Gallery. We're a block away from downtown, with its grand gold rush buildings and featureless mall, which feels windswept even on a calm day.

La Trobe's Bendigo campus has a small art centre in town, and I'm here to give a lecture as part of the campus's Pride Week. Thanks to an enthusiastic counsellor and an impressive student group, Rainbow

Eagle, there's a lot of queer activity on campus this week, including a flag raising ceremony outside the Union Building. There's a moving talk by a transwoman and an overly partisan one by the federal Labor member, who then raised the rainbow flag. I'm uneasy that an apparently straight woman does this: how would we react were a man to raise the flag for International Women's Day—or a non-Indigenous person raise the Aboriginal Flag? Is this the same unease I feel when commercial business floats march ahead of community groups at Mardi Gras?

We move inside out of the cold, and Senator Janet Rice (Greens Victoria) and I are ensconced on comfortable couches on a dais in the middle of the union building for what's billed as *No Dumb Questions: Panel Discussion on the next 50 years of LGBTIQ and equity*. It's an odd event; there is no audience as such but the centre of the hall, which rather resembles the waiting room of a provincial railway station, is taken up with stalls supporting Pride Week, and some of the stall holders are asked to join us on the couch, including a local police officer and a member of the University Labor Club. I'm not sure how much of the conversation can be heard, but I like the informality, the very ordinariness, of taking us into the centre of campus life. I quickly realise that expressing irony or doubts is not well suited to these events. I thank Prime Minister John Howard for putting gay marriage on the agenda through changes to the Marriage Act in 2004, which inserted the phrase that marriage was "between a man and a woman". One of the young men at the Labor stall heard this as praise for Howard, and I'm not sure he was persuaded otherwise.

More controversially I wonder at what age can kids be certain that they have been assigned to the wrong gender, but to ask that question is seen as transphobic. The term trans* now covers a continuum of ways of experiencing one's body, from seeking full surgical reassignment to a refusal of any form of stable gender identity. There is much about the trans* experience that I do not fully understand, and I should acknowledge that. Like other sexual liberationists I assumed that discomfort with one's gender was an expression of sexual repression, which has proven to badly misunderstand the range and subtlety of how people understand their gender. As the sociologist Raewyn Connell, who herself transitioned over a decade ago, said: "I am one of the group about whom Dennis expressed the 'personal belief (hope?) that we would disappear. But since he also contemplated with approval that the homosexual as we know him/her would disappear, I have forgiven him."[5]

I think back to the early days of queer organising at Sydney University in the 1970s, when it seemed both risky and self-promoting to come out in public, and the police were feared and detested. A lot has changed in forty years, which was the theme of my lecture that evening. I was introduced by the deputy mayor, a retired teacher with a shock of wild white hair and a laconic wit; the audience was small but engaged. And the questions were smart, ranging from marriage to bisexuality, and my insistence that we are all potentially bisexual, thus making the 'bi' category largely irrelevant.

Marriage, again, is central to the much grander event the following Thursday evening at the National Gallery of Victoria. Several hundred-people are seated under the translucent Leonard French ceilings to listen to former High Court Justice Michael Kirby give an address as part of La Trobe University's fiftieth anniversary. As usual Michael is eloquent, a great teller of stories, and skilful with the politician's trick of turning any question to the one he wants to answer. But I am uneasy with the emphasis he and his two respondents place on the marriage issue as demonstrating lingering homophobia within Australian society. Most Australians support same sex marriage; resistance to 'marriage equality' comes from a successful alliance between Christian fundamentalists and right- wing politicians, who so far have managed to prevent a free Parliamentary vote.

I accept that 'marriage equality' is symbolically important, but I am sceptical that it will change a great deal. Unlike other countries Australia already has strong de facto recognition of same sex couples,

---

5   Raewyn Connell, 'Ours in Colour', Carolyn D'Cruz & Mark Pendleton (eds), *After Homosexual*, UWA Publishing, 2013, p.42.

and better anti-discrimination laws than most countries. In his speech Michael speaks of his own very long-lasting relationship and extolls it as a model for a good life. My concern is that the stress on marriage as the ultimate goal of equality sends a message that happiness can only be attained through conventional coupledom. Constantly emphasising this compounds the feeling that anyone who is not in a long-term relationship has failed.

I've known Michael Kirby for half a century. I have memories of going to a national student conference, a young and naïve undergraduate from Tasmania, and being overawed by the two grand old men from Sydney, namely Michael Kirby and Peter Wilenski. Peter later became head of a series of government departments before dying in 1994. Michael has become one of the best known public gay figures in Australia, but in the formative days of gay liberation he remained carefully discrete, and only came out publicly after his nomination to the High Court. This discretion allowed him to play an extraordinary role in Australian, indeed global, public life, and to become a role model for a new generation. But Michael and I are temperamentally very different; he is a genuine conservative, of a type rarely seen in our public life, where most self-styled conservatives are bad tempered reactionaries with little concern for social cohesion.

Both events emphasised how much has changed over the past few decades, which, in part by accident, has been the focus of much of my writings. My first book—*Homosexual: Oppression and Liberation*—had some success and gave me momentary recognition. It also set boundaries to what I might do, although I have written several more mainstream political books, one of which, *Rehearsals for Change* (1980), was used for some years as a text in secondary school civic classes. The book was republished in 2004 as part of a short-lived foray at Curtin University into reviving books by 'Australian public intellectuals'. In a generous introduction Carmen Lawrence echoed my belief that a more equal society requires us to work both within and beyond party politics, a significant comment from someone who had been both a state premier and a senior federal minister.

Bridging the gap between sexual and mainstream politics was harder for earlier generations. Gore Vidal complained that his career as a politician was marred by the controversy around his early 'gay' novel, *The City and the Pillar*. I never quite believed his protestations; he must have foreseen how a novel that acknowledged homosexual sex would be received in 1948. And although Gore publicly claimed to be bisexual—his retort when he was asked about his first sexual partner was that he was too polite to ask—in practice he was homosexual, and fond of hustlers. When I stayed with him at Ravello he organised a hook up for me on the beach at Amalfi, a service he claimed to have also performed for Princess Margaret.

I'd met Gore through his 1968 book *Myra Breckinridge*; a zealous Customs official confiscated a copy of Sanford Friedman's *Totempole* and *Myra* in a package I had posted to myself from the States, and the Council for Civil Liberties agreed to make this a test case of Australian censorship laws.[6] I wrote at the time: "The case of Altman v. Collector of Customs was heard in a small cell-like court room with pea-soup green walls and a large fan. Present were the judge, his clerk, lawyers representing myself and the Customs department, several reporters, a middle-aged woman and several men from the Department with short cropped hair and large brief cases seemingly filled with copies of the books in question."

The Judge upheld my right to import *Totempole*, and Customs were instructed to pay me one dollar, its nominal value. *Myra B*, however, he deemed offensive, with passages of "just plain dirt". Ironically a couple of the sentences relied upon by Customs' lawyers were present in the British expurgated version, freely available in Australia.

Gore mentions the case in several interviews but confuses *Myra* with his earlier novel, *The City and the Pillar*. When he visited Australia a few years later I appeared on a television program with him, and subsequently was taken out to dinner; over the next few decades I visited him in Rome, Ravello and Los Angeles. So much has been written about Gore since his death in 2012, but his public persona—known to

---

6   Nicole Moore, *The Censor's Library*, UQP, 2012, pp. 269–74.

millions through television—hid the reality that he could be surprisingly kind in person, and a very generous host. And while the public Gore mocked romantic love there was little doubt that he loved deeply his lifetime partner Howard Austen, with whom he lived for fifty years. A few years before he died I took Anthony to Gore's house in the Hollywood Hills for lunch. This was a two storey Mediterranean villa not far from the Hollywood Bowl, presided over by a fierce Filipino steward who served us lamb chops. We sat in the ornately furnished lounge room, with its hand carved fireplace and occasional tables, boasting signed photographs of Princess Margaret and various Kennedy and Hollywood celebrities. At one point, I left them to go to the bathroom, and Gore told Anthony, whom he had just met, that he had been miserable ever since Howard's death. As I look back over that sentence, I realise that Gore died only four months before Anthony; I heard the news sitting in Los Angeles Airport, waiting to fly home from an International AIDS Conference, still unaware of Anthony's cancer.

I can't claim to have known Gore well, but he had a major influence on my life. As Samuel Delaney, the pioneering gay science fiction writer, observed after he met W.H. Auden: "The great writer, once met, however fleetingly, ceases to be a passing, passive interest and becomes an active object of study."[7] Gore was a dominating presence and a generous host, with a strong sense that he was the best President the United States never elected, though even he might not have been able to imagine President Trump. When I was invited to write a book for a short-lived series on 'celebrities' I decided I would write about Gore, which seemed a way to straddle American history, politics and sex. The resulting book, *Gore Vidal's America* (Polity 2005), was fun to write but had little impact; in retrospect, it was a mistake to write about an author who was so prolific and so fond of telling his own story.

The book was finished in the first half of 2005 when Anthony and I were at Harvard, and Gore became strangely obsessed with what I was writing. I had given him a copy of the final draft of the manuscript,

---

7   Samuel Delaney, *Motions of Light in Water*, Paladin, 1990, p.149.

with the proviso that he could correct matters of fact not opinion. There followed several long phone calls from Mulholland Drive, during which Gore took umbrage at various sentences, which failed to paint him in his own lights. He devotes a short chapter in his memoir *Point to Point Navigation* to my failures, ending with a classic Vidal quip: "I am chided for not doing enough about AIDS; but my virological skills are few". At one point he picked me up on a criticism that he had been insensitive to racial prejudice. "What do you expect?" he asked, "I am a product of my time." Gore seemed to never read anything of mine except when I wrote about him, and then he read ferociously.

We were living, not very comfortably, in one of the historical student residences of Harvard, while I taught a class on global sexual politics, stretching the boundaries of what might be considered Australian Studies. Our nights were frequently interrupted by boisterous parties at the offices of the *Harvard Crimson* across the street and by midnight fire drills, when we all gathered, freezing in assorted bed clothes, outside the building while campus firemen checked whether it was safe to return. The wealth of Harvard was overwhelming, which made Gore's decision to leave his estate to the University he had never attended particularly bizarre.

When my book appeared, the publicists arranged two bookstore events with Gore, and I was exposed to the full ferocity of his ego. Gore occupied a stage in ways that made it clear anyone else was, at best, a Greek chorus. If it is fashionable to claim the death of the author, an appearance with Gore meant the invisibility of the author. We spoke together at stores in Beverly Hills and San Diego, where my publicist tried not to blanch at the wines Gore ordered for dinner. I learnt much from Gore Vidal, not least that if one craves fame one can never be famous enough. In that week we spent together in 2005 there was something very sad about his constant need to reassure himself of his importance, and the sudden bursts of anger about hurts and rivalries going back over a long career.

The last time I saw him was a week later at a PEN dinner in Los Angeles, where he was the guest of honour. He sat patiently at his table as writers of whom he had clearly never heard were rewarded. At the very end of the dinner I introduced him to someone whose work he did know, science fiction writer Ursula le Guin. His face lit up with pleasure, and the charming, courteous and witty Gore of old returned. At his best, there were few who matched him as the perfect dinner companion.

May 20: Berlin

I am in Berlin for a week of hanging out with friends and open to the surprises of a relatively unknown big city. I first visited Berlin before the Wall came down, and crossed over to the East several times, thrilled by the illusion of entering the world of John le Carre. Foreigners entering East Berlin were required to buy a certain number of Ostmarks, which had little value in the West, and I spent some of mine on a large collection of East German stamps which I bought from an elderly woman in a small and poorly stocked general store. Their triumphal multicolours proclaimed a socialist future in a city where stark Stalinist blocks of apartment houses cramped the streets. Even the winds felt colder than on the brighter streets of the West.

Several decades later I'm back in Berlin, those same streets constantly busy with trucks and cranes as new apartment blocks and chic cafes slowly erase the gap between East and West. New since my first visits is the splendid Jewish Museum, designed by Daniel Libeskind, which links the old baroque Kollegienhaus to what at first viewing resembles an enormous and undisciplined beach shack. Now other memories of Berlin surfaced, such as the looming ruins of the Kaiser Wilhelm Church on Kurfurstendamm, and the moments when certain U-bahn lines surface and run parallel to city streets. I have a fragment of the Wall which Anthony brought back from a trip he made to Europe a year before we met. Anthony had trained as a biologist, and he had many photos from the Berlin Zoo, one of the few places that I recall from each of my visits. But the unreliability of memory is such that maybe what I remember is through Anthony's photos, not my own, which lingered on the fantastical architecture of the enclosures more than on the animals incarcerated within.

In 1993 the International AIDS Conference was held in Berlin, and I was there, as part of the emerging network of global community activists. I was billeted with a sweet German leather queen, who was extremely houseproud; fail to replace a plate at the right angle and a look of pain crossed his face. The Conference took place before effective therapies against HIV had been developed, in a period of anger, fear and grief, and Berlin itself made little impression, though my diary records a visit to the New Action Bar near Nollendorfplatz, a bar that still exists.

I recall the advice of Christopher Isherwood and Penelope Lively and start searching old diaries to place my first visit to Berlin. My diaries tell me I flew in and out of the now demobilised Tempelhof Airport and went to the opera—I have vague memories of an Offenbach operetta, exasperating as my limited German failed to follow the humour. But they also tell me that my first visit was at the end of 1992, three years after the Wall fell, and with it the official destruction of the East German mark. Yes, I did buy a stamp collection from somewhere in the former East Berlin, but my memory of crossing the frontier and having to change money is false.

There are many reasons why I might have constructed a story involving the physicality of the Cold War, whose imagery is familiar to everyone older than forty through news and film. In my case there is an extra and personal explanation; in my twenties I had a German boyfriend, a little older than me, who was one of the last people to flee East Germany before the Wall was erected. Unconsciously I suspect I have colonised his memories as a way of inserting myself into the tumultuous history of Berlin.

This time Berlin is less melodramatic. With friends from Melbourne I visit monuments of twentieth century totalitarianism. I trudge the length of the former Stalinallee, strangely deserted on a Sunday, with its unyielding rows of eight story apartment blocks, and Anthea Caddy and I go out to the Olympia Stadion, built for the 1936 Games, where Anthea lingers, longingly, above the pool, its natural limestone belying the stark neoclassical structures of the larger fascist edifices. Anthea is at least a generation younger than me, a former neighbour with whom I've bonded over the past few years so that we see each other as family. She's a contemporary sound artist, whose career has brought her to Berlin, from where she is constantly in demand for festivals across Europe: we compete to see who has been to the most countries. She's absurdly modest about her work, which has involved acoustic sculptures in the Snowy Mountains and an abandoned oil tank in Estonia. When I ask about her performances Anthea assures me that I would be bored by them.

One day I walk through linden-shaded trees to Charlottenburg, where both my parents had lived, at different stages in their lives. My mother's father, Aaron Patkin, had been a social democrat in the dying era of Czarist Russia, a colleague of Kerensky, who was imprisoned first by the Tsarist government and then made stateless by the Bolsheviks. When she was three her family moved via Poland to Berlin, where they lived for some years until, shortly before the rise of Hitler, they moved to Melbourne where distant relatives had established what was becoming Australia's largest department store. My father came from Viennese Jewish aristocracy; his mother was the daughter of a successful banker, and a contemporary of Freud and Mahler who told me she had a bundle of correspondence with Alma Mahler that she'd destroyed. When her three children fled Vienna she stayed stubbornly in the city, relying on the protection of her then husband and her conversion to Catholicism, finally leaving during the War and managing, with the aid of nuns, to move to Geneva. In my first year at University my family made a trip to Europe to visit my grandmother who had moved back to Vienna after the end of Russian occupation and lived in an apartment on top of the grand building on the Ringstrasse, the grand boulevard that encircles the centre city, that had been her family home. For my parents this was a difficult visit, and my father had a slight heart attack, almost certainly related to the stress of returning to the city that had expelled him.

One of the exhibitions in the Berlin Jewish Museum is a collection of dioramas, in which there is a large photograph of refugees disembarking in Sydney shortly before the outbreak of World War II. The men in the photo—they are almost all men—are dressed in suits and ties and look appropriately sober; the end of the voyage must have been frightening, as the unknowns of exile loomed ahead of them. My father is not in that picture, but he could have been; he arrived in Sydney in 1938, having chosen Australia ahead of Mexico and South Africa.

My parents were introduced shortly after the War began, and although both spoke perfect German we grew up with English the language of the home, in a time and place when it was still uncommon to hear anything but English in public. They rarely spoke of Berlin; my sister Vivien remembers my mother talking about her school, my father told me he had seen Marlene Dietrich sing in a nightclub, perhaps in the very streets where I've been walking. I heard Dietrich at the end of her career when she tottered on stage in Sydney in 1975, though I was not at the performance where she fell and broke her hip.

One evening friends take me past the apartment block where Christopher Isherwood lived for almost four years, in one of the neat bourgeois areas of the city, bordering on what was then and is again the gay centre of Berlin. But Isherwood's Berlin lives on, despite war and occupation; the streets around Nollendorfplatz are still a gay centre, marked by rainbow flags and an improbably large number of very neat leather shops. I eat several times at a gay restaurant, serving meals that seem like fantasy versions of German food—Die beste Rinderroulade der Stadt !!! as their menu boasts—and the waiter who serves us, for I brought several friends to the Elefant, could have strolled out of one of the bars in Isherwood's Berlin stories—or Emanuel Litvinoff's 1958 story of Cold War Berlin, *The Lost Europeans*.

On hot nights men overflow onto the footpaths from the many bars, but during the day the streets around my hotel are surprisingly empty for a big city. It feels different when I spend a day in Hamburg, and sit, not that comfortably, outside a café on the Lange Reihe, stretching towards the lake, where the street is full of couples, gay and straight, many of them with children: I'm next to a seemingly heterosexual couple with two infants, but a man walks by who seems, to my inadequate eavesdropping German, to be the lover of the father, or perhaps of the couple?

May 25–28: Brighton

Unplanned, this has become a tour of the southern English coast: Brighton, Deal (Kent), Torquay. Each city is very distinct, though they share a strange mix of Victorian grandeur and slightly decaying seaside grunge. Even Brighton, now fashionable as a cultural and tourist destination, loses its splendour quickly when one drives away from the seaside and 'the Lanes', the latter a jumble of untidy cafes, shops, backpackers, an economy of unnecessary things where one might, with luck, uncover something collectible.

Over the past twenty years I've been in Brighton four times and there's a familiarity to the long expanse of pebbled beach, lined by long lines of Regency terrace houses in dusty stucco white. Many of these terraces have become bed and breakfast hotels, and I'm staying in one, with a view over an oblong patch of green where a few sunbakers have encamped, just down from St James Street where the pubs are already filling in mid-afternoon. As a Jewish puritan I'm a little shocked by the drinking culture of England, the seriousness with which women and men of all ages seem to approach social drinking and the subdued violence that I feel walking past pubs. At St Pancreas Station I hear a woman, loud on her mobile: "My top three priorities are work, family and drink."

This time I'm in Brighton two weekends before the unnecessary British election of 2017, and even Labour stalwarts are remarkably pessimistic about their chances at this point. Brighton is the hub of three marginal constituencies: one Labour, one Green, one Tory—the last of which will swing to Labour. I talk about the elections—along with the vexed politics of trans* identities, with the anthropologist Andrea Cornwall, who's out on the hustings for Caroline Lucas, the sole Greens member in Westminster. Her fear that large numbers of students were enrolling to vote for Jeremy Corbyn didn't hurt Lucas in the end, though it helped swing some seats in university towns to Labour. It's a familiar discussion for me, as I live in that part of Melbourne where Greens and Labor battle it out for several inner-city seats, and my last book, co-edited with historian Sean Scalmer, dealt with the dilemmas for some of us in choosing between them (*How To Vote Progressive in Australia*). Our electoral system means this is a very different choice to the American election last year when the effect of the Greens candidate, Jill Stein, was to siphon off votes from Clinton in crucial states.

I've arranged my weekend to link up with an old friend, Robin Gorna, whom I first met when she was a young AIDS worker in Oxford, and later worked with during her time in Sydney as CEO of the Australian Federation of AIDS Organisations. Along with Rob Moodie, one of the founding directors at WHO's Global Program on AIDS, we co-chaired a large regional AIDS Conference in Melbourne in 2001. At dinner Robin recalled our ferocious email wars at the time, though neither of us could remember what they were about. The conference was managed by an extraordinary secretariat, headed by a very smart American lawyer, Tom Seddon, who had come to Australia to play rugby; rugby had damaged his body, the intemperate politics around the International Gay Games had left him more savvy in dealing with multiple egos.

The Sixth International Conference on AIDS in Asia and the Pacific brought 4000 people to Melbourne in the aftermath of the September 11 attacks; and the collapse of Ansett Airlines immediately afterwards. Delegates' flights were cancelled, visas became harder to get, but the Conference opened in splendour at the Exhibition Buildings on October 5, and my major diplomatic duty was to escort the Queen of Bhutan, most elevated of our 'first wives', to the front row. I later discovered that she was the third wife of the then King of Bhutan, all sisters, which presumably made royal duties somewhat less onerous. At the turn of the century a number of leaders' wives had taken up support for HIV as their cause, and we gathered a group to speak at one session: "None of them were ever elected to anything", whispered Joan Kirner, former premier of Victoria, to me as they took their places on stage. There were more significant government officials at the Conference; at one point I saw the Health Minister of Nepal sitting on the floor, surrounded by all the delegates from his country. He told me afterwards that was the first time he had spoken with someone who was openly HIV-positive.

There is an intimacy when one is driving with someone, and Robin and I make several long trips through the Sussex Down, the first of which was to attend a literary festival at Charleston, former home of some of the Bloomsbury Group, set in a perfect English garden. Despite constant attempts to make them more contemporary, writers' festivals are not unlike academic conferences, except that they attract crowds, usually older and female, willing to pay to hear their favourite authors. That afternoon the Irish author Colm Tóibín was surprisingly funny talking about his latest book, *House of Names*, the story of the Greek Queen Clytemnestra and the murder of her husband Agamemnon, not an obvious subject for wit.

After her time in Australia Robin held several key positions in the international HIV world, and we were colleagues again when she became Executive Director of the International AIDS Society, whose main purpose is to host the ever-growing International Conferences. For those of us who became part of the international AIDS circuit, international conferences become yardsticks of progress and personal life, often interwoven. There are moments of public drama, such as Nelson Mandela's appearance at Durban in 2000 or the announcements of breakthrough therapies in Vancouver in 1996. There are moments of personal achievement in speaking in plenary sessions at the conferences in Yokohama in 1994 and Bangkok in 2004. And there are moments when conferences change our lives: Anthony and I spent some of our first time together at the first Asia/Pacific Conference, a small gathering linked to the Australian national gathering in Canberra in August 1990. Six years later, in Vancouver, Robin met the man who would become the father of her twin sons, Julian Jayaseelan, whom I'd known for several years because of his work at Pink Triangle in Kuala Lumpur. On one visit Julian was engaged in empathetic pregnancy exercises in Kuala Lumpur while Robin was back home in London, which seemed a harbinger of his largely absent fatherhood.

Over three decades AIDS has developed its own elites, networks and institutions, fuelled by a mix of altruism and ambition which collectively created a movement that has sped up biomedical research and slowed the progress of an epidemic that has already killed 38 million people. Talking with Robin re-emphasised for me how central AIDS was in our lives for many decades, even if, unlike those who are positive, we could take time off. AIDS engendered new passions, alliances, skills that brought together the most remarkable group of people I've had the privilege of knowing. We became comrades, in all the socialist optimism of that term, and as comrades do, fell out amongst ourselves, fought over imagined differences, swore, forgave, loved, suffered, died, got bored, were obdurate, pig-headed, confrontational, egotistical and, in the end, changed forever through the scars of struggle.

In the heat of the car we traverse shared conflicts and lives, unpicking old wounds which shrink in perspective. Our second, and longer drive, takes us to Deal in Kent, once the busiest port in England, where a long-time mutual friend, Simon Watney, has retired. The Downs give way to the grimness of coastal Kent, its seaside strips less wealthy and ornate than those of Sussex, where we find Simon in an old cottage that looks as if it had wandered out of the green room of a production of *Mapp and Lucia*, E.F. Benson's caustic novels about social climbing in a Sussex town.

An art historian and a friend of legendary figures such as Duncan Grant, Angela Carter and Derek Jarman, Simon Watney became an early British AIDS activist, wrote *Policing Desire*, one of the first books on the epidemic, and developed close links with American treatment activists. His was a politics born of urgency; he begins *Policing Desire* by writing of an old friend who died at the beginning of 1986. By the time Simon visited us in Melbourne in 1991 he was already consumed with rage at the failures of the political and medical systems in Britain and the United States. That rage subsided, but occasionally resurfaces in attacks on the idiocies of Brexit and the limits of the British health system.

It's a sunny day, here on the edge of Britain, and we walk out onto the pier, a workman like structure used by local fisherman, and with a functional café at the end. But even in sunshine Deal suggested novelist Wilkie Collins's remark: "Is there any prospect of desolation ... which can rival the repelling effect on the eye, and the depressing effect on the mind, of an English country town in ... the transition state of its prosperity."[8] Simon frets about the amnesia of the gay world and touches on the fears we all have as we age, that we are forgotten by new generations hungry for recognition and intent on discovering the world for themselves. Too often we forget how like them we once were, that we too dismissed anything that happened before we experienced it, as unimportant. Simon has hordes of papers from his activist and artistic life that he wants to pass on, but there appears to be little interest. He has saved a huge pile of envelopes with commemorative stamps for me, and I spend the train trip back to London carefully tearing small margins round the stamps so I might soak them off when I return home.

May 31: Torquay

Why Torquay?: a need to get away by myself, and the lure of a leisurely train trip through English countryside, green with a lustre one rarely sees in Australia. But also a long standing romance with the idea of the English Riviera, fed by my obsession with Agatha Christie. She was born, grew up and married here, and Torquay, thinly disguised, is the site of several of her books. The town, far bigger than I'd imagined, contains a few understated bronze plaques which follow her life around Torquay.

I'd grown up reading Christie, but it was my friendship with the poet Dorothy Porter that made me see Christie as more than comfort

---

8   Wilkie Collins, *The Woman in White*, Penguin Classics, 1999, p.425.

reading. Conversations with Dorothy were as wide ranging as her poetry, likely to touch on astronomy, ancient Egypt and possible new pandemics, but usually she would ask which 'Aggie' I was reading; taking for granted that one returned to Agatha much as one might to a favourite macaroni cheese. Back in 1999 we'd spoken together at an 'Agatha Night', organised by Sisters in Crime, a boisterous group of mystery fans who met at the back of a well-known 'spaghetti bar' in St Kilda. Between us we 'queered Agatha' before academic fashion overtook us; pointed to the surprising number of spinsters and unmarried gentlemen in her books—and, stressed Dorothy, *no children*. Recently I met a twenty-four-year-old art student who has thrown himself into reading all of Agatha Christie, for reasons that he struggled to explain.

When Dorothy died, nine years later, her partner, the novelist Andrea Goldsmith, gave me her collection of 'Aggies', which I've added to over the years. Many years earlier James Baldwin spoke of a grim hotel in Hamburg where reading Christie had nursed him through a lonely night. (Matt Brim has pointed out to me the reference in Baldwin's *Just Above My Head* where the character, Jimmy, "is reading, as one always does at such moments, something by Agatha Christie, and will have got to the end of it before realizing that he has read it before."[9]) Whenever I travel I seek out Christies in translation; I am fondest of the Turkish edition of *Murder on the Orient Express*. To my surprise there seems to be no Christie memorabilia on sale in Torquay, which voted almost two to one to leave the European Union. Somehow this seems to echo the very deep distrust of foreigners that Christie ascribes to so many of her characters.

But I relish the anonymity of this very English, red-faced town, the battered fish and chips, complete with mushy green peas; the dowager grandness of my hotel, with its ornate deco lobbies and airline breakfasts. I've spent many hours discussing the joys and traps of travelling alone, of those moments when one suddenly realises no-one would notice if you were to pass out in a hotel room, of the challenge of walking into a restaurant alone, and looking as if it's by choice. One friend

---

9   James Baldwin, *Just Above my Head*, Michael Joseph, 1979, p.593.

admitted, somewhat shamefacedly, that her solution was makeshift picnic dinners in her hotel room. But at its best, dining alone can be a small luxury, and one that should be treasured.

June 1–5: London

My generation of Australians grew up with constant references to Britain and learnt the streets of London from Monopoly sets. We read English books—Enid Blyton, then when I was a little older, Arthur Ransome's *Swallows and Amazons*, Rachel Compton's *William* and W.E. Johns' *Biggles*, all of them anchored in complacent middle-class English assumptions. From there I graduated to Agatha Christie, who was a favourite of my Melbourne grandmother, and P.G. Wodehouse, whose humour was nicely pitched at adolescent bookworms. The only Australian book I recall was Nan Chauncey's *They Found a Cave*; she lived north of Hobart beside a small wildlife sanctuary and was the first author I ever met. Checking her life I discover that her husband was a refugee from Germany, which is presumably how my family knew her.

London is both a foreign and a familiar city, triggering off memories that are often images from fiction rather than lived experience. I go into Foyles Bookstore on Charing Cross Road and remember my high school French teacher, who came from England, and grew nostalgic talking about the bookshops of London. Now, half a century later, I prowl through Foyles, and surreptitiously snap a picture of one of my books, inconspicuous on a top shelf in the politics section.

I walk through Bloomsbury, and drop in at *Gay's the Word*, London's queer bookshop since 1979. My generation of queer writers saw these bookstores as integral to our worlds, and the first shops were products of political commitment as much as of business entrepreneurship. The first openly gay bookshop was New York's *Oscar Wilde* on Christopher Street, just up from the Stonewall Inn, whose owner, Craig Rodwell, moved through the Mattachine Society to the more radical gay movements of the 1970s. I barely knew Craig, whom I remember as rather dour; in his book *The Politics of Homosexuality*, Toby Marotta suggests he modelled the store on a Christian Science Reading Room, although it was smaller and less brightly lit than most of their rooms. In Toronto, Jearld Moldenhauer founded *Glad Day Books*; I look back to photos he took on my first visit in 1972, when the bookshop and the magazine, *The Body Politic*, shared premises, and I stayed with some of the collective in a ramshackle three-story house in about-to-gentrify Cabbagetown. During the 1970s *Body Politic* was an important inspiration for embryonic gay movements worldwide and survived several attempts to prosecute it for obscenity.

The very grand British Library is holding a reception for the opening of 'Gay Love, Law and Liberty', marking fifty years since the partial decriminalisation of homosexuality that followed a number of scandals and the response of the Wolfenden Committee. At a time when gay public figures have become commonplace one forgets that fifty years ago even the most private behaviour was subject to imprisonment, extortion and blackmail, a time summed up in *Victim*, the 1961 film in which Dirk Bogarde, courageously, plays a married lawyer who confronts the blackmailers of his lover. *Victim* was the first English language film to utter the word 'homosexual'; there is a poster for it in the Library collection, along with a program from the contemporaneous play, Sheelagh Delaney's *Taste of Honey*, first produced in London in 1958.

As an undergraduate I was active in the University of Tasmania's drama society, the Old Nick Company, and I organised a public reading of the play, responding, I am sure, to the inclusion of a gay character who, predictably, finds himself alone at the conclusion. I had come across the play on a family trip to Europe while I was still a gawky teenager, and my copy is annotated with production notes; but while Geoff is a secondary character, and described by Vito Russo in his book *Celluloid Closet* as "pathetic, sexless, childlike", his very existence caused splutters from American film critics when Tony Richardson's version of the film appeared in 1961. The cover of the play-script depicts the central character, the young woman Jo, alongside her black sailor boyfriend, itself slightly shocking at the beginning of the

1960s. The person we cast as Geoff was himself gay, though I was not to discover this until some years later, just as I, at the time, was still largely unaware of my own sexual desires.

The crowd at the Library is mixed, some veterans from the early British gay movement, when 'gay' was understood to include women, but also some much younger and respectably dressed people, only one of whom could be described as gender-bending. I'm surprised that I know a few people there, including the queer activist Peter Tatchell, who tells me determinedly that he remembers a meal with me in St Kilda in 1987, and that we disagreed about the possible independence of East Timor. The vagaries of memory: have I forgotten that conversation because I was wrong?—or has Peter remembered a conversation that may not have happened? Lots of alcohol and *no food*: I leave as others seem happy to keep drinking the free wine, and take refuge in an unremarkable sushi train restaurant that seems half populated by solitary diners.

An image from a 1971 Gay Liberation Manifesto leads a younger legal scholar to ask my memories of that year, when I visited London and sat in on an early meeting of the collective who established *Gay Left* magazine. Two days later I have lunch with Jeffrey Weeks, historian and gay liberationist, whose *Coming Out*, first published in 1977, is a crucial work in writing the history of contemporary homosexuality and its politics. Jeffrey and I have oddly similar trajectories: we both were caught up in the liberation movements of the early 1970s and found ways to incorporate our experience into academic life. Jeffrey's scholarship around sexuality has been pivotal, marked by judiciousness and the ability to read widely across a number of disciplines.

Here we are: two elderly and successful academics in a Greek café on Upper Street, looking back over what will soon be a half century of writing and activism. I am always slightly embarrassed when I am described as an activist; I've never been arrested and have skipped more demonstrations than I've attended. Activism demands a certain ability to suspend doubts, to be totally committed to the slogans of the day, whatever their limits. Yes, writing is itself a form of activism, and often provides a platform for public appearances. But it is also deeply individualistic and can sit uneasily with the activist need for certainty.

What made us activists? In my case it was a series of accidents, of ambition mixed up with affirmation and some altruism. Had I not been in New York at the end of 1970, had I not shared an apartment with someone, now largely forgotten, on the fringes of the embryonic gay liberation movement, had I not been in search of a topic for a book … but there is the reverse speculation: what if I hadn't written that first book, had stayed closeted, had built a more conventional academic career? Most of our lives resemble the film *Sliding Doors*, though I hardly see myself being portrayed by Gwyneth Paltrow.

Predictably, and probably for the better, much of what we wrote and struggled over has now been largely forgotten, moved into archives where the occasional doctoral student might wander, and feel mild surprise at how many current debates are prefigured in earlier movement circles. There's a line in a song from Mike and the Mechanics: "Every generation blames the one before". But my sense is that current young queer activists are far more generous to those of us who were liberationists in the 1970s than we were to our homophile predecessors. Maybe every generation needs the certainty that comes with the arrogance of ignorance.

On June 3 came the terror attack at Borough Market in which eleven people died. I'd been in the Market the evening before with old friends and colleagues, Rajyashree Pandey and Sanjay Seth. Raj had taught Japanese, Sanjay Politics, at La Trobe for many years, and we'd bonded over departmental lunches and meetings. Like Anthony they both smoked, and I have memories of the three of them sneaking out from departmental events like naughty school children for increasingly forbidden puffs. Sanjay grew up in Sydney; Raj was born outside Bombay, studied at Oxford, has lived in Calcutta, Canberra, St Louis, Melbourne and now London. None of which, she mused, really feels like home. And as we age, finding a place that feels like home becomes increasingly important.

We don't really discuss our work: only when I come back to Melbourne will I read a remarkable interview with Sanjay from Lisbon, where he speaks of himself as "the bastard child of [Sir Thomas] Macaulay". Raj recently published a book with the wonderful title *Perfumed Sleeves and Tangled Hair*, which I promise to read. But unlike writers, academics rarely speak of their work; maybe the reason they—we?—are so fond of conferences and seminars is that we need the artificial constructs they provide to talk about our work. A Vice Chancellor once told me that the most constant complaint in his emails was about parking, a reminder that academic life is a workplace like most others.

June 8: Lausanne

The research part of my trip has brought me here, to take part in a European Conference on Politics and Gender, where I'm speaking on two panels. But the first evening is set aside for dinner with Jeff O'Malley, who's visiting Geneva. I'd stayed with Jeff in his small apartment in Geneva sixteen years ago, when he was working with Jonathan Mann, at the World Health Organisation's Program on AIDS. Jonathan resigned because of lack of support from the Director General, and took up a position at Harvard, from where he managed the 1992 International Conference—relocated from Boston to Amsterdam because of the US ban on HIV-positive entrants—and founded the journal, *Health and Human Rights*. He had connected with the mysterious-sounding Bolivian Countess Albina de Boisrouvray, after she founded a major foundation in honour of her only son who had died in a plane crash in Mali. With her support Jonathan established the Global AIDS Policy Coalition, and at Jeff's urging I was invited to join. Consequently, I met Albina, who turned out to be remarkably unlike the social heiress of legend, but deeply committed to development work and blasé about her wealth. At one point, Anthony and I went to her apartment in Paris and were served a decent, but frugal breakfast.

In Sion the Coalition met at a hotel owned, I suspect, by Albina, and rode in a helicopter over the Swiss Alps. I look at photos from that trip and try to remember what we discussed at our several meetings.

The most tangible outputs from the Coalition were two large reports, *AIDS in the World*, although my hunch is Jonathan and his colleague Daniel Tarantola would have produced much the same without the Coalition. In retrospect, we were a group of hand-picked 'experts' from around the world, mainly African women and white gay men, who provided another veneer of respectability to Jonathan's endeavours. (In a tragic irony Jonathan died in a Swissair plane crash in 1998.) Of all the conversations that swirled around our meetings I remember best an intense moment with Noreine Kaleeba, one of the founders of the first AIDS organisation in Uganda, who was speaking of a visit to San Francisco: "It reminded me of home", she said. "The same sense of death and desolation all around."

At the Lausanne Gender Conference, I come out as old: I am on a panel with three scholars half my age and looking at the room I repeat my now hackneyed line that as we age our lived experiences become a new generation's history. The Conference is largely comprised of youngish women, who spend a lot of time fretting over the whiteness of the meeting. Around twenty percent of the attendees are men, largely gay: there are so many queer panels that it would be impossible to go to them all. In my usual conference sloth I miss most of the papers but am assiduous at attending lunch and dinner.

The second evening there is a fondue evening, served in the glass box building where we've been meeting, a black and white structure ringed by fields in the outskirts of Lausanne. Only in a very rich country could bread dipped in boiling cheese be regarded as a delicacy. Already there is the quick bonding that marks Conferences at their best, heightened by the fact that there is now a community of queer political scientists in Europe. I view them as a third generation, following the 1970s sexual liberationists and 1980/90s AIDS and queer theorists. But my own generation built on a hundred years of writing about sexuality, even if we were largely ignorant of the early homosexual movements. Today academics are trapped by the growing professionalisation of academic life, the pressure to publish in a selected group of journals and to write in a disciplinary language that isn't the language of the activists they often write about. There's a timidity about politics reflected in the carefully chosen language—'intersectionality' is in, 'queer', interestingly, is not. Though critical of queer theory in its heyday, now I strongly prefer the term to the portmanteau 'LGBTI', increasingly used as if it were a proper noun. "Then", said one person on our local gay radio station, "I entered into an LGBTI relationship." If one thinks what the letters stand for this is clearly very improbable.

I once wrote that queer theory was "the bastard child of the gay and lesbian movement and postmodern literary theory, which like other unwed mothers has been very loath to acknowledge the father." Looking back on that sentence it seems to me both accurate and a not very well concealed grievance at being overlooked in the new scholarship which seemed more aware of literary than political antecedents. I remain irritated by the overly academic language with which queer theory is too often expounded. But the term 'queer' is a useful shorthand for capturing unconventional forms of gender and sexuality, even if it is sometimes vigorously rejected by older homosexuals who remember it as a term of abuse.

I become fascinated by the problem of language: here we are in French speaking Switzerland—less than a hundred kilometres to the east it switches to German—and the conference is conducted entirely in English. Other than the British most people here are effectively tri-lingual and are genuinely puzzled when I ask them about the experience of having to do most of their academic work in a language that isn't their own. (In Brussels earlier that week two young Flemish academics had been adamant that publishing in their own language was an academic cul-de-sac.) Only one person I spoke with seemed bothered by the dominance of English, a young German who was determined to publish in German although his English was flawless. But the dominance of English also means a homogenisation of writing, an over reliance on ideas and analysis that comes from North America. Most of the people I encountered at the Conference seemed a lot more interesting than their papers suggested. No-one uses PowerPoint when they are talking about their lives.

While I am in Lausanne the British are voting, and predictions that Theresa May will win a sweeping majority are quickly dispelled. Back in my hotel room I struggle to stay awake to watch the first results come in, but the exit polls are remarkably accurate. The Tories seem to be back, but greatly weakened; the Left is thrilled that Corbyn turned out to be a natural campaigner, and not the disaster many in Labour had feared. Like Bernie Sanders in the United States he tapped into a widespread desire for more than politics as usual, and a willingness to embrace change more radical than that proposed by the establishment Left.

June 10: Paris

This trip ends in Paris, and another election: the first round for the Legislative Assembly. On the Sunday, the streets between Bastille and the Seine are choked with runners for a major charity event. The Boulevard Henri IV is closed to traffic, and there are several small stages with loud music; at the entrance to the metro a few disconsolate passengers try to work out how to cross the blocked streets. I wander through the Marais, now almost deserted, and perch in a café near the town hall of the fourth arrondissement. Opposite the café a couple of gendarmes keep watch over a polling place inside the imposing nineteenth century stone building, which is flanked by an ordered line of posters for the candidates: not only those of the major parties, but those for animal rights and various splinter groups, both left and right.

This is the fourth election I've experienced since Malcolm Turnbull called an early election in Australia last July and, like Theresa May, almost lost his gambol. It is also the least problematic. Emmanuel Macron had easily won the Presidency the previous month, and his La République En Marche was expected to repeat this in the legislative elections. Not surprisingly turnout slumped. From my seat in the café I saw only a trickle of voters, almost all elderly, approach the polling place; but none of the countries I'd been in seemed to take elections as seriously as Australia. "Not a sausage sizzle in sight", as I posted on Facebook from Paris. But I was in the heart of Macron territory, and the results seemed a foregone conclusion.

In Australia we do elections well, and the ABC coverage is as good as anything I saw in the US, Britain or France. Of course, different systems produce different possibilities, and the complex voting systems we use—plus the reality of releasing figures as they are counted, rather than waiting, as do the Brits, for the final tally—allows for geekish invention. Nor do other countries have our endearing habit of naming constituencies after individuals: at each redistribution an Australian electorate is named after any recently deceased Prime Minister. Far more inventive than American naming: locating Barton or Gwydir may not be as immediately apparent as California 16 or, indeed, the third constituency of the Loire, but the names carry their own resonance. The Americans rarely show maps indicating voting patterns on television, though they do colour code states as the Electoral College vote is tallied. But while red has traditionally been the colour of the left, Americans have come to paint Republicans as red, Democrats as blue, as little bound by international precedents as they are in retaining miles for distance and Fahrenheit for temperatures.

July 3: Melbourne

Mario's is one of the oldest cafes on Brunswick Street, now far hipper than when it was founded shortly after I moved to Melbourne, thirty-two years ago. I am here with Benjamin Law, eating humming bird cake. Ben burst onto the literary scene in 2010 with his first book, *The Family Law*, about growing up gay and Asian in Queensland in the 1990s—now in its second series for television—and has become a very successful journalist, columnist and general gadfly. He is, as I like to remind him, the most charming self-promoter I have ever encountered, and always fun to hang out with.

Ben and I first met on stage at several events, including a remarkable debate in the Sydney Town Hall about same sex marriage, when we joined the Russian-American journalist Masha Gessen in disagreeing with Janette Winterton about the virtues of monogamy. When

I published *The End of the Homosexual?* in 2013 Ben interviewed me in the top room of an Oxford Street bar, one of the surviving gay places on what may still be Australia's best-known gay strip. Today we're discussing his forthcoming *Quarterly Essay* on the Safe Schools controversy, and what this tells us about larger socio-political changes. The Safe Schools program, which provides schools with resources to prevent bullying on the grounds of sexuality or gender expression, was originally funded by the Abbott government in 2014. Now it has come under increasing criticism for allegedly indoctrinating children with radical views on gender and sex.

When Ben was in school the Queensland Parliament decriminalised homosexuality; now the state government is planning to pardon men convicted under those laws. Ben came out into a world where his behaviour was legal; I came out into a world that still defined homosexuality as crime, sin and deviance. The progress in two generations is extraordinary, even if confined to what we used to call 'the West'. But there is a subterranean backlash, played out largely within the Murdoch press and the ranks of the Liberal Party, and we talk about the vicious campaign that the Safe Schools program unleashed, including direct threats to my colleagues at La Trobe who are involved in delivering the program. Just as the sexual liberationist movements of the 1970s were strongly influenced by ideas from the United States, so it seems the cultural warriors of the American right are feeding the paranoias of those who feel threatened by changes to the sexual/gender order. At least in Victoria the state government is maintaining its commitment, but the Turnbull government has refused to re-fund the program despite the recommendations of a review ordered by his own Education Minister.

July 13: Melbourne

Took one of my oldest friends, Danny Vadasz, to a belated birthday dinner. Expensive restaurant, which was disappointingly bland, but had the advantage of spaciousness and quiet.

I first met Danny in the late 1970s, while I was living in Sydney and he was one of a group of Melbourne activists who established *Gay*

Community News. *GCN* was modelled on its namesake in Boston and the Canadian *Body Politic* and saw itself as an alternative to the more commercial *Campaign*, which had started publication in Sydney a few years earlier. Under Danny's leadership *GCN* eventually morphed into the glossier, more explicitly male *Outrage*, which became the major gay publication in Australia for the next several decades. When I moved to Melbourne in 1985 I gravitated to the orbit around *Outrage*, and its sister street paper, *Melbourne Community News*, drawn by the same mix of camaraderie and politics I'd found in the gay media world in New York. The newspapers were swallowed up in a messy and acrimonious takeover of gay publications in the 1990s.

There is surprisingly robust material in some of the now ageing *Outrages*, which should be anthologised and made available to a younger audience. But when I push Danny to reminisce about his time running a gay publications group he talks less of the content and more of the world before fully computerised layouts, when fax machines seemed harbingers of a new technological future. Within a decade they were outmoded.

We talk about a couple of movement veterans who never managed to fulfil the ambitions of their youth. Movements have their costs, and not everyone becomes an activist without making major sacrifices. There's a ruefulness in Danny's discussion of his time in the gay movement, a sense that much of what we did is forgotten in the triumphalism of current assertion. Unlike many of his contemporaries Danny is not much drawn to nostalgia; he has successfully negotiated two senior positions in very different areas since the collapse of Bluestone Media at the turn of the century. Rather complacently we congratulate ourselves on professional lives well lived, in part because of the support—and pressure—of coming from refugee families. "Yes", said Danny, "We have the Holocaust genes." Growing up in refugee families creates a certain mixture of ambition and anxiety which we recognise, often subconsciously, when we meet other outsiders.

July 20: Melbourne

It's three years since I stopped grieving for Anthony, who died in November 2012. Grief is too heavy an emotion to live with forever; sadness at loss never totally vanishes, but there's a moment when it ceases to be the dominant theme of one's life. For me that moment came during the International AIDS Conference in Melbourne. It was cold and sunny that week, with a crystalline brightness to the city, very different to the Conference two years earlier in Vienna, when I sat in shorts on a late evening terrace, sharing a drink with Francoise Barre-Sinoussi, one of the co-discoverers of HIV, unwilling to leave despite constant attacks by mosquitoes. Francoise had joined the Governing Council of the International AIDS Society shortly before she was awarded the Nobel Prize for Medicine. I had come to know her gradually, aware of the awe with which many of my colleagues approached her. Her husband died a few years before Anthony, and several years later over dinner in a restaurant in Paris she assured me that in time grief gives way to memories of time together. Oddly I remember the restaurant as smoky, even though Francoise abandoned me at one point for a quick cigarette outside.

I'd been consistently sceptical about holding the AIDS Conference in a country with a small and well managed epidemic, but to my surprise I enjoyed the week enormously. Without bitterness or regret I recognised it was time to withdraw from almost thirty years of AIDS activism, and—perhaps connected to this—that I no longer needed to cry over Anthony's death. Maybe relief came from the intensity of interaction with so many people from across the world, the sense of passion that grew from the huge toll of death and illness that so many in the halls had experienced. Behind the tall glass walls of the Convention Centre were echoes of emaciated bodies lying on narrow pallets that I'd seen in hospitals in Soweto and Ho Chi Minh City, and memories of too many people who'd died far too young. But there was also glamour: for many of us participation in the AIDS world was an entrée to celebrity and attention. The AIDS world is marked by a churning mix of altruism and ambition, and the huge Conferences become showcases for both.

The official histories of the Conferences mark progress in biomedical science, which has been extraordinary. My memories are more self-indulgent. At the 1996 Conference in Vancouver I was with Marina Mahathir at an event where Elizabeth Taylor, already in a wheelchair, appeared, and we were elbowed aside by muscle boys determined to get close to the icon. Two years later the Conference was in Geneva, and I spoke on a late afternoon panel with the then Miss America. She had, at best, a rudimentary knowledge of HIV, while helpful with grooming tips backstage. But behind the frivolity there was anger and passion, even if this was so tamed that the Melbourne Conference had timetabled a demonstration six-months in advance, without any sense of who we might demonstrate against.

Every day for a week I took the train to the city, walked along the Yarra River to the massive Convention Centre which had become its own small city, complete with the 'global village' of community stalls and the larger, glossier commercial exhibition section, where pharmaceutical companies entertained in padded chairs, and well-groomed attendants offered free espresso and ice cream. The large halls housed a parade of celebrity speakers—Bill Clinton, Richard Branson, Helen Clark, Bob Geldof—surrounded by long stretches of poster presentations, earnest summaries of research findings and community programs reduced to a few metres of butcher's paper.

My main commitments were off-stage. In a downtown bar, I chaired a discussion about international queer politics, then, a few nights later, a discussion about the cultural responses to the epidemic, with a panel of writers and performers in the Wheeler Centre, home for year-round literary discussions, which has helped Melbourne join the fast growing UNESCO list of cities of literature. It is a sign of how the AIDS world has developed that discussion of 'culture' was not part of the main Conference program; in my introduction, I referred to those early markers of the epidemic like the musical album, *Red, Hot and Blue* and the AIDS Quilt; above all the play *Angels in America*, which had recently been restaged in Sydney. My hunch is that *Angels in America* is the greatest work of art to have come out of the epidemic. In a sprawling two-part drama Tony Kushner reaches across the country like a contemporary Walt Whitman, mixing lived reality and metaphysical exploration. Historical figures—Roy Cohn and Ethel Rosenberg—rise from the dead, alongside angels, sprung from myths of both the Kabbalah and the Book of Mormon. It's a play deeply embedded within the American experience; indeed, I was cautious when Roger Hodgman at the Melbourne Theatre Company asked me whether I thought they should stage it. My caution proved wildly wrong, and *Angels* has been restaged several times since in Australia. The play takes on a new relevance today; at least in the rich world far fewer people are dying of AIDS, but the brutal politics of Roy Cohn live on in the Trump Administration.

On the Wednesday, I organised a small dinner for visiting friends. We took over a small café on Gertrude Street owned by my friend Krystos, a yoga teacher, and we sat, ten of us, looking out onto the street where the local Council had painted a rainbow flag. K even produced a menu, appropriately in pink, with its choice of fabulous fish pie or Marrakesh vegetable stew. This is what we, in conference-land, call *networking*.

July 22: Noumea

Flying back into Melbourne after a weekend away in New Caledonia with Ed. He's become a passionate scuba diver and was up at six to go out on the reefs; I followed a couple of hours later and enjoyed the pleasure of sitting in cafes by the sea. New Caledonia is a remarkable remnant of imperial expansion, of the Faustian pact that the conquered inhabitants have made with their French overlords, who settled in the islands to the point where the richer parts of Noumea recall a somewhat fading resort town on the Mediterranean. We are staying in Anse Vata, which coils around an azure bay, once a swamp and then headquarters for American troops during World War II. In the last year of the War this was the second busiest port in the Pacific.

Now Anse Vata is another strip in the global tourist map, and where the troops gathered are now manicured lawns sloping down towards the narrow beach front.

"What", Maggie Smith (as Lady Grantham) might ask, "Is a holiday?" A successful holiday is one which there is little to write about; a diary is not the place to describe the beauties of the islands, which tourist brochures can provide, nor to explain the tortured relationship between Kanaks and settlers. One sees glimpses of the contradictions of settlement constantly: on the east coast, at a township called Yate, not unlike small towns in the Queensland scrub, there is a small gendarmerie flying a French flag, and a general store which was closed for a two-hour lunch break. Go into the centre of Noumea and one is aware that this is a Pacific city, half sleepy tropical despite the orderly street grid and statues of empire. New Caledonia is part of the French Republic, but it is not France.

In many ways this was an almost perfect holiday but left me feeling some of the exhaustion of ageing. Michel Foucault died at the age of 58, so he never lived to experience the increasing burden of healthy old age on 'care of the self'. I think of this as I look at the list of appointments that face me in the next few weeks: GP, audiologist, osteopath, dentist, ophthalmologist … Foucault's was a more philosophical vision of self-care, but he would have agreed that the body needs to be carefully tended.

I met Michel Foucault in Paris in April 1977, in the Cinema Olympic, which was owned by Frédéric, President Mitterand's gay nephew. Paris's first gay film festival, the 'semaine homosexuelle', was organised by a radical gay group, and received considerable media coverage. The festival re-screened some classic English language films—*Victim*, *The Killing of Sister George*, *Staircase*—as well as the very confronting *Hunting Scenes from Bavaria*, a 1969 German film in which a man is literally hunted down for supposed homosexuality. I struggled to keep up in a session on the homosexual struggle; the debates included one on pederasty which received considerable press coverage at the time.

There was a film screening in a full cinema, and I was sitting on the steps when a somewhat older man came and sat beside me. After the film we talked a little, introduced ourselves; only after he left did I realise who he was. My partner during the seventies, Barry Prothero, had already discovered Foucault's writings in Sydney; I doubt that I fully understood the extent to which he was overturning the easy assumptions of liberal positivism. But he was charming, unpretentious, and a few weeks later invited me to dinner, to the spacious apartment in the thirteenth arrondissement where he wrote some of his books. Michel cooked, but I barely remember the apartment, now familiar through the diaries of Mathieu Lindon who has written of his relationship with Foucault.[10] There was a pro-Iranian demonstration outside on the rue de Vaugirard, and we disagreed about the advent of the Ayatollah's leadership of the revolution, which he welcomed enthusiastically. I like the description of him in Laurent Binet's semiotic novel, *The 7th Function of Language*: "At once sturdy and slender. He has a determined jaw with a slight underbite and the stately demeanour of those who know that they are valued by the world."[11]

Over the following decade Foucault became probably the most famous intellectual in the world. When I lived in New York in the early 1980s there were constant stories of his life, and his forays, both intellectual and sexual, into California. As was the case with Vidal I knew several people who claimed to be his 'best friend', and probably, for a time, they were. He shared an ambivalence towards the gay movement with many intellectuals of his generation. (In some accounts he suggested the name *le gai pied*, the radical gay paper which started publication a year after the festival.) Like Susan Sontag and Patrick White, and, of course, Gore Vidal, there was simultaneous attraction and disdain when confronted with the possibility that their own sexual lives might be understood politically.

Back to holidays: less than two years ago I also fled the cold of Melbourne, this time to northern Australia. I look back to an account

---

10   Mathieu Linden, *Learning What Love Means*, Semiotexte, 2017.
11   Laurent Binet, *The Seventh Function of Language*, FSG, 2017.

I wrote, sitting at a long table at the rear of a beach resort in the Queensland tropics:

> It is warm, but surprisingly dry; no sign of the tropics but for a lone great egret surveying the visitors with the air of a slightly jaded matron. The resort is usually confined to gay men, but tonight it is in transition; over the weekend it will become the site of a swingers weekend, only open to heterosexual couples, and the organisers have arrived to make preparations. The Sunday night, they tell me, will be ABC: an 'anything but clothes' event.
>
> "Wear a towel" I suggest to one of the men, who's already tantalising the room in skimpy shorts and singlet, displaying a neatly tattooed bicep. The woman who choreographs the event starts talking to us about the advantage of using gay spaces; the weekend is known as "the only straight in the village" said her partner in an aside. Already it's clear that the event is heavily controlled, and admission is only for heterosexual couples who pass strenuous checking. The emphasis is on partying and acting out fantasies; the website seems heavily angled towards straight men, even though swingers clubs usually struggle to attract as many women as men.
>
> The two couples here are perhaps in their early forties, too young to have experienced the 'sexual revolution' of the 1970s, clearly affluent and remarkably self-confident. One of the women flashes her latest I-watch, talks of her running exploits. Much later that evening, her partner having discreetly left the bar, she will hit on one of my friends: "I had to tell her I wouldn't know what to do" he told me rather abashed the next morning.
>
> The image of an old cover from *Nation Review* flashed into my mind: I wrote a long review of Gay Talese's book *Thy Neighbour's Wife* for a 1980 issue, and the cover image was a very orange picture of two heterosexual couples frolicking in a

frothy hot tub. This was just as a herpes epidemic was leading to proclamations that the sexual revolution was over; several years later the onset of AIDS seemed to echo this warning in graphic form. The explosion of internet communication has meant possibilities for sexual experimentation that the swingers in Talese's book could barely imagine; in one generation we have moved from the liberalisation of laws banning pornography through the era of porn videos to a global self-help industry in which everyone is potentially performer and watcher at the same time. *Playboy* is currently seeking to reinvent itself, having discovered that men will no longer shell out ready money for images of female nudes, even when presented as self-improvement.

In some ways the Queensland resort is itself a throwback to an earlier time, a period when gay men needed to seclude themselves from the larger world. Indeed the men there seemed less concerned with sexual experimentation than were the swingers about to arrive. But what the swingers' website proclaims as "an exciting new lifestyle" felt strangely passé, even if the bodies are better and the participants more assured. It was rather like watching the re-made fortieth anniversary version of *The Rocky Horror Show* and being reminded that we spoke of genderfuck before Judith Butler gave us a performative framework to conceptualise it.

What has triumphed, at least in western liberal democracies, is a smooth blending of sexual freedom and neo-liberal economics: when the swingers claim to be a "sexy, open minded, liberal club", I doubt they had politics in mind. Any notions of the necessity for social revolution as a precondition for sexual liberation now seem outdated romanticism; capitalism has proven remarkably comfortable with rapidly changing sexual mores. The couples at my table were all successful small business people, the women as confident in the marketplace as their male partners. My hunch is that one of the major shifts in the past few decades has been towards greater self-confidence and assertion by young women, even if it takes forms uncomfortable for many feminists, such as an emphasis on style and fashion. Maybe ageing sentimentality leads me to see young men today as more likely to be uncertain and struggling to figure out how to perform their lives.[12]

One of the blessings—or hazards?—of being an older single gay man is meeting guys from very different worlds. Age matters—there are certain experiences that are shared by one's generation—but so too does class, ethnicity, education, even though the institutions of gay male life tend to flatten these out, making physical types and sexual tastes seem the central sorting blocks. But I've become increasingly aware of the cultural gaps, the references to what I assume are taken for granted that reveal huge crevices in knowledge and experience.

There are many young gay men—I can't speak with assurance of women—who are struggling with their sexuality, with careers, with fears of a world which seems to hold no place for them. And despite stereotypes they do not necessarily come from religious or ethnic backgrounds that are homophobic, nor can they necessarily articulate what frightens them.

July 27: Melbourne

Lunch with Nicholas Gruen: he is a public policy maven, whose father had come as a boy to Australia on the *Dunera* in 1940. This was the ship that brought over 2000 refugees, mainly Jews, to Australia in 1940, who were interned in Hay and Tatura, and went on to have a remarkable influence on postwar Australian life. Several of the Dunera Boys were important figures in my life, above all Henry Mayer, professor of Government at Sydney University, and a crucial figure in inventing an Australian political science. Henry was central in my appointment to Sydney University in 1969; and when, two years later, I decided to write about the embryonic gay movement, he was very supportive at a

---

12   'Is the Personal Still Political?', *Meanjin* 75:4, Summer 2016: 414.

time when this might not have been a safe choice. While I was writing *Homosexual*, Henry was on leave at Berkeley and sent me clippings about the gay movement from local Californian papers. He was a workaholic, a man who was both generous and fickle, likely to turn on people for imagined failings which were never explained. Several generations of academics owe him the impetus for their careers.

Nicholas's father, Fred Gruen, was twenty years younger than my father, but came from the same milieu of educated upper-class Viennese Jews. Inevitably we compare family histories: "Do you identify as Jewish?" Nicholas asks. It's a good question. In the census, I tick 'no religion', as do 30 percent of Australians, but, yes, being the son of Jewish refugees is central to who I am. My parents were both agnostic, and we had no religious upbringing, except for the very watered-down version of Christianity that pervaded my Quaker School. But there the majority of staff, and the great bulk of students, were not Quakers; the most overt religious lessons came through the antipathy of our English teacher to Catholicism when we studied Shaw's *Saint Joan*. But Jewishness is not Judaism, and as I grow older I recognise that much of how I navigate the world comes from growing up with parents from Jewish backgrounds, in both cases non-religious.

July 28: Melbourne

I've done several radio interviews this week for a forthcoming issue of the *Griffith Review*, in which I have an article on populism. Neither has left me satisfied: the word is so vague, and any attempt to narrow it down leads to greater confusion. For me the essence of populism is authoritarian leaders who claim to speak for "the people", and in so doing vilify minorities and disregard the checks and balances of liberal democracy. But the term gets too easily abused; for the Right, any suggestion to redistribute wealth gets denounced as populist, for the Left, populism is used to describe all forms of racism and discrimination.

I watch the news each evening as I would watch the next episode of a soap opera, amazed at what twists the writers can yet invent. (For the record, my current watching includes the Scandinavian black comedy

Black Widows and Netflix camp teen drama *Riverdale*.) A year ago I was part of the consensus that Trump was unelectable. It's almost exactly a year since the Republican Convention awarded him their nomination. I cannot imagine where he will be a year from now. The powers of a President who behaves as if he were the world's greatest *capofamiglia* is frightening.

August 5: Melbourne

Went with Carol D'Cruz to an exhibition of Soviet-inspired Australian constructivist art at the Heide Gallery. Heide was the home of art patrons John and Sunday Reed, whose house and grounds have become a significant small art gallery, complete with kitchen gardens (their mushrooms are big and fleshy, quite unlike those served in inner city cafes). The art was striking: who knew that the artistic experiments of post-Revolution Russia would find an echo amongst Australian artists several generations later? But removed from the optimistic turmoil that produced the Russian originals they seemed too formalistic, cold if striking with their bold red and black lines.

I met Carol towards the end of my full-time position at La Trobe, and came to know her in that fateful year, 2012, which was both the best and the worst of times for me. With three colleagues Carol organised a conference to celebrate forty years since the publication of my first book and threw herself into that Conference at a time when she was suffering through a messy break up with a long-term partner. The organisers made the very smart decision to exclude me from all planning of the event, though they had several quiet conversations with Anthony to check on several of the invitees.

The Conference itself spread over three days, beginning with a big event at Federation Square, where I sat on stage with the two visiting keynote speakers, Jeffrey Weeks from London and Alice Echols from Los Angeles. There was something both embarrassing and touching at seeing images of myself projected onto huge overhead screens, and both feelings grew over the next two days as almost two-hundred people came together in earnest discussions ranging from the personal to the hyper-academic. As Carol helped me to understand, the Conference was both about me, and *not* about me. Looking back over the abstracts I knew perhaps a third of the participants, many of whom were younger academics enjoying the possibilities of a queer gathering. I sat in on a couple of sessions, enjoyed Neville Hoad's reminiscences of our sharing "the bus of shame" which ran from the University of Chicago, where we met in 1996, to 'Boystown', the rainbow coloured few blocks of gay life in the northern reaches of Chicago. Neville is a ferociously smart literary scholar from South Africa, whose acerbic tongue hid a sweet temper; we had adjoining rooms in the former Chicago Theological Seminary, one of the ugliest buildings on the campus, with linoleum floors and harsh neon lights. Many of the papers from this Conference, plus some others, made their way into the collection Carol edited with our friend Mark Pendleton, now at the University of Sheffield, called *After Homosexual*.

The dilemma with writing a successful book when one is young is that one is constantly striving to go beyond, while struggling to keep up. Books have an impact as much because of timing as any intrinsic quality; I was lucky to be in the right place at the right time, as was true twelve years later when I lived in New York in the early days of the AIDS epidemic. I've also been lucky that at several crucial points in my life more senior academics have acknowledged the worth of writings that combine the personal and the analytic. During my time at La Trobe the University was consistently supportive of public engagement in ways that are increasingly difficult for younger academics.

August 6: Melbourne

Memorial service for Graham Carbery, who founded the Australian Lesbian and Gay Archives nearly forty years ago. I barely knew Graham but he was one of my tribe, and the event was in part a tribute to what has become one of the largest such archives in the world. I'd never known the romance of Graham's life: he left home to join the navy as a teenager, worked as a postman and a football umpire, put himself through university in the post-Whitlam days of free university education, long vanished. By the time I came across him, in the heady days of the 1970s National Homosexual Conferences, he was teaching post-secondary students. Graham was relaxed about his homosexuality and refrained from ever dramatising himself; he'd become briefly famous in 1980 when an incident involving a Victorian Football League player led to him being outed in the press. As a former colleague said at the service: "Imagine walking onto a field in front of fifty to sixty thousand people, and being booed as a poofter ..."

Like several other such events I've been to in the past few years there were few tears, more a sense of a life well lived and now complete. No religion; no music; but a hall full of people, looking out onto a football field on a strangely sunny afternoon. It was a very Melbourne event; years ago, historian Jim Davidson, who was present, put together a collection about the difference between Melbourne and Sydney which he'd called 'St Petersburg or Tinsel Town?' (Unfortunately, the book finally took the anodyne title of *The Sydney Melbourne Book*.) When I lived in Sydney through the 1970s, we were certain that we were the gay centre of the gay world, an impression fostered by the extraordinary success of Mardi Gras, which has become the most iconic queer celebration in the country, though far smaller than events in cities like Sao Paulo and Madrid. But Davidson's title reminds us that Melbourne has also been home to many of the key people and events in queer Australia.

August 10: Melbourne

The Senate has rejected a plebiscite on marriage equality for the second time; there will be a postal ballot conducted by the Australian Bureau of Statistics. The government is determined to spend a large amount of money to discover public attitudes, but not require Parliamentarians to accept the result. As I wrote: "It is a decision that undermines the authority of parliament, and simultaneously shows contempt for the people whose views are sought. Sir Robert Menzies would have been horrified by the idea of same-sex marriage—but even more, I suspect, by this perversion of Westminster democracy." The 'no' campaigners are thrilled, the marriage equality groups have been in some disarray. The reality is that we need to campaign hard to get maximum return of a 'yes' vote in a system that is clearly flawed and is not binding on Parliament anyway.

The right-wingers in Cabinet have been clever and have out-manoeuvred the equality movement. Because 'ballots'—i.e. survey questions—will be mailed to the known addresses of registered voters, many people who have moved, or are travelling, will miss out, and these are likely to be disproportionately young. I dropped in at the office of one of the movement's leaders, above a small drag cabaret bar in Collingwood, velvet booths and too loud music. Upstairs he a fellow activist were wading through emails and messages, fretting over the built-in biases of the postal vote. It seems that a few initial calls to boycott the poll have been stopped, but the movement now needs to recalibrate quickly.

August 12–13: Bendigo

Back in Bendigo, for its writers' festival. I am interviewed by a legendary ABC presenter, who ends the session by telling us that people "like Alan Turing—and Dennis Altman—are normal". I am so struck by the phrase that I write it down; this could be a well-meaning liberal heterosexual forty years ago. I check later with someone who'd been in the audience that I'd heard right. "Yes", he says, "Thought it was strange at the time …" I should be angry at being positioned as the object of other people's tolerance, the self-congratulation that is expressed in statements of support, but outrage is too easy an emotion. Last night, in response to journalist David Marr's assertion that Australia was a very British nation, an Indigenous woman writer eloquently responded that he had ignored and insulted her people. Had she been less indignant she might have realised that David's comment was in part the explanation for why Indigenous Australians have been so oppressed. But attacking David for pointing to the ongoing dominance of British assumptions in our political culture was easier. As in the marriage debate, I am troubled by the too easy recourse of those I see as political allies to yell victim rather than engage with their opponents.

There are too few moments such as these at writers' festivals, where the general mood is quiet self-congratulation and polite nodding of heads at similar worldviews. But the hunger for public discussion is extraordinary: this festival offers ninety events spread over a long weekend, and they fill the halls up and down View Street. I enjoy the serendipity of these events, the casual encounters over breakfast and in the green room with other writers, the moment of sudden drama in the sessions, the unexpected reference to a book one immediately wants to read. At writers' festivals everyone shows off, none more so than the person who sits through interminable sessions ready to leap up with a question that is, in fact, a statement.

I'm part of one of those amorphous panels that festival curators concoct to give their guests that last, obligatory appearance, discussing 'Tomorrowland' with a renowned expert on artificial intelligence and a rather ferocious science fiction writer. Not surprisingly we dart between technological optimism and political pessimism; the spectre of conflict between the United States and North Korea looms over us. (That evening, when I get home, I will see the disturbing reports of right-wing terrorists attacking demonstrators in Charlottesville Virginia). I suggest that the best way to relieve the crushing tentacles of metropolitan growth is to relocate the state capital to Bendigo, and build a fast train connection to Melbourne Airport, but the audience take to this with less enthusiasm than I'd hoped.

My fellow panellists seem somewhat taken aback at my enthusiasm for dystopian science fiction. I'm struck by a comment that in every dystopia there is a hidden utopia and, not surprisingly, think of Margaret Attwood's *Handmaid's Tale*, the television version of which is currently hot. There are right wing science fiction writers, but the genre has also been the site of considerable radical speculation, as in the extraordinary novels of China Mieville. Over the last month I've been reading both Mieville and Hilary Mantel on revolutions: his meticulous account of Russia, *October* (2017), her massive novel on France, *A Place of Greater Safety* (1992). Both books are forbidding, with their huge cast of characters and factional disputes, and both writers write sentences that evoke the world of St. Petersburg and Paris, summoning up the truth in ways unknown to academic writing.

Ride back to Melbourne with novelist Steven Amsterdam and his partner Cory. I met Steven last year because I read his novel *The Easy Way Out*, and, knowing we had a whole web of mutual friends and contacts, asked him to brunch. The novel is a whip-smart story about euthanasia; smart because Steven, himself a palliative care nurse, doesn't polemicise. The right to die has been a constant issue here and, like same-sex marriage, one where the politicians consistently lag behind the majority view.

I'm a strong if admittedly inactive supporter of the right to die movement. After Anthony died I wrote a piece for the weekend Fairfax papers, which led to my being asked to speak on a panel about euthanasia at the Perth Writers Festival three years ago. It was a confronting event; three of us—the founder of Exit, Philip Nitschke, novelist Lionel Shriver and I—up against that most charming of Jesuitical moralists, Frank Brennan, with feminist author Anne Summers keeping order. Philip Nitschke is a genuine hero, whose career has been derailed several times by his insistence that consenting adults have the right to make decisions about how their lives should end. I'd anticipated a zealot, but for someone who is constantly reviled and surveilled he is remarkably relaxed. Last year Philip asked me to speak at an Exit International Conference, where Anne and I again spoke together, and I was able to catch up on the current debates, most importantly to reflect on the distinction between medically administered euthanasia and death chosen and controlled by the individual herself.

I plan to go to an Exit workshop with Andrea Goldsmith. I first met Andrea when she was living with her partner Dorothy Porter, who died of breast cancer in 2008. When Anthony was diagnosed, and especially when he died, Andrea was there, guiding me into the world of widowhood which has its own rites and special knowledge.

There are deep secrets about living with a dying partner that we cannot reveal, even to ourselves.

We have come to be unacknowledged partners in each other's lives, sharing a liking for music, reading, gossip. Andrea is one of those rare people who listen carefully to what is said, even if prone to then state forcefully how one should react. We meet regularly for coffee, and I've eaten many good meals in Andrea's house, walking distance from mine. Two years ago, Andrea, then abroad, had been shortlisted for the Melbourne Prize for Literature and asked me to stand in for her. I sat towards the back of the auditorium, as various dignitaries made long and repetitive speeches about the importance of Culture and Writing, and was ready to leave when she was announced the winner. "Yes" I cried, leaping up to run down the stairs to the front, half aware of the shock on people's faces as they wondered what this strange elderly man was doing when he clearly was NOT Andrea Goldsmith. Luckily the Chair knew why I was there, but in the confusion I received the award without reading the words Andrea had carefully given me in preparation.

August 18: Sydney

"I'm not sure that's me" said Meaghan, squinting at the photograph. It's a slightly blurred snapshot from 1977, two women standing under trees by a river, taken when I lived that year in Paris. I've brought it to a reunion dinner with old friends, Meaghan Morris and André Frankovits. I've known Meaghan since the heady days of the early 1970s, when gay and women's liberationists gathered in a house on Glebe Point Road, with interminable meetings and roneo-machines, darting forth at night to paste the inner suburbs with posters. André was part of 'the Push', that group of anarchists and heavy drinkers who dominated Sydney's Bohemian worlds until new social movements and the Whitlam government made them seem increasingly irrelevant. Both have had distinguished careers, Meaghan as one of the founders of cultural studies in Australia, André as a leader of several human rights bodies.

They've taken me to dinner to an old Labor haunt, a vast Greek restaurant in central Sydney, pictures of sun-swept Greek islands on the walls, and waiters who flirt with the women and shake hands with the men. Meaghan examines the photograph again: "Yes", she says "I remember the cardigan." We debate who the other woman might be, and later Meaghan identifies her as Brigitte, "a strangely ethereal literary/philosophical soul, a lesbian traumatised by growing up in a provincial aristocratic family from Lyon". I'm not concerned that I have no memory of her, though am more puzzled by the names that reoccur in my diary from that time whom I've also forgotten. I seem to have had a short affair with Bernard, whom I met in a café on the Rue St-André des Arts, where there was a juke box, and the hot number was 'Don't cry for me Argentina' from the musical *Evita*. I have a photo of him, long dark brown hair and sweetly serious, sitting in one of the rattan cane chairs outside the café, but I am surprised at how often he appears in my diary. I wonder what's happened to him, and whether he has any clearer memories than I of our encounters in that intoxicating Paris spring.

There was an extraordinary group of Australians that year in Paris, some of whom I've crossed paths with over the following decades. The one I knew best is now dead: Philip Brooks, a film-maker from Hobart, whose brother was a friend at University. Philip is the inspiration for one of the characters in Helen Garner's *Monkey Grip*. When he died in Spain fourteen years ago Helen described him as: "an Eros figure who would blast a path through one's careful daily orderliness and be gone again in a shower of sparks, leaving wet towels on the bathroom floor and a mess in the kitchen, but also a breathless sense that one had just been spun round, reinvigorated and filled with fresh heart."[13] With his partner, Laurent Bocahut, he made several documentaries, most significantly *Woubi Cheri*, a story of trans women in Abidjan.

The last time I saw Philip was in Melbourne, where he was filming his last film, *My Own Private Oz*, an exploration of returning to Australia a quarter of a century after he left for London. He told me

---

13 Helen Garner, 'Obituaries', *Sydney Morning Herald*, January 25, 2003.

that that he'd left Australia because he couldn't be open about his homosexuality with his friends, to which I replied that he should have chosen his friends more carefully. It's tempting to believe that attitudes have changed sufficiently that no young person today feels impelled to leave their home because they are scared to acknowledge their sexuality. The changes are real and tangible, but they are also incomplete. I think of the forty-year old runner, University educated and with no particular religious background, who lived with constant anxiety that his homosexuality would become known, to parents, colleagues, unspecified "people". "I know" T— said, when I tried to reassure him, "I know it's all in my head."

As I write these words my Facebook feed is full of anguish as anti-gay hate mail starts showing up on lamp-posts and on line, the inevitable collateral of this silly referendum-turned-plebiscite-turned-public-opinion survey that was invented to resolve the government's deep divisions over the marriage issue. The past two weeks have been dominated by the threats to decency symbolised in the murder of a woman protester in Charlottesville just over a week ago, and Trump's ambivalent response to the new confidence of the Alt-right in the United States. I'd like to dismiss the fringe hatred that the marriage vote is unleashing but given the history of poofter bashing in Australia it's hard to be confident that everyone is safe.

August 22: Melbourne

My third official meeting as a 'mentor'. I've come to this role through Out for Australia, an organisation of young queer professionals who link people across generations, ostensibly so we older ones can help the career and personal development of the younger. In the two cases where I've been matched up I feel I've learnt more than I've imparted, and P—, currently a law student, seems self-possessed in a way none of us were at his age. Both he and Z—, an aeronautical engineer, are well educated, smart and very good at negotiating the line between deference and friendship: that they even want mentoring is a sign of their self-confidence.

P— and I discuss a couple of recent documentary films we've both seen, and I recall Eric Hobsbawm's comments about living in "the twilight zone between history and memory".[14] I re-lived some of my earliest time in New York's pre-AIDS West Village watching David France's documentary, *Death and Life of Marsha P Johnston*. P— was thrilled to discover the role of trans* leaders in the gay liberation movement. He is sceptical about the forthcoming marriage poll, dismissing the equality movement as conservative and heteronormative, and uninterested in anyone but themselves. "Think of the message a 'no' vote would send" I urge, even as I agree with some of his criticisms.

On the news this evening Trump is rallying his supporters in Phoenix, promising to build "the Wall" along the Mexican border, along with angry bombast against the media and even some fellow Republicans. In *October*, China Mieville quotes Lenin: "One must always try to be as radical as reality itself." But what do we do when reality is more frightening than anything we can imagine?

August 26: Melbourne

Up early to speak at a panel on populism at Melbourne Writers Festival. This is the contribution of *Griffith Review* and the panel is chaired by the remarkably energetic founding editor, Julianne Schultz. She makes the point that populism and popular are different concepts, a distinction that seems lost on at least one of the questioners. But it's an enthusiastic audience, and one which seems clearly disturbed by current developments and the rise of popularly elected authoritarian rulers.

A couple of people come up to me afterwards with questions, and I'm unnecessarily abrupt, a pattern I too easily fall into. But I have coffee with Sophie Cunningham, author of both novels and non-fiction, whom I first met when she was a young editor as I wrote *Defying Gravity*, and we reflect on the changing terrain of identity politics. It's true that identity politics have become a minefield, where I often

---

14   Eric Hobsbawm, *The Age of Empire*, Abacus, London, 1994, p.3.

feel constrained to defend its excesses against right-wing attacks. I'm reminded of the awkward ABC television panel show, *Q and A*, when four of us queers were paired with the Reverend Fred Nile, who's led the anti-gay movement for forty years. (Nile's sat in the NSW Legislative Council on and off since 1981.) Being forced to confront him pulled the rest of us together, but also meant any intelligent discussion of different perspectives within the queer world was impossible. But attacks on identity politics too often assume that everyone starts from the same starting point. The American liberals who sigh for the pre-identity politics of Roosevelt's New Deal obliterate the reality that it privileged white men in almost all its programs.

I take the tram up Swanston Street to the State Library, where people are gathering for what will become the largest marriage rally to date. I wander through the crowds, a mix of ages, genders, ethnicities, with lots of prams and dogs. With Carol D'Cruz I listen to the first of too many speeches, then we duck into the multi-layered complex across the road.

We're in a food court at Melbourne Central, and the young man behind us is talking at full volume, exuberant from the excitement of the demonstration. I realise that this debate is so passionate because it's involving people on multiple levels. For many it is their first encounter with politics; but it is also pushing people to come out as queer in ways they may not have expected. Even people who seemed totally comfortable with their sexuality are suddenly confronted by discussions with colleagues, friends, family, that are unnerving. I hear stories of first-generation Chinese Australians talking to parents who've been receiving anti-marriage pamphlets in the mail, of snide remarks overheard that reveal a colleague to be deeply prejudiced.

That evening I go with Andrea Goldsmith to a concert version of Massenet's opera *Thaïs*. Written in 1894, it's the story of a courtesan won over to God by a young monk; and the libretto seems to foreshadow Freud in its constant tensions between sexuality and repression. We want a staged version, preferably lush and erotic, rather than the formal setting of a concert stage. I look round the audience, wonder at the way in which music written a hundred years ago still has resonance for so many people. One reads constant stories about the decline of opera, but I am more impressed by its staying power, by the reality that on any given night there will be literally hundreds of fully staged works played across the world. The cast singing tonight have sung in operas not only in the traditional operatic houses, but also in Guangzhou, in Edmonton, in Macau, in Mexico City.

I realise how lucky I was to grow up hearing classical music, and there are pieces—Tchaikovsky's *Capriccio Italien*, Rossini overtures—I associate with my Melbourne grandmother; others, such as Beethoven's *Emperor Concerto*, with my school. Growing up in Hobart there were few occasions to go to opera productions. But I would listen to operatic highlights on radio when we stayed with my grandmother in Melbourne—commercial radio has long since abandoned classical music. When I first visited Vienna in 1961 I saw a few operas, large scale, rather lumbering productions that suited a city still living off its imperial past. At one point in Wagner's *Flying Dutchman* I started to cry, though I no longer know what fears or desires had been tapped. At its best opera crosses the right and left spheres of the brain, appeals to both our emotions and our reason. When the music matches the action—the prisoners emerging from their underground cells in *Fidelio*; Violetta dying in *Traviata*; the two queens confronting each other in *Maria Stuarda*—this is, for me, the pinnacle of cultural imagination.

August 27: Melbourne

More body maintenance: I visit my masseur who works at the local gay sauna. M's qualified in myotherapy and does lots of gentle manipulation of my neck and upper back. He's worked at a couple of 'swingers' evenings', and confirms the stories I've already heard, the dearth of single women and the limits in the numbers—and surveillance—of single men who want to attend. "They drink a lot more than gay men who come here" he muses. "And they are a lot tidier."

September 1: Melbourne

I am on the thirty-fifth floor of a city building, the lights of the city carpeted below. In the thirty years or so that I've now lived here Melbourne has become a big city, the buildings that impressed me as a child in Hobart—one of our school texts referred to the Gothic forty-metres Manchester Unity Building as one of the great buildings of the Empire—now dwarfed by glass and concrete shards.

I'm here for a reception at the Melbourne Writers Festival, and the room buzzes with the noise of 150 egos. I move away from excited accounts of interviews and reviews and am introduced to several visiting writers from the Philippines. There's a lilt to Filipino English that immediately engages me: "I was a little in love with your country," I say, rather self-consciously. "Though I only know Manila."

I'd visited Manila three or four times during the 1990s, each time struggling to adjust to a massive metropolis choking for air, crumbling relics from the times of Spanish imperium side by side new skyscrapers, with shacks and corrugated iron shanties crowded into every available crevice, overflowing onto the potholed streets where young girls too young for motherhood crouched and begged, babies in their arms. On one trip a storm lashed Luzon, and brownouts slashed power across the city; on another I took a boat ride down the Manila River, the city unfolding into the river bends.

On an early trip in 1991 I wrote of staying at:

> a small guesthouse several blocks from Manila Bay, close to both the American Embassy and the posh Manila Yacht Club. Outside, the hotel roosters tethered to small poles scratched the ground, and small dogs and cats ran in and out of cramped hovels. Nearby is the zoo, a metaphor for the city, just as the immaculate Singapore Zoo represents the extent of that country's wealth and sophisticated surveillance. A small number of seemingly bored and unhappy animals—lions, giraffes, monkeys, a crocodile, even a donkey—live in small dank concrete enclosures, too dispirited even to complain. The zoo is surrounded by squatters, and even within its walls one

sees neat lines of washing hung out to dry. Zoos have their own particular smells, but in Manila the stench of unsewered water overwhelms that of the animals.

Inhumane and cramped zoos are not the preserve of poor countries. When I lived in Paris I was shocked by the enclosures at the Jardin des Plantes, made worse by the chic surroundings of the left bank: no washing lines there. I cringe reading those lines about the Manila Zoo today, but they grow out of the difficulty of coming to terms with being confronted simultaneously with splendour and misery.

At that time the best-known gay bar was the Library, established by Andrew de Real in 1986 on Adriatico Avenue in Malate, a café sized room with crumbling school books lining the walls. During one early regional AIDS meeting a group of us including Marina Mahathir, daughter of then Malaysian Prime Minister, went to the Library. Marina was a little diffident about entering the bar; her security guards, provided by the Philippines authorities, were even more so, and stayed outside, chatting awkwardly with the improbably young men who in turn guarded the bar. Security for Marina was not confined to the Philippines; some years later I took her to dinner in Melbourne, and we were accompanied by two very polite local police, who sat at a table discretely placed to be out of earshot but within, I assume, firing range.

On my next trip I was dispatched as the official emissary of La Trobe to visit several Manila Universities, and duly returned with two signed agreements for cooperation. At the University of the Philippines, a massive campus set within sprawling and not very well tended gardens, it was clear that my visit was no more than a ritual, although whichever ranking dignitary received me was happy to sign onto an agreement that was clearly one of several hundred. I had more success at Ateneo de Manila, founded by Jesuits in 1859, and one of the best Southeast Asian universities. Not only did we sign an agreement, but the following year a small group from La Trobe spent a few days on their campus inaugurating an exchange program which continues today. Like the University of the Philippines, Ateneo's main campus is set in the sprawling suburbs of Metro Manila, alongside one of the main city roads with its proliferation of fast food outlets, roadside stalls, and constant traffic, including the omnipresent Manila jitneys, half bus, half jeep, covered in garish designs and slogans. We were housed for three days in austere rooms, with hard, narrow beds and the frowning images of Catholic martyrs and saints patrolling our sleep. But we shared conversation and meals with staff from Ateneo; in one discussion about HIV a couple of European Jesuits claimed that Filipinos engaged in less casual sex than did Westerners, a claim met by knowing smiles of amusement from a couple of local academics.

"I used to encourage people to visit the Philippines", says one of the visiting writers, "but not now, with our President ..." I nod, aware that Prime Minister Turnbull has just spoken of Australian military support against ISIS fighters in Mindanao, thus making us complicit with a regime that is encouraging extra-judicial killings. Both of us are slightly embarrassed, feeling we should apologise for what is done by governments in our name. For all the rhetoric about our closeness to Asia there is a remarkable lack of interest in Australia in the decline of democratic freedoms in the Philippines, Thailand, Cambodia.

On the late-night news tensions are increasing in Korea. Pessimists remind us of the way tensions between the United States and Cuba during the Kennedy years came close to unleashing a nuclear confrontation.

September 5: Melbourne

I am reading my friend and colleague Judith Brett's *Enigmatic Mr. Deakin*. I first met Judy when she was a young graduate student in England, wrote occasionally for her when she edited *Meanjin* in the early 1980s, and encouraged her to come to La Trobe, where we were colleagues over several decades. I've heard stories about Deakin over the past few years, as she's been working on the book, but I didn't expect to be as enthralled as I am.

In 1887 Deakin sailed to London via Ceylon, Aden and the Suez Canal; my first trip to Europe followed the same route, three quarters of a century later. Within a decade, developments in jet aircraft made the sea voyage unsustainable, but in 1961 my family spent several weeks at sea, travelling on a P&O liner. Like Deakin we stopped at Colombo and Aden, where my father proudly haggled for a suitcase which promptly fell apart as soon as we set sail. Seaboard life was a lot less formal than it would have been for Deakin, but there were probably similar rituals, such as the silly partying on crossing the Equator, and the fancy-dress evenings. We disembarked in Marseille, and took a slow train to Paris, my first real sight of a European city. The continuity between Deakin's world and mine as a student was in some ways greater than between the early 1960s and today.

Coffee with Todd Fernando, who's writing a doctoral thesis on Indigenous homosexuality. He's charming and smart, and not quite thirty. We talk about the importance of generations, and whether the experience of Indigenous Australian queers is necessarily different to that of others. I suggest that there are three generations of gay men, marked by major shifts in social attitudes towards homosex: those, like me, who came of age when we were criminalised and feared disclosure; those who came of age in the early years of AIDS, when the equation of sex and death was commonplace; and those, like him, whose experiences came in a period of much greater social liberalism and effective HIV therapies.

My generation first learnt about our possible selves through books; his through film. Now adolescents have access to enormous amounts of imagery and information through the internet and seem to be 'coming out' earlier than before. My nephew, Peter, came out on Facebook while still at school, and his mother rang to tell us as we were watching Kurt come out to his father on the television show *Glee*. Yes, dividing whole populations by generation is of limited use: the talk of the 'baby boomers' ignores the deep divisions of class and education that marked the experience of the Vietnam War, when young men both went to war and were imprisoned as draft dodgers. But certain experiences are linked to age, whatever else divides us, and this becomes more marked as technological change hastens.

I am increasingly asked what lessons radicals today can learn from my generation, perhaps a reflection of the strange nostalgia of the Left that showed itself in young voters flocking to support Bernie Sanders and Jeremy Corbyn. The most important is that while gay liberation asserted our identity as homosexual, we also saw ourselves as part of a larger move to transform society, rather than only concerned with our own immediate goals, although reassuring ourselves that it was fine to be homosexual was central to everything we did.

Much like the feminists of the time we lived our politics, and for gay men that meant casual sex which was as much about creating community as it was about instant gratification. On an informal speaking tour through the States for my first book I was billeted with a couple of guys in Cincinnati who asked me politely with whom I'd prefer to sleep, as if a shared politics was enough to produce desire. What we did share was a sense that we needed to declare our sexuality, confront the demons, both internal and external, that plagued us. In one of the first gay liberation books Peter Fisher wrote: "Many people will go to enormous lengths to avoid seeing themselves as homosexuals, no matter how extensive their homosexual activity may be."[15] Peter was one of the founders of the Gay Activists Alliance; I recall a scrawny young man with a mass of curly brown hair who took me back to his basement apartment near Columbia University one night.

Gay liberationists scorned the older world of bars, carefully screened from the streets, and cautious street cruising; instead we organised dances and used meetings to hook up. One of my memories of the early 1970s in New York is of leaving a performance of *Lucia di Lammermoor* at Lincoln Centre to take the orange number one train uptown to a gay dance at Columbia, the strains of bel canto melding into jubilant disco. The world of gay liberation was very small, and when I look back at the writing of the time I am reminded how interconnected we all were, long before the development of large community organisations and openly gay professionals. Today there are medical clinics that advertise to 'the LGBT community' with glossy promises of thicker

---

15   Peter Fisher, *The Gay Mystique*, Stein & Day, 1972, p.15.

hair and whiter teeth; then we swapped names of sympathetic doctors and told stories of unsympathetic treatment in VD clinics. We had virtually no role models, unlike kids who today struggle with 'coming out'; the few depictions of lesbians and gay men in popular culture invariably presented us as either comic or tragic.

Vito Russo, whom I first met when he waited on me in a West Village restaurant, has written at length of the ways in which homosex started to infuse movies in the 1960s. He would gather friends in his apartment in Chelsea to show us clips from movies he was beginning to discover. The first film I remember that spoke to my sexual possibilities was John Schlesinger's *Darling*, even though the homosexual character was secondary. We were struggling to make sense of ourselves, with little guidance, grasping at whatever pieces of information came our way, the few novels *(Giovanni's Room; The Well of Loneliness; The City and the Pillar)* and those few psychology texts that didn't condemn us. I was outraged by David Reuben's best seller, *Everything you wanted to know about sex ... but were afraid to ask*, which repeated old stereotypes and invented a couple of new ones, such as the claim that "food seems to have a mysterious fascination for homosexuals". (His publisher refused to buy the British rights to my first book because of my criticisms of Reuben). For us what was crucial was *coming out*: by declaring our sexual identity we believed we could change everything.

Gay Liberationists—we stressed the capitalisation to distinguish ourselves from the more single-issue gay *activists*—were determined to position ourselves as part of a broader radical movement and insisted on our ties to the black movement. Leonard Bernstein attracted Tom Wolfe's scorn when he courted the Black Panthers; the New York Gay Liberation Front sent a contingent to several Panther sponsored conventions in late 1970. I have a vague memory of confusion and frustration at the November Revolutionary People's Constitutional Convention in Washington DC, where the gay liberation contingent gathered at St. Stephen's Church in multifarious caucuses and rap sessions but remained largely irrelevant to the main meeting. The DC police imposed various restrictions on the larger meeting, which failed not only to incorporate sexual liberation but to present a united front for radical back activism. Perhaps fittingly the longest entry in my diary for those few days is about the long shared ride back to New York City where: "We got lost three times and it was a very long trip." Indeed.

It's wet and cold, but that evening I drive down to the Lesbian and Gay Archives to hand over a collection of magazines and T-shirts. The Archives already possess a tantalising collection of ephemera, and I've brought a hand knitted sweater with the image of Lou Reed (from his album *Transformer*) knitted into the fabric. I admit that I have no memory of where it came from, and Nick Henderson, queer history's most professional archivist, promises to track it down. Some years ago I contributed a rather decaying collection of matchbooks from gay venues, souvenirs of an epoch when every bar and restaurant was wreathed in cigarette smoke, and handed out matchbooks with their logos and addresses. Nick made a slide presentation which I used as the basis for a talk a few years later.

September 6: Melbourne

Back in Mario's, this time with cartoonist and activist, Sam Wallman, who talks about union organising among migrant workers on the fringes of the economy. He's been meeting with people from the Rohingya community, currently under siege from Burmese troops.

Sam has been asked to do cartoons for the *New York Times*, now setting up their Australian site, and we talk about the constant Australian fear of becoming too American. I wrote about this a decade ago, in a little book called *Fifty First State?*, which Russ Radcliffe at Scribe had commissioned. This was during the Presidency of George W Bush, and lasting anger at the disaster of the second Iraq War. Since then we've lived through Julia Gillard's romance with Barack Obama and Hillary Clinton, the Anglophilia of Abbott and the initial strained relations between Turnbull and Trump. But there remains the reflex, slowly developed since World War II, of seeing the United States as our ultimate protector, to whom we need pay homage through providing troops for its overseas adventures. I always found it odd that

Australian troop have been sent to Afghanistan by five successive governments as part of a deployment by NATO, which is, after all, an alliance of North Atlantic states. But if Australia can send contestants to the Eurovision Song Contest, is mine an outmoded concern with geographic specificity?

The pages of my copy of *Fifty First State?* are slightly faded, a reminder of the transitory nature of political commentary. Looking back, I see that talk of Australia being Americanised can be traced back to the Gold Rush of the 1850s. We live in a constant state of anxiety about our national identity, ever alert to the need to proclaim our Australianness even while seeking approval from London and New York. Were I rewriting that book today I would need to pay more attention to global warming, to the rise of China, to the seeming decline of global commitments to human rights and democratic norms. But the dominant theme, our obsession with the United States, continues, even though writing in 2006 I anticipated neither a President Obama nor a President Trump.

September 7: *Melbourne*

Kate Millett died today. I bought her *Sexual Politics* at Honolulu airport in 1970 and was influenced by it as I have been by very few books (she is the most cited author in my own first book). Millett's call for "a cultural revolution" and her final hope that: "We shall even be able to retire sex from the harsh realities of politics, but not until we have created a world we can beat out of the desert we inhabit", echoed the utopian language of the time, but more than other feminist writings she paid considerable attention to male homosexuals, and broke through the reluctance of early second wave feminism to acknowledge homosexuality in general. I heard her speak late in 1979 in a packed lecture theatre at Columbia University, when Millett was pushed to declare herself as bisexual; she had already come out at a meeting of the lesbian organisation, Daughters of Bilitis.

Some years later Kate founded a feminist art colony in upstate New York and I visited her with Joshua Sippen, whose family lived close by. In a note she wrote to Carol D'Cruz in connection with the *After Homosexual* project, she recalled Josh and me in Bermuda shorts. Kate was gentle and soft spoken, but the drawing she gave me, a Japanese style abstract, was harsh in angry red. Water damage sadly destroyed the print many years ago. The collective funded themselves by growing Christmas trees, which surrounded the grounds in short tubs.

When she wrote *Sexual Politics*, Kate was married to a male Japanese sculptor; when she died she was survived by her wife, Sophie Keir. Kate's life and work symbolised the changes in attitudes to sexuality over the past half century, but also the danger of forgetting that sexuality is fluid, malleable, and heavily influenced by social possibilities.

September 17: Melbourne

Why was I so dissatisfied with Raul Peck's film, *I Am not your Negro*? It's a very evocative documentary, based almost entirely on Baldwin's own words, and taking off from the book he planned to write about the intertwined deaths of three black leaders: Medgar Evans (shot 1963), Malcolm X (1965) and Martin Luther King (1968). Peck juxtaposes images of Baldwin speaking, in halls on and television, with cuts from American films and advertisements, to draw parallels between the hegemonic racism of Baldwin's America with its persistence in police brutality today. There has been consistent praise for the film, modified by the reluctance to acknowledge Baldwin's homosexuality as central to his politics. This disturbed me, because it also meant eliding the real resistance to Baldwin that came from many black Americans *because* of his homosexuality, which is a constant theme in his novels, if not his essays. But to speak honestly of the homophobic attacks on Baldwin by writers such as Ralph Ellison would further complicate the idea of racism as the singular curse of America. (In his essay *Notes on a Native Son* Black Panther leader Eldridge Cleaver attacked Baldwin with a homophobia that was extreme even for its time). Baldwin risked being beaten up both as a black man and gay, and although it is easier to hide one's sexuality than one's race this carries its own penalties. A couple of years ago I went with a younger Korean man to buy wine at the local bottle shop. "They were looking at us", J— said to me, "Because I'm Asian." Well, perhaps. But perhaps, too, because we were two men together, or because of the age difference.

Baldwin inspired me more than any of the other great gay writers of his generation. I must have already read, surreptitiously, *Giovanni's Room* before I first went to the US; my own, now tattered Dell paperback of *Another Country* was bought as soon as I arrived at Cornell. I had not yet met him when I wrote *Homosexual*, but he was clearly a significant inspiration; a few years later I sat, nervous, in a small radio studio in Sydney and spoke for half an hour with him on a late-night program, marvelling at the rich cadences of his voice, an amalgam of black ministry and hints of British camp. He spoke of his despair at the state of America, the deep layers of racism and violence that reverberate through his most recent novel at the time, *If Beale Street Could Talk*.

Baldwin was then living in France, and I used the excuse of a research trip to Europe—I was lazily researching the international student movement, a more interesting topic than I'd expected—to visit him in St Paul de Vence, a village inland from Nice. Oddly—for I am not very visually aware—I recall the day in vivid colours: a two-storey stone house, off-white against the angry blue of the Provencal sky, the green fronds of palm trees, the red and gold and purple of a garden bursting with flowers, where we sat and spoke for several hours. His driver took me back to Nice, where my diary tells me I read Agatha Christie in French, possibly inspired by our conversation.

Seven years later I re-met Baldwin at an event in New York organised by Black and White Men Together, a group founded in 1980 in San Francisco to allow gay men to cut across racial barriers. The meeting was held in the West Village building that housed America's first gay synagogue and was apparently his first appearance before an acknowledged gay audience. The meeting was followed by a dinner in Brooklyn, which became increasingly riotous as the evening wore on. My diary reminds me I went home with someone from the dinner, but he has long faded from memory.

September 18: Melbourne

I spend the morning chatting with colleagues at the University where I taught politics for a quarter of a century. La Trobe's Bundoora campus sits in the northeast suburbs of Melbourne, surrounded by a moat, and the occasional wading bird, a cluster of brown-brick buildings set around a central meeting square. I came to La Trobe when Australian Universities were transitioning from aping Oxbridge pretentions to becoming corporate enterprises, in which students become clients and layers of professional bureaucrats replace part time academic administrators. As Universities compete for swelling student numbers with expensive television ads and massive hoardings, the numbers of people employed who actually teach and research—which all Universities agree is their primary mission—declines, and teaching is increasingly put on-line or farmed out to casual staff, ambitious young doctoral graduates who drive endlessly between outer suburban campuses trying to find a permanent foothold.

It's good that tertiary numbers are increasing, but successive governments have ignored the extra resources needed to support students without the comfortable cultural capital of most cabinet ministers. Graduation ceremonies at La Trobe are moving because of the enormous pride of families, often first-generation migrants, whose child is the first in the family to go to University. When I came to La Trobe we spoke of the "Agora Greeks", and for a time it seemed as if an invisible line separated 'wog' and 'Anglo' students. Now the student body is considerably more varied: more female, more multi-racial, in part because our universities are increasingly hostage to an international student market, which could be disrupted in ways that would literally bankrupt the sector. But the diversity also reflects the reality that the northern suburbs of Melbourne are among the most ethnically varied parts of the country.

In my lifetime the Australian population has trebled and diversified enormously. The first stamps issued by the Commonwealth of Australia in 1913 showed a kangaroo superimposed on a map of the continent, coloured white to proclaim the policy of excluding non-Europeans.

When I was an undergraduate in the first half of the 1960s, unease about the White Australia Policy was growing. My parents attended a public meeting in Hobart, and I was very proud that they supported ending the policy. And the University Union sponsored several debates, at one of which I first met Gough Whitlam, then Deputy Leader of the Opposition, who was deliberately daring the party to discipline him for demanding changes to its policy. I recall a debate between the poet James McAuley, then Professor of English in Tasmania, and John Marriott, already a long time Liberal Senator. In tones that foreshadowed Pauline Hanson, Marriott spoke of preserving our national character; in response McAuley, a leonine presence with considerable charisma, responded that to thrive, national character needed to constantly change.

McAuley was already an established poet and right-wing political figure when he came to Tasmania the same year I enrolled as an undergraduate. He never taught me, but because I was active in student politics he courted me, and I fell under his spell, as he carefully negotiated an end to the black ban placed on the University's Philosophy department after it sacked Sydney Orr for alleged sexual misconduct with a student. The case played out for a decade, a tawdry episode which involved an alleged shooting attempt on Orr just before Christmas 1959. As his house was only a few hundred metres away from ours we were properly titillated. McAuley had learnt politics through his involvement with the anti-communist movement that led to a split in the Labor Party and the creation of the Democratic Labor Party, but he was less interested in my Labor sympathies than in bringing the student union on side in resolving the Orr case. He sat with us in the University cafeteria, sharing stodgy English puddings, and allowing us the illusion that we were part of the careful settlement being hammered out at the end of 1963. (Cassandra Pybus's account of the matter, *Gross Moral Turpitude*, virtually ignores any student role in the process.) It's a sobering reflection that I first encountered politics through someone whose positions on the Vietnam War would place us on bitterly divided sides later in the decade.

Few students today have the sort of informal contacts with academic staff that we took for granted, and which so enriched university life. Now universities have become massive business operations, run by ever expanding bureaucracies, in which personal contact is increasingly replaced by online transactions. And, as Sally Wood has pointed out, the student press mattered. Thanks to her book I know that I was "the SRC's nominated censor on the staff of *Togatus*", a position I had long forgotten.[16]

September 25: Melbourne

Coffee with former colleagues of Anthony's at the Australian Research Centre in Sex, Health and Society, based at La Trobe. Anthony had begun his academic career studying the reproduction of crocodiles, which took him to Darwin; after years camping out by dangerous rivers, he refused to ever camp again. He drifted into health research, and after moving to Melbourne at the end of 1990 became one of the founding staff members of what was then the Centre for the Study of Sexually Transmissible Diseases, now ARCSHS. In his career he published almost two hundred papers, with 136 co-authors. He was the lead investigator of the major empirical study of Australian sexual behaviour, often referred to as an Australian Kinsey report,[17] which involved hundreds of detailed phone interviews across the country, all managed by a group of women based in Newcastle, New South Wales. After his death his co-investigators invited me to contribute to one of the papers, so I became his official 137th collaborator. On one paper he included the names of our cats among the acknowledgements, fairly certain no-one would notice.

AIDS opened up new possibilities for sexuality research, a natural progression from my involvement in gay politics. In 1983 I was invited to the University of California, Santa Cruz, where I co-taught a course

---

16 Sally Percival Wood, *Dissent: The Student Press in 1960s Australia*, Scribe, 2017, p.96.
17 See the special issue of the *Australian and New Zealand Journal of Public Health*, 27:2, April 2003.

on gay and lesbian politics with Politics Professor, David Thomas. The Santa Cruz campus had been created by Governor Ronald Reagan, it was said, to house students away from any major metropolitan centre. Santa Cruz was a sleepy seaside town and the campus nestled in the redwoods, a mile or so away from the main drag which led down to the beach. But it was also a university which sought to develop new and interdisciplinary approaches, and one of the first to offer a subject in Lesbian and Gay Studies. One of my duties was to deliver a public lecture, which was chaired by Sheldon Andelson, a gay businessman and major Democrat funder, whom Governor Jerry Brown had appointed to the University of California Board of Regents. There was dinner at the Chancellor's house with Andelson, who said that raising money for politicians was a hobby, but also a way to legitimise being gay. Four years later he died, as did so many men of his generation.

Teaching gay politics was not without its tensions; when the personal and the political overlapped there were tears, anger, outbursts of petulance. For the only time in my academic career I had a brief affair with one of my students, not then frowned upon as it would be today. Luckily G— was remarkably sensible, and we avoided any of the problems that could have arisen. I had more problems with my co-lecturer, who at one point stormed out of the classroom, for reasons I no longer remember.

What did we teach? I look back at the curriculum and it seems a combination of my preoccupations at the time, reflected in my recent book *The Homosexualization of America* and David Thomas's intimate knowledge of the gay politics of the Bay Area. We brought several visitors to the class, mainly women; lesbian historian Lillian Faderman gave a guest lecture, as did Gayle Rubin and Peggy Cruickshank, who was teaching a similar subject at San Francisco State. (Faderman and Rubin would each write several of the most influential works in queer studies.) And David invited a small group from the Sisters of Perpetual Indulgence, gay men who had formed a counter-order to both raise money and satirise the Catholic Church, arguably the most powerful force for homophobia in many parts of the world. A group of Sisters in Sydney would become one of the most visible presences at queer demonstrations for many years.

Santa Cruz had elected one of the first openly gay mayors in the United States, John Laird (Mayor 1983–4), and it was already known as a queer centre; we played gay volleyball on the beach once a week, and went to post-game barbecues in the hills, which felt a more comfortable gay world than the frenzied sex slums and intellectual hothouse back in New York. I recall sitting in the sun and reading episodes of Armistead Maupin's *Tales of the City*, which appeared daily in the *San Francisco Chronicle*. He was writing what became the fourth book of the series, *Babycakes*, where Michael, the central gay character, comes across an advertisement for an "I'm Safe" piece of jewellery—what 'safe' means is not defined—and throws it away: "It was too much", he thinks.[18] Many of us felt that way at the time.

In the fall of 1983 my agent, Peter Ginsberg, had brought me together with the editor Loretta Barrett at Doubleday to write a book about the unfolding crisis. I had already been reading voraciously about epidemics and epidemiology; in New York I went to Gay Men's Health Crisis training for 'buddies' and crossed over to Brooklyn to talk with a soft-spoken Haitian physician, who saw his community as completely overshadowed by the gay organisations that were developing. I was taken around the AIDS wards in San Francisco General and given considerable help by a couple of Congressional aides, who were working to craft the first official federal responses. My diary records the names of many of the first generation of AIDS activists and researchers, of meetings and conferences which I can barely remember. Along the way I wrote several journalistic pieces, one for the *Village Voice* which the journalist Richard Goldstein edited ferociously, and I hung out in the Doubleday offices, using their phones and computers.

I seem to have written much of *AIDS in the Mind of America* without any fixed abode: I was moving, restlessly, between New York, Santa Cruz and San Francisco, trying to maintain the relationship with Joshua. At one stage Joshua had intended to become a therapist and

---

18   Armistead Maupin, *Babycakes*, Harper & Row, 1984, p.55.

seemed to have a far more intimate relationship with his therapist than he allowed to me. In due course I decided that I, too, needed therapy, and arranged appointments with a psychologist who lived, predictably, on the Upper West Side, and had offices arranged so one client never caught a glimpse of another. I saw my therapist in a rather desultory fashion for a few months, arranging to coincide with nearby visits by one of my best friends, theatre critic Don Shewey, who reminds me that when we first met, in the offices of the *Soho News*, I "had a flower stuck, ironically, behind one ear." We would meet after our respective appointments and eat in one of the Upper West Side's Cuban Chinese restaurants. Perhaps my greatest satisfaction with therapy was the illusion that it made me a genuine New Yorker.

While I was in San Francisco the Australian Health Minister, Neal Blewett, visited to learn more about the developing epidemic, and I spent time with him and his advisor, Bill Bowtell, who would become a central figure in the Australian response. I organised a meeting for them with some of the leading AIDS figures in the city, and found myself taking notes, which presumably are carefully secreted somewhere in government archives. I'd known Blewett for many years as a fellow political scientist and had spent time with him in Adelaide where he was professor of politics at Flinders University, before his election to Parliament in 1977. He became Health Minister during the first two Hawke governments and was central to Australia pioneering one of the world's most innovative responses to the AIDS epidemic. He was then married to Jill; she died in a domestic accident in 1988, after which Neal moved in with a man he'd originally known at University, the anthropologist Robert Brain. I should have guessed that Neal was bisexual after he stayed briefly at my place during the 1980 election campaign, but Neal, though he found a trashy gay novel on my bookshelves as an escape from the campaign trail, had perfected the art of discretion. He outed himself to Prime Minister Paul Keating in 1994 when he was appointed High Commissioner to London; it was a mark of how far things had changed that Keating, who voted against decriminalisation of homosexuality back in 1973, was unfazed that his representative in London had a male partner.

In April 1985 I was at the first International AIDS Conference in Atlanta, where Reagan's Secretary of Health, Margaret Heckler, spoke of developing a vaccine against HIV within two years (over two decades later none has been yet developed). As home of the Centers for Disease Control, Atlanta was the site for much of the first research on AIDS. There were several thousand people at the Conference, which is regarded as the founding event of the International AIDS Society, on whose Council I would later sit. I hung out with a group of guys from London, where the Terrence Higgins Trust had been already set up, and was taken around 'gay Atlanta', with its very clear demarcation between 'white' and 'black' gay bars.

By the spring of 1985 the book was done; we sat around a table in the mid-town Doubleday offices trying to come up with an appropriate title. One chapter was called 'contagious desire'; I regret not using that. (The British publishers settled on the name *AIDS and the New Puritanism*.) That week I came to meet Loretta, who was taking me to lunch to celebrate the imminent publication of the book, when the elevator doors almost closed on Jackie Kennedy, then an associate editor at Doubleday. As we descended 37 floors Loretta introduced me as one of their authors; I remember nothing of what I said. My lasting image is of Jackie walking away down the long marble corridor towards Park Avenue, seeming much smaller than she did on television. Reading through the acknowledgements to that book conjures up vivid memories of living between the coasts, even if some of the names have faded to a quiet sepia.

The following winter I was back in the US to promote the book, which meant a number of radio interviews and bookshop signings in the midst of a particularly brutal winter, although I did get to Miami for a few days.

So many young men died. A couple of years after I left Santa Cruz, I visited one of my students, Michael Perlman, half asleep in a hospital ward overlooking a cruelly blue ocean. Michael was only a decade younger than me, once lean and intense, now gaunt with pain. "It's not fair" he said bitterly, but illness and early death never are. Michael died in 1989, in that awful period when obituaries and funerals crowded the pages of gay papers.

Writing this now unlocks a long list of young men whose lives touched mine in various ways, and who should now be growing old with me. How does one choose whom to remember? When Terry Bell died, at the end of 1989, I went into the back garden and cried: Terry had been a gay liberationist, a few years younger than me, who combined a ferocious politics with an easy sexuality. "Very beautiful" was Gore Vidal's verdict, when Terry interviewed him on his visit to Sydney. In the mid-1970s he was one of the founding editors of the short-lived journal *Working Papers in Sex, Science and Culture*, along with my friend Meaghan Morris, which introduced Australian readers to current French psychoanalytic thought. I lost touch with Terry, and I know his role as an activist during the epidemic through the work of Robert Ariss, who died himself five years later.

Robert and I were members of one of the government's advisory committees on AIDS, and he used to stay with us when meetings brought him to Melbourne. He was writing the doctoral thesis which would be published posthumously (*Against Death: The Practice of Living with AIDS*). The most revealing moment in that book is when Robert allows himself into the narrative and tells the story of being interviewed about the slowness of the pharmaceutical approval process: "'But I don't feel angry' I confessed with some embarrassment. He (the journalist) looked rather disconcerted, and after a few more futile attempts … packed up his equipment and continued on his quest for a vocal angry gay activist".[19] Robert was an intensely private person, and his funeral was a clumsy event, his parents slipping in and out of a side door to avoid meeting any of his gay friends. I realised, too late, that too much of his life remained unsaid.

---

19   Robert Ariss, *Against Death: The Practice of Living with AIDS*, Gordon and Breach, Amsterdam, 1997, p.192.

Two of my former lovers died of AIDS—Barry Prothero and Antoine Pingaud—and I feel slightly guilty that they were not the names who surfaced immediately. But they died far from me, Barry in London and Antoine in Paris, and we had become strangers. It is one of the myths of gay life that former partners become best friends, when often the burning out of an affair allows buried resentments and criticisms to surface, so that it is too painful to remain in touch. Years after we broke up I stayed with each of them, first with Barry in London, where he lived in an untidy squat, then with Antoine in Paris, in the small apartment he'd bought in the rapidly gentrifying Twentieth Arrondissement. Both visits underlined the distance that grows quickly once love fades: I wrote a short story at the end of 1980 called 'The End of All My Affairs' that is too raw to quote.

September 28: Sydney

Richard is sure he remembered my trip to Ulan Bator. That is now fifty years ago: Richard Walsh was International VP of the National Union of Students, and we were supposed to meet at an international students' meeting in Mongolia, obviously a Soviet front. He has even recorded a memory of my "droll report ... I had merely missed unbelievable cold, modest hospitality and predictably tendentious speeches".[20]

In fact, the meeting was in Leningrad, and I have two black and white photographs of the delegates, young men dressed in ties and ill-fitting suits, on the banks of the Neva. We gathered in the draughty high-ceilinged dining room, partitioned so the party minders ate slightly apart, all of them men and far older than the students they claimed to represent. The hotel was Soviet grey, with shrivelled old women keeping guard on hard chairs placed at the end of the corridor. We were taken to the Summer Palace of Catherine the Great, glimmering rococo blue and silver buildings in carefully pruned gardens, and to visit a youth camp, where I blurted out my surprise at how happy

---

20   Richard Walsh, 'From Ulan Bator to literary fame', in Carolyn D'Cruz & Mark Pendleton (eds), *After Homosexual*, UWA Publishing, 2013, p.15.

everyone seemed. Looking back, I can see my interest in international activism stoked by those first long, smoky meetings in Leningrad.

We are sitting at the north end of the city, a windy promontory of offices on the approach to the Harbour Bridge. Richard is still working in publishing and has called for a remaking of our political system in a small book, *Reboot: a democracy makeover to empower Australian voters*. In the face of his critique I find myself defending existing institutions in a surprisingly Burkean fashion.

I first met Richard through intervarsity debating, at about the same time as he co-founded *OZ Magazine*, a blast of satire at the end of the Menzies era. When he was editor of *POL Magazine* he published the first piece I ever wrote on homosexuality, an anonymous comment on the play *Boys in the Band*, which had been reviewed very unsympathetically in a previous edition. A couple of years later Richard became chief executive of the distinguished but moribund publishers, Angus & Robertson, and bought the Australian rights to my first book.

Richard's memory of another trip is more accurate: in the late 1970s we drove together from Paris to Frankfurt to attend the Book Fair. En route we stopped in Strasbourg, where the car needed attention. Richard recalls me flirting with the garage guy, but he is not sure in which language.

I'm in Sydney to receive an honorary degree from Macquarie University. As everything else changes, our universities cling to British ceremonial for graduation ceremonies, and I enjoy donning the scarlet hood and cloak, ready for a cameo appearance at Hogwarts. We proceed up the aisle, followed by the bearer of the mace, and I am tempted to giggle. Luckily the Deputy Chancellor, Elizabeth Crouch, has the skills of a minor royal, and the ceremony proceeds seamlessly, and with a certain dignity as almost 200 new graduands cross the stage, anxious in high heels and new suits, and doff their caps to the Chancellor.

Flying back to Melbourne I'm struck by the tailfins: of the planes lined up at the airport; other than Qantas they are all Asian or Middle Eastern. One of my long-abandoned collections was of airline timetables, from a period when most major European lines flew to Australia and companies like Emirates and China Eastern were still to be imagined. It's a reminder of how the world has changed since a boyhood lived during the dwindling of European empires. An early political memory is the Bandung Conference in 1955, when Indonesia's President Sukarno hosted Asian and African leaders in the first steps towards building a non-aligned movement in the Cold War. As an earnest schoolboy I wrote an essay, long lost, about the significance of the meeting, possibly for a competition on the ABC's children's program *The Argonauts*, which shaped several generations of Australian children. The following year came the events around Egypt's annexation of the Suez Canal and the Russian invasion of Hungary, and I started to follow international politics more seriously.

October 3: Melbourne

Already the number of ballots returned in the marriage poll exceeds the participation rate in most democratic elections. But we still need to keep campaigning, say the Equality folk. They repeat this, perhaps too often, in the ritzy upstairs room at Crown Casino where nearly 300 people have gathered for an evening of *fun*raising. For $150 we get to graze and drink with other supporters, and to bid on auction items ranging from Marquee tickets for the Melbourne Cup to personal consultations with a bridal couturier. The most generous estimate of what the evening might return is that it could buy a couple of minutes of advertising on prime TV time.

I feel old and short: the crowd are primarily young professionals, the men mainly gay, the women more ambiguous. Genuinely moving speeches from Campaign director Tiernan Brady, who'd been central in the Irish campaign to amend the Constitution to allow gay marriage in 2015, and Labor Senator Penny Wong, who talks a lot about 'Australian values'. She and I spoke on a panel last year when I acknowledged that despite my cynicism about marriage I could hardly be on the same side as Cardinal Pell against Penny Wong. The crowd tonight seem like any random group of young urban professionals, very few of them veterans of earlier queer movements. "The most interesting question", I remark to Tiernan, "is where all these energies will go after the ballot". "Into community organising," he says, "Not politics."

This was not the world we expected getting on for fifty years ago when the contemporary gay movement emerged, and we took tentative steps towards claiming equality. 'Equality' then meant the end of criminalisation and enforced psychiatry, but it also meant a sense of community with others who were oppressed and a desire to radically transform society. Now the marriage movement seems bent on assimilation into society as is, and brave talk of creating new forms of family and community have largely disappeared.

October 8: Melbourne

There are over 400 people in the grand foyer of the Melbourne Town Hall for the inaugural Coming Back Out Ball. This is the brainchild of the extraordinary Tristan Meecham—dancer; performance artist; event entrepreneur—who sought an event to honour "LGBTI elders". More women here than men, most of us over 60—"The women", I'm told, "are happier to acknowledge they're ageing"—a three course meal and a string of legendary performers. Gerry Connolly welcomes us in his drag persona as the Queen; Carlotta, founder of the Kings Cross drag show *Les Girls* more than half a century ago, totters onto the stage in impossibly high heels; Robyn Archer, cabaret artist and artistic director, sings Lorenz Hart's 'Bewitched, Bothered and Bewildered', noting that she, a gay woman, was singing an ostensibly heterosexual love song written by a man who hid his desires for other men. And Deborah Cheetham, Indigenous opera singer and composer, who took the theme song from *Evita* and turned the lyrics into a song for marriage equality, brings us all to our feet. Tristan, a compact man in tuxedo with *Kinky Boots* platform shoes, gives an emotional speech of thanks to his elders, a phrase that makes the Peter Pan in me cringe.

Drag queens, acrobats, sequins, dinner suits, wigs, a couple of people on walkers, and one man with his guide dog: this was a snapshot of the queer world, past and present, but it built upon an extraordinary week. The Ball culminated a two-day workshop on "LGBTI Ageing and Aged Care", which had drawn 200 people to a Collins Street hotel, many of whom were here tonight. Early gay liberation meetings took place in small rooms or university campuses; now our events sprawl across the City, and the Town Hall displays rainbow flags.

The day after the Ball social media lit up with enthusiastic comments. My own post mortem took place in a large gilded Italianate café, with three gay men: Nick Henderson and I tantalise the others with glimpses of the evening. I start talking with Dino Hodge about his life and work in the Northern Territory, some of which is recorded in his book *Did you meet any Malagas?* (1993). I'd met Dino when I visited Anthony in Darwin in the winter of 1990, and we went to the 'Queen's Ball'. The evening featured a visiting drag star from Sydney, who unleashed a series of racist and sexist jokes. "Darwin has changed", remarked Dino, and so has the country: none of the events I've been to over the past week could have happened even twenty years ago. Ironically the marriage poll has revealed huge wells of acceptance, often in unexpected places, such as the Rugby League Grand Final crowd who cheered US rapper Macklemore's 'Same Love', to the fury of the no campaign.

There's anger in 'the community', but alongside a certain sentimentality, expressed in constant messages about caring for each other. This has led, probably inevitably, to a certain amount of hyperbole; at an opening event of the Melbourne International Arts Festival the Director spoke of this as "the most difficult time for the LGBT community ever", which ignores the far darker times of police persecution and AIDS deaths. There's also, to be honest, something of a search for victimhood. Yes, the poll has unleashed some nasty and threatening cases of homophobia, including several random acts and threats of violence. But hunting down every instance of overt support for the 'no' case, and posting it constantly on social media, conflates hatred with resistance to change, and only furthers the feeling of being under siege. That a skywriter smokes "Vote No" over Sydney Harbor is not, itself, homophobic, and best left to fade away.

But the campaign picks at old scars, and thousands of people across the country feel they are forced to relive adolescent traumas, to come out again, in the spotlight of national attention. One of my friends spoke at length of her fears about talking to her family, above all her deeply religious mother, and her relief when her mother told her she'd voted yes. I want to dismiss the fears and anxieties every mention of the no case provokes when I come across words from Nelly Sachs:

> We are so sorely hurt
> We feel that we must die
> If the street throws a harsh word at us.[21]

October 13: Melbourne

The Forum on Flinders Street is one of the world's great kitsch theatres. Built in 1929 in the Moorish revival style, popular in the late nineteenth century for theatres and synagogues, it features a cavernous hall, lined with pseudo-Roman statues, and a deep blue ceiling studded with lights. For two weeks the Forum is home to the anti-Trump centrepiece of this year's Melbourne Festival, Taylor Mac's very queer *History of Popular Music in America*. Over twenty-four hours—four slabs of six hours—Mac sings, camps, dances, talks, involves the audience in the history of the United States, backed by musicians, dancers, acrobats and anxious recruits from the audience, whom he drags on stage as living props.

Tonight's show covers the second half of the nineteenth century, complete with an audience re-enactment of the Civil War, in which our weapons are gestures and ping-pong balls. The festival publicity didn't tell us that he calls his show a "radical faerie realness ritual"— nor that 'judy' eschews gendered pronouns. But as Nic Holas wrote on Facebook: "Last night, I embraced my queer siblings from all over the country. My privilege meant I knew many people in the room already. And I know what we're going through. We came together,

---

21   https://nellysachsenglish.wordpress.com/2013/04/29/.

and it felt like the beginning of a healing." Mac's queerness proclaims itself throughout the show; huge hooped dresses and Versailles-style wigs are homage both to traditional drag and contemporary trans* affirmations.

It's a tricky business, negotiating the journey from drag to trans*, and one which I've never fully understood. My earlier assumption that transsexuals, as we then called them, would disappear as gender roles became less restrictive, and people accepted varied forms of sexual desire, reflected a much simpler understanding of gender than has proven the case. Historical, anthropological and psychoanalytic evidence of the ability of humans to experience diverse and changing patterns of sexual desire are increasingly reduced to an identity—'bisexual'—which only makes sense in the framework of a hetero/homo binary. But if we take the trans* critique of gender seriously this particular binary ceases to mean anything.

It is fascinating how apparently upfront trans* critiques are being used in popular culture to reinforce conventional heteronormative attitudes. The musical *Kinky Boots*, which played in Melbourne last year after triumphs in New York and London, is largely a feel-good glossy version of an old style drag show, with men dressed up as women to reinforce conventional notions of sex and gender. Australia does drag pretty well—Dame Edna, *Priscilla*—and for all its talk of acceptance and diversity *KB* could easily play in the Gladstone Bowls Club. Lola, played here in a stunning performance by Callum Francis, insists that he is a drag queen who likes women; his apparent love interest, factory owner Toby Francis, ditches his fiancé, but for another woman.

But trans* people, as Lola acknowledges in an aside, are not drag queens or cross dressers, but rather people who wish to challenge the gender identity ascribed to them thorough biological characteristics. Some believe they are really a man or a woman and need reshape their bodies to accord with this reality; others are happy to present as neither. In fact there is not a single genuinely trans* or gay character in the entire show, and the ensemble numbers are high energy Broadway musical, without any hint of sexual pairings that would discomfort the

Christian Right. The publicity suggests we come away with greater love and acceptance, but we also come away with the idea that boys might dress up as girls, but in the end they go home with girls, even if they get kicks from knee high stiletto boots on the way. There are no drag kings in *KB*: the women in the show are there to be worshiped, wooed and, occasionally, to upbraid the men.

Last year I went to a queer Midwinter Ball in the appropriately plush settings of Crown Casino, where the entertainment included one of the longest drag numbers ever: men in dresses; men in skimpy shorts showing off their bodies. But the grand finale paired drag queen with muscle boy in ways reminiscent of nineteenth century ballet. Performing gender can allow heterosexual coupling of the most conservative sort.

The audience for Taylor Mac doesn't strike me as predominantly queer, whatever that term now means; it's young, white, leftist. But the show clearly speaks to the mix of anger and affirmation unleashed by the marriage debate. Unlike many visiting Americans, Mac acknowledges this is Australia and we might miss some of the references; judy deems us all Americans for the night. An attempt at local relevance falls flat when we are asked to mock Governor Macquarie, and few in the audience recognise the name. No matter: we are in the presence of a charismatic performer, able to swing from choreographing large audiences to quietening us with a song. And if some of the history is new to most, the music is deeply familiar, underlining the extent to which we are all part of the American multitudes. When Taylor Mac sings *Hard Rain's Goin to Fall*, or even the minstrel songs of Stephen Foster, the songs resonate more than the references to Governor Macquarie.

October 15: Melbourne

Social tennis in the Edinburgh Gardens. One of my earliest childhood memories is watching my parents play tennis with other Jewish refugees in Sydney, and like many other Australian children I learnt tennis from my father on local school courts, and my parents regularly complained that the school did little to encourage me, preferring to push me into reluctantly participating in team sports, which I found frighteningly violent. Given how much has changed over sixty years it's reassuring that the rituals of weekend tennis remain, even if the copious food is likely to be catered, rather than the home-made salads and cakes of my childhood. There's something oddly comforting about the sense of continuity the day brings.

Is nostalgia an inevitable part of ageing? My Melbourne grandmother, who grew up in the Russian part of Poland, told a story about seeing her aunt using a telephone; and thought she was speaking to herself. When we moved to Hobart in the early 1950s there was a waiting list for phones, and my parents had to trudge to the nearest phone box to make calls. Now we expect to be constantly linked through wireless, and people sit in cafes half alert to the constant beep of their phones. It's common to bemoan the loss of social skills through the ubiquity of the smart phone, but I've discovered there's an intimacy that's possible through texting, and I appreciate the connection with the broader world that is offered me by my friends on Facebook, most of whom I actually know.

October 22: Ballarat

Ballarat, like Bendigo, is a regional city superimposed upon the wealth of the nineteenth century gold fields. Old bluestone and brick buildings, major edifices of Victorian wealth, give way to cheap concrete and deserted malls; grime covers some of the stateliest buildings. The town is growing, they tell us, but it has an air of quiet resignation, broken by a couple of hoons roaring down the main street in their cut-off cars.

I try to explain why I prefer to be introduced as a writer rather than an activist. I'm in Ballarat for the first local writers' festival, and a small group of people have come to the Museum of Democracy to listen to me in conversation with film-maker Lucinda Horrocks. I speak of writing as grappling with nuance, contradictions, ambiguities, while activism need speak in certainties, to use shorthand to rally support.

This discussion follows a larger panel discussion on 'fixing democracy', where Sam Dastyari, the energetic Iranian-born Labor Senator, talks of his fears that our politics are becoming increasingly polarised, so that sensible compromise becomes more difficult. Once again, the spectre of Trump hovers in the background, even though none of us on the stage invoke him. Sam speaks of our politicians increasingly having to shore up their base, rather than seeking to reach out to a larger public, but I wonder how accurate this is. As party loyalties decline politicians need to work harder to hold the support of people with diverse priorities, and while this makes for a shrillness in public life, governments still need to find ways of engendering majority support. I suspect Sam is reflecting the uncertainty in all Western countries about the viability of a political system based on nineteenth century institutions and twentieth century parties.

My optimism about Australian politics is neatly challenged that afternoon by a question about why there is continuing refusal to allow the less than two thousand people, now in horrendous detention on Nauru and Manus for four years, to come to Australia. I acknowledge this represents a downwards spiral by our political leadership, who justify their stance by public opinion polls, rather than seeking to change the narrative.

Lucinda pushes me to explain how I came to write about the gay liberation movement, and I talk of arriving in New York for a few months in the fall of 1970 and needing a place to live. Through an advertisement in the *Village Voice* I ended up sharing an apartment with a painter called Adolph Garcia in the East Village. Adolph lived in a sprawling seven-room apartment on Second Avenue, decorated with his paintings of feet—naked, half-shod, elaborately pedicured—which had become a meeting place for the new gay newspaper *Come Out*. The writer Paul Goodman came by one day to be interviewed, and was particularly taken by this particular fetish. Goodman was then well known, above all for his book *Growing Up Absurd*—but who reads Goodman now? In his novel *JD*, Mark Merlis conjures up someone who may or may not be Goodman, and who never accepts his homosexuality nor his replacement by other gurus of the Left, but Goodman would be an important influence on me, as he was on

Susan Sontag, who wrote a moving obituary after his death, praising his "direct, cranky, egotistical, generous American voice".

Without much effort on my part, I was suddenly involved in one of the collectives that made up the larger gay movement in New York, and started attending meetings of the Gay Liberation Front, as well as the Gay Activists Alliance, established by people irritated by what they saw as leftist political posturing in the Liberation Front. In practice the gaps between the two groups were hardly significant; for me they merged into a new and exhilarating world, in which politics and friendship and sexual adventure merged in the possibilities of a complete transformation, a world in which being homosexual would be both central and unremarkable.

That fall, *Harper's Magazine*, edited by Midge Decter, who later became a prominent neo-conservative, had published an article by the critic Joseph Epstein titled 'Homo/Hetero: The Struggle for Sexual Identity'. In it Epstein wrote: "I do think homosexuality an anathema, and hence homosexuals cursed … If I had the power to do so, I would wish homosexuality off the face of this earth." When the Gay Activist Alliance's request to publish a rejoinder met with no response, the group organised a sit-in, and some of us submitted our own pieces to *Harper's*, none of which were published. From this incident I resolved to write a book about the new gay affirmation and began trudging around New York City in search of a possible publisher. I spent long grey days typing out proposals, and hand delivering them to offices, walking through the grimy wind tunnels of midtown Manhattan where publishing then resided.

I was friendly with Australian rock journalist Lillian Roxon. Lillian was constantly unhealthy—she died aged 41 of asthma—and enormously energetic; she took me to parties at Max's Kansas City, and to Elton John's first New York concert, where he was the back-up act to Leon Russell; she also sent me to meet Harris Dienstfrey, co-founder of the short-lived publishing house, Outerbridge & Dienstfrey. Harris saw the possibilities of the book I was touting, and, gulp, I signed a contract, negotiated for me by—another gulp—my first literary agent.

It was Harris who suggested calling the book 'Homosexual'; I added the words 'Oppression and Liberation'. I regretted not using the title of the last chapter, 'The End of the Homosexual?', which became the title of another book, forty years later. But if I first conceptualised *Homosexual* in New York I wrote the first chapter in Los Angeles, staying in a tacky motel along the beachfront at Santa Monica where I was to join my Australian boyfriend, Reinhard Hassert, who would spend New Year with me in the States. I still have a matchbook from the Beach Auto Hotel "overlooking the Blue Pacific", the back of the cover a picture of "pistol packin mamma!".

While I was in the early stages of writing *Homosexual* I wrote a 'letter from New York' for a short-lived radical journal back in Sydney which reminds me, forty-five years later, of my enthusiasm for the counter-culture, even if I was more spectator than participant. With the ebullience of youth I wrote of the collapse of the Amerikan Dream—yes, we used the 'k' deliberately—and the emergence of a new consciousness. New York then was a far grottier and more dangerous city than it is today: "There is, in the offices of Random House, a conference table that cost $40,000 to buy. Meanwhile, four miles downtown, the city notices proclaim: 'Keep the lids on your trash can. Starve a rat today'." And I wrote tentatively of my occasional boyfriend, who'd renamed himself Dusty, had been thrown out of college for shooting up, and now hung on the fringes of Andy Warhol's Factory. We'd met at a Gay Night at the Alternate University, a short-lived experiment offering courses in the preoccupations of the New Left, ranging from 'revolutionary Cuba' through to organic food and self-defence. "If there's heavy bleeding" said one woman briefing a group on first aid in demonstrations, "Stop it and worry about infections later." I remember lying on a tattered sofa with Dusty as he read my horoscope, fascinated by the fact that our birthdays fell on the same day and unsure how to factor in the major time differences between Sydney and Ohio.

I've written elsewhere about the ideas and itinerary of that book.[22] Thanks to a lukewarm review in *Time* magazine and a more enthusiastic

---

22   See Introduction and Afterword, *Homosexual: Oppression & Liberation*, UQP, 2012.

one by Martin Duberman in *The New York Times*, the book survived its first publication by an obscure publisher to become a mass-market paperback. It was subsequently translated into several languages, most recently—in 2010—Japanese. One of my translators, perhaps into Italian, told me he had improved on the writing.

Looking back, there was a naïve millenarianism around the early gay movement (a Christian term, looking forward to a thousand-year age of peace and righteousness), reflected in some of the Utopian language I quoted. *Come Out!* declared itself "a revolutionary homosexual group" bent on "abolishing existing social institutions". Today's activists, as I've noted earlier, seem more determined to join those institutions.

October 25: Melbourne

Last Sunday there was a flash mob dance for marriage equality in the centre of the city. Two of the dancers are in the studios of JOY 94.9, Melbourne's queer radio station, breathless at re-living the exuberance of a mob of people dancing in the city streets. It feels like the early days of gay liberation, or perhaps Mardi Gras: "I've never been political", one of them confides to me, a reminder that most people do not think much about politics, and the marriage debate has thrust thousands of people into an unfamiliar world in which governments suddenly impinge on their very sense of who they are. People are opening-up about difficult discussions with their family, hurts that they have carried for half a lifetime that now re-surface. One friend speaks of his parents never displaying a photo of him with his partner, even when they automatically did so for their straight children.

Interesting, too, to talk to straight supporters, some of whom are far more invested in same-sex marriage than I am. I recall a former Labor Cabinet minister expostulating in fury that Julia Gillard did not support SSM; a couple of years later I spoke at a rally with Opposition Leader Bill Shorten, who was genuinely passionate on the issue. Is there some element here of atonement for earlier attitudes, an unspoken acknowledgement that they ignored all the underlying structures of homophobic prejudice, what Christopher Isherwood called "annihilation by blandness"? Misogyny, as Julia Gillard said of the attacks on her as leader, does not explain everything, but it is always present. The same remains true of homosexuality. When Christos Tsiolkas published *Barracuda*, a novel about a competitive swimmer, I was struck by the reluctance of reviewers to discuss the sexual anxieties and desires of the central character; yes, *Barracuda* is a novel about class, sport and private schools, but Danny's life makes no sense unless one ponders his sexual confusions.

November 1: Melbourne

On my local train, there's a two-year old in his stroller scrolling through an iPad. He is presumably not reading the headlines that three members of Trump's campaign team have now been indicted. The Trump team claim this does not discredit their claims to have had no illegal links with Russia, but on the ABC *Q and A* program, former Prime Minister Kevin Rudd claimed Trump was "nuts". Coming from Rudd this was a frightening insight into the way in which many of the global liberal elite see the President of the United States. When choleric right-wing shock jock, Alan Jones, objected, Rudd stuck to his assessment. Meanwhile the Australian government stumbles from one misstep to another, as questions of parliamentarians' citizenship reach Gilbertian proportions. When the Australian Constitution was drafted at the end of the nineteenth century no-one imagined that the clause excluding dual citizenships from Parliament could debar those born in Scotland, Canada or New Zealand: our citizenship then was assumed to be British. Now increasing numbers of Parliamentarians are forced to resign because they hold dual citizenship. (In the following year fifteen MPs and Senators will stand down because of doubts about their eligibility to hold office.)

Sexual harassment allegations against actor Kevin Spacey dominate the news. A few days ago, *Buzzfeed* reported claims that he had molested a fourteen-year old boy, leading to a string of allegations, fed by a new sensitivity to sexual harassment. A couple of days later Spacey came out as gay, hardly a surprise to most people, but a rather disingenuous way of asking for support. Netflix, for whom he played the central character in *House of Cards*, has removed him from future episodes. I understand the reaction, especially as new charges come to light from his time in Britain, but I think of the numerous claims against Donald Trump during last year's campaign, and how easily they were brushed aside. As usual, morality is selective.

Our notions of sexual harassment have changed, and that's all for the good. But there's a danger that the revelations of sexual misbehaviour can create a new puritanism, one that conflates coercion with consent, and brands anyone who enjoys sexual adventure as somehow morally deficient. Senator Sarah Hanson-Young recently sued fellow Senator David Leyonhjelm for attacking her as a misandrist who liked shagging men: "It's slut shaming," said Hanson-Young. Similar attitudes have surfaced in debates about making condoms, and more recently PREP, available for people who want multiple sexual partners.

Hypocrisy is the one constant in attitudes towards sex. A recent *New Yorker* cartoon showed a youngish woman talking to a man on an anonymous middle-class sidewalk: "OK: so we'll have sex and if that works out we'll go out for a nice dinner and maybe a movie." And six pages later a book reviewer muses about the new possibilities for sexual contacts created by the internet.[23] As more gays and lesbians—I accept the common mix of an adjective and a noun to describe us—yearn for monogamous coupling, it seems the mores of the gay male world are becoming universalised. Tinder followed Grindr, just as demands for marriage followed demands for anti-discrimination. 'Love is love' is the slogan of the marriage equality movement, which makes sense, rhetorically at least, but part of me hankers for the ways in which my generation talked of sexual liberation rather than monogamous coupling. The liberation movements of the 1970s found inspiration in John Rechy's "sexual outlaws" and Erica Jong's "zipless fucks", recognising that love, sex and companionship were not necessarily all found in the same person.

---

23   Laura Miller, 'A Family Affair', *New Yorker*, August 7 & 14 2017.

November 4–8: Melbourne

According to the main commercial news channel 87,000 people attended the Derby Day races; 1000 marched to protest continued detentions on Manus and Nauru. Standing with friends at the State Library lawns the turnout for the demonstration seemed disappointingly small, the same people who've been demonstrating against the downwards spiral of Australian asylum seeker policies for years, even the same banners: Greens, church groups, socialists. (But no rainbow flags, of which more later). But the march unfurled the full length of the CBD, stretching down to the intersection outside Flinders Street Station, overshadowed by a huge sign for *The Merry Widow*, where a police line gradually withdrew to allow the streets to be fully blocked. The people who marched looked like a cross-section of the Australian population, fuelled by anger and frustration. Of all the protest signs my favourite read: "We are not rocks for you to block the sea with".

The images are horrific: refuges who have been held on Manus Island, off the northern coast of Papua New Guinea, are refusing to vacate the centre which the government is closing. These are men who came to Australia some years ago seeking asylum and fell foul of the national obsession with 'stopping the boats'. They claim that moving into the Manus community will endanger them, and external observers agree. Pictures of young men holding up their crossed arms as they beg for a last-minute reprieve are painful to watch, though they appear to have no impact on the government or its supporters.

The anthropologist Margaret Mead spent considerable time on Manus, and during World War II it was occupied by Japanese forces. Now we know it as a jungle prison, holding over 600 men, refugees from a series of repressive regimes and hostages to an Immigration Minister who seems to delight in parading his toughness. Already six men have died while under our protection, many more are broken, their hopes for survival slowly choking. I join the chorus of anger and indignation against government policies, but it has no seeming impact. For years we have spoken, marched, given money, supported legal challenges, lobbied the major political parties, and yet the situation worsens. I write to a few federal Labor politicians, and several reply, acknowledging the anguish but not yet ready to just say what is clearly necessary: *Bring Them Here*! Tomorrow the Prime Minister will refuse the offer of the New Zealand government to immediately accept 150 asylum seekers.

Across Federation Square, in the Koorie Heritage Trust, a small group of us meet two visiting activists from Black Lives Matter. Rodney Diverlus and Patrisse Cullors are charismatic, charming and very aware that they are in another country, as they politely address a motley collection of potential donors and Indigenous leaders. I am uncomfortable that Indigenous North Americans are ignored in the conversation, and at one of the local speaker's references to "the black diaspora" as including Aborigines and Torres Straight Islanders, but I also feel unable to raise this. Patrisse's demand that in a majority white society we need to take responsibility for talking about racism amongst ourselves, rather than lecturing those who experience it, hits home. I slip away, anxious to see what's happening in the Flinders Street intersection, where about 200 protestors remain, and traffic wearily bypasses them without, it seems, any incident.

A few days later about forty of us gather outside the State Library to express queer solidarity with the 600 asylum seekers held on Manus, who are being threatened with movement to as yet unfinished camps. This was a deliberate reaction to the absence of rainbow flags at the demonstration last weekend; here we stand behind a banner proclaiming, in rainbow colours: 'No Pride in Detention'. A few hours later I am on air for JOY 94.9, stressing that some of the men on Manus are homosexual, and fear persecution if they are forced to settle in Papua New Guinea.

November 15: Melbourne

It seemed fitting that the evening before the marriage survey result was announced there was a queer event at the Loop bar, a narrow space jammed in a city laneway, which was rather ambitiously titled 'Thinking

LGBTI History for the Future'. A large, occasionally boisterous panel, intended to suggest the breadth of current queer activism, in which the only veteran of what we used to call the Gay, then Lesbian and Gay, movement seemed already outdated. Not as outdated, however, as the intimate drinks event from which I'd escaped, in a discreet Carlton terrace, ornate with signed photographs of operatic divas and cupboards of petite porcelain dolls. Mainly older men, with those slightly exaggerated camp mannerisms that hide a lifetime of concealment and hurts. I signed the visitors' book and made my excuses.

Thousands of us gathered outside the State Library to hear the results of the postal vote on marriage equality. The live feed from Canberra almost collapsed, but the figures came across clearly: over 60% of the 12 million people who responded had voted yes. There were cheers, speeches, rainbow flags, jubilation; a group of us went for coffee and prosecco to the Library café, where the staff were flirting their relief. Did I think, someone asked, that this was a moment when the Zeitgeist shifted?

There have been many moments in my life when social attitudes towards homosex have shifted, and times when people have mobilised to create change: this was true of moves for decriminalisation in New South Wales and Tasmania, painfully real during the early years of the AIDS epidemic. Today felt like a major milestone, but I don't think that the Zeitgeist shifted, rather that several decades of slow shifts towards greater acceptance came together, and most Australians recognised this. By 7.30 that evening long lines snaked down Victoria Parade from Trades Hall, overwhelmingly young and not very queer. Certainly, the mood of celebration and relief was real, but it felt as if everyone under thirty from inner Melbourne had turned up whether they had been part of the campaign or not. I joined friends in the line, but the noise and the crowds drove me away.

November 27: Melbourne

Over the past fortnight we've seen the marriage poll, the passing of very limited right to die legislation in Victoria, the brutal evacuation of the Manus detention centre and the return of the Labor government in Queensland, in an election which the Australian Christian Lobby referred to as "a referendum on radical gay sex and gender programs, abortion and euthanasia". Fearing a conservative rout in Queensland the front page of the *Weekend Australian* decried "the demise of politics"; their house intellectual, Paul Kelly, pontificates that the "Coalition sinks deeper into the valley of despair." Both conservatives and radicals feel the world has turned for the worst, with constant references to Trump/Brexit, which has become a shorthand term for the decline of a certain sort of polite bipartisan neo-liberalism. At a forum during the week Nur Warsame, the only openly gay Imam in Australia, quoted the Italian Marxist Gramsci: "The old world is dying and the new world struggles to be born".

Gramsci, who died after persecution by the Fascist regime in Italy in 1937, was discovered by New Left thinkers in the 1970s, which also felt a period of collapsing certainties and increasing brutality. His writings are elliptical and fragmentary, but through their use of terms like hegemony and civil society gave us a framework which still resonates today: "I'm a pessimist because of intelligence, but an optimist because of will."

This evening I visit my myotherapist, who comes from New Zealand. "I admire your country" I tell him, but he misses the reference. I explain it's because successive governments have offered to take in some of the refugees held in our offshore camps, but it's not an issue he's thought about much. When I point out that the total number of people held on Nauru and Manus would be fewer than the numbers of international arrivals at Melbourne Airport any morning, he shrugs.

November 30: Melbourne

The opera singer hits notes in *Advance Australia Fair* that I'd never known were there. Apparently, a former singer, Joan Carden, wore a red ribbon when she sang the anthem at an AFL Grand Final twenty-five years ago, thus launching the symbol of AIDS resistance into popular consciousness.

2017

About sixty of us are sitting in the humid upper floor of a Chinatown restaurant to commemorate the quarter century of the Victorian Red Ribbon. I'd never realised there *was* a distinctive Victorian ribbon, but apparently it differs from the more usual global image, having deleted a loop at the top, while retaining a safety pin, to demonstrate 'safe sex'. We listen to long descriptions of the creation and ongoing life of the ribbon in Victoria, while eating bland Chinese banquet food. A former Liberal state minister is at my table and I ask why he voted against the assisted dying legislation, which has just gone through the state Parliament. "Not sufficient safeguards" he says, while acknowledging he found himself in unexpected alliance with conservatives. He defines himself as a state patriot, with seemingly little time for his counterparts in Federal Parliament. Victoria, he claims, has been consistently cheated by federal governments of all persuasions.

There are almost three generations in the room: men who were adult long before the AIDS epidemic began through to some who were not yet born. Already events like this feel like meetings of returned veterans, with those of us who lived through the deaths trying to explain the emotions of the time to far younger folk for whom AIDS has become a manageable and largely preventable condition.

December 1: Sydney

I'm in Sydney for a family weekend: over the next two days we'll drive across Sydney as the weather changes from hot and humid to rain, and the beach at Bondi lies empty, pummelled by unending waves.

There's an exhibition of Robert Mapplethorpe's photographs at the Gallery of New South Wales, sparse images in black and white of beautiful young men, flowers, celebrities. The flowers bore me; the images of sexy black men bother me because we are told nothing about their lives, as distinct from those of the more celebrated women he photographed.

Most of the photographs date from the years I lived in and out of New York when Mapplethorpe was chronicling the avant-garde art scene and the underground sex worlds of New York. The years between the gay liberation movement at the beginning of the 1970s and the onset of AIDS a decade later are viewed in a certain strand of gay nostalgia as 'the golden age'. It's hardly surprising that those who lived through the period might see it this way; in retrospect all youth is golden. What is surprising is the extent to which men not then adult—perhaps not yet born—have accepted the idea and are slightly disappointed when I try to disillusion them.

For me the entry to New York's so-called golden age came one day in November 1977 when I had brunch with Michael Denneny, Edmund White, Doug Ireland and Chuck Ortleb. Between them the four men represented an extraordinary agglomeration of gay cultural power: Denneny, the slightly acerbic editor who turned St Martin's Press into a crucible for queer writing; Ireland, the cherubic faced, smart leftist journalist who knew everyone and would die of diabetes and a stroke in 2013; White, then a fresh faced and largely unknown novelist (Michael was about to publish his novel *Nocturnes for the King of Naples*); Ortleb, editor of *Christopher Street Magazine*. Three years later Ortleb and Denneny would found *The New York Native*, the cutting edge of gay journalism until it collapsed in a frenzy of denialism that HIV was the cause of AIDS.

Looking back what strikes me is the immediate intimacy of gay literary and political New York. The radicals of the early 1970s were gradually winning respect in a broader world, but there were still few enough people who were open about their sexuality for it to establish a common bond. It seemed possible, then, to know everyone; my diary mentions meeting the German film director, Rosa von Praunheim and the Argentinian writer Manuel Puig. I have no memory of Praunheim, whose film *It Is Not the Homosexual Who Is Perverse, But the Society in Which He Lives* was an important influence on the German gay movement, and I desperately wanted to meet Puig, because he had footnoted me several times in his novel *Kiss of the Spider Woman*, an unusual device for a novel. I met a small, depressed man in a downtown apartment, described by Suzanne Levine in her excellent book about Puig as "replicating the monkish austerity of his room in Buenos Aires".[24]

---

24 Suzanne Jill Levine, *Manuel Puig and the Spider Woman*, FSG 2000, p.272.

The overwhelming attraction of the New York gay literati world was sufficient for me to resign my lectureship at Sydney University and move to New York in 1981. The ten years at Sydney had been exciting, marked by bitter disputes within Philosophy and Economics, which led to a student strike and both departments splitting between traditionalists and radicals. But the prospect of thirty more years in the same institution was stultifying: I wanted to live out the fantasy of becoming a real writer. In a farewell article I wrote for the now defunct *National Times* there is a note of bitterness about the ways in which American academic modes were being grafted onto British nostalgia: "The American social scientist, with his pocket calculator, his crass unawareness of the broader implications of what he is doing, and his general lack of interest in cultural matters … is becoming the model … and government pressure for universities to become more 'efficient' and 'productive' can only foster this development."[25]

The temptations of writing were seductive. In 1980, the year I left Sydney University, I met film-maker James Ricketson and we plotted a film about a romance between a gay and a straight man. James then lived at Palm Beach, on the northern tip of the Barrenjoey Peninsula. I stayed with him several times over the year, including his wedding the following year, when the singer Joni Mitchell was a guest. She and I went down to the beach the morning of the wedding, and she talked about her time in Crete and her fondness for the sun, which had given her skin an ochre tinge. James and I developed a treatment, and a proposal for the New South Wales Film Corporation, who paid us a $3000 advance for a script then entitled *But What If True Love and Happiness are Not the Same Thing?* I still have copies of the treatment, eight pages of laborious typescript, but that was the end of the project. Our lives veered off in very different directions, taking James most recently to Cambodia where he faced dodgy charges and was released after several months in prison.

This was Sydney at its idyllic best, but the lure of New York remained. I would spend the next four years adrift in Manhattan, living off a

---

25   'A Farewell to Sydney University', *National Times*, April 27 1980.

small post-University income and in various temporary apartments. I think it was Susan Sontag who said that writers need live off their wits, and there was an edge to the very temporariness of my New York life, which began and ended with two men, very different, with both of whom I lived briefly. I met Adrian Driggs during the summer in Julius', the oldest continuous gay bar in Greenwich Village (it appears in several films, including *Boys in the Band* and *Can You Ever Forgive Me?*). At the far end of the bar, in a dark, long salon framed by sepia photographs of various sports events, sat the man with golden hair who would become my New York boyfriend for the following tumultuous year.

Adrian was a lawyer, who lived in a small neat apartment near the United Nations, in that peculiarly anonymous stretch of Manhattan between Grand Central and the East River crowded with condos, coffee bars and consular offices, even a functioning service station. Ours was a tormented relationship, a holiday romance that I made the mistake of trying to make more permanent. I spent a couple of months sharing his flat, then moved to an old apartment in the West Village which was leased by the sister of a friend who dislodged me for a couple of nights once a month when she came into the city. It was the sort of apartment one might imagine Audrey Hepburn renting when she was breakfasting at Tiffany's, complete with a copper bathtub in the kitchen in which my friend Mark Blasius, a political scientist then teaching at LaGuardia College, stored six live lobsters in preparation for a birthday dinner. The apartment was on top of a five-storey building, and several of us waited, listening anxiously to the loud puffs of Doug Ireland as he laboured his way, wheezing, up the stairs.

Mark was one of my three or four 'best friends', which in pre-mobile days meant long hours on the telephone, sometimes rehashing what we had just told our therapists. One of the oddities for me, coming from suburban Australia, was that men who lived in small cockroach-lined apartments would, for a short period during the summer, become shared tenants of glorious summer houses on what became globally known as *the* gay resort, Fire Island. At that time there were two gay sections on the island: the older camp houses at Cherry Grove, linked by a strip of scrub and sand to the more fashionable Pines, where a trip to the store might mean crossing paths with several Broadway celebrities, sometimes wandering home, stoned, from a night in the Dunes. Thanks in part to Larry Kramer's novel *Faggots* the island came to symbolise unlimited sexual hedonism, but it was also a place to escape the Bombay heat of a New York summer, to cement friendships and, even, to write.

My New York in the first term of Reagan's Presidency was defined by two extraordinary groups, the gay literati clustered around *Christopher Street* and the *New York Native*, and the hothouse intellectual world of New York University's Institute for the Humanities, presided over by the sociologist Richard Sennett. The link between the two was Edmund White, a man of southern charm and northern ambition, ruthless in his pursuit of celebrity and celebrities, and capable of both great generosity and sudden barbs of wickedness. Edmund was one of a group of gay writers who made up what became known as the Violet Quill. Urged on by Doug Ireland, who was then an editor at the *Soho News*, a spunkier version of the *Village Voice*, I wrote a piece called "a movable brunch—the fag lit mafia", of which Christopher Bram later wrote: "This bitchery was the first bit of fame for the group."[26] But gay writing was beginning to encroach on high culture; there was excitement when the *New Yorker* published what was thought to be its first overtly gay short story (David Leavitt's 'Territory') in 1981—and some chagrin amongst other New York writers.

Edmund is one of three surviving members of the Quill, and I last spent time with the others, Andrew Holleran and Felice Picano, at a Saints and Sinners Festival in New Orleans in 2015, a queer literary festival wrapped within the larger Tennessee Williams Festival. The festival takes place in the Beaux Arts Monteleone Hotel in the centre of the French Quarter, whose stultifying nineteenth century rooms, with their dark panelling and elaborate décor, seemed to match the slightly dour feel of the event. I spoke on two panels, notable for the

---

26 Christopher Bram, *Eminent Outlaws Twelve*, 2012, p.196.

lack of connection between the presentations, and wandered around the Quarter, loud with buskers and tourists. I have never enjoyed New Orleans, which remains a deeply segregated city and one with more drunken yobs on the street than anywhere else I have been except perhaps St. Petersburg. Both Andrew and Felice were extraordinarily welcoming; without necessarily articulating it we recognised that we shared a history of both triumphs and tragedy. But I felt very much an outsider at this festival, where no one showed any interest in what might be happening outside the borders of the United States.

Edmund White was a central figure at the Institute for the Humanities, which I once described as the *New York Review* at lunch, perhaps because of memories of seminars dominated by the presence of Susan Sontag, her legs sprawled across the table as she munched sandwiches and repartee with equal ferocity. I barely knew Sontag when in a moment of rashness I agreed to speak about 'dandyism' in a small seminar. Naively I had forgotten that Sontag wrote of dandyism in her iconic 'Notes on Camp', and I suspect she was angered by my too easy equation of dandies with homosexuality. Susan turned her well-rehearsed wrath on me for what was self-evident fatuousness; I retired hurt; and Edmund took me to dinner, having seen others who had experienced Susan's barbs. Looking back, I realise this was a rite of passage; some months later Susan and I went to dinner together, my main memory of which is a Lower East Side Chinese restaurant which specialised in offal, and a discussion which touched for a time on opera. What I glimpsed that evening was something of the ferocious determination with which she was constructing herself as a cultural icon, a ferocity that seemed shared by so many of the people I came across in New York, where every transaction, even at the bank or post office, demanded concentrated ambition.

Occasionally I went to evenings at Sennett's house, where men gathered around the piano, in an arch approximation of a Proustian salon, and Sennett spoke of his developing friendship with Michel Foucault. There are echoes of those moments in both Sennett's novel *The Frog Who Dared to Croak* (1982) and White's *Caracole* (1985), the latter of which caused a celebrated split between him and Susan Sontag, who recognised herself and her son, David Rieff, in the novel. Many famous people passed through the Institute; I met Nadine Gordimer while I was trying to decide whether to leave New York, self-evidently the centre of the gay literary world, and return to Australia. "But there are no centres anymore" said Gordimer, a great comfort to me when a year later I did decide to return to Australia.

The nicest person at the Institute in the early 1980s was the writer Barbara Ehrenreich, who lived with her then husband and two children out on Long Island and invited me to several long family meals. Barbara had trained as a cellular immunologist, but she abandoned academia to become one of the most consistent progressive social analysts of American life over the past fifty years. At that stage she was writing about sex and relationships, reflected in her book *The Hearts of Men*, and we shared a certain cynicism about the standard myths of finding true love and happiness. We last met over coffee at the Smithsonian Institute in Washington on a cold sunny morning in 2012, but my lasting memory is of going with her twenty years earlier to see the anti-nuclear film *The Atomic Café*, and her stories of growing up under the shadow of the Cold War. This was in the first years of the Reagan Administration, when we still feared the possibility of war with the Soviet Union. His rapprochement with Gorbachev was as unexpected as Trump's with Kim Jong-un, and somewhat more substantial.

My first year in New York was taken up with the final edits and publication of the book that would become *The Homosexualization of America*; "Better", Vito Russo had said to me one day, "to call it *The Americanization of the Homosexual*", and in retrospect he was right. I worked on the book with Michael Denneny, the toughest and most demanding editor I've encountered, but then our lives and our work crossed over, so that it seemed perfectly natural that some of the work was done in Michael's shared holiday house on Fire Island. Of all the books I've written this one involved the most intense collaboration with an editor, Michael being even more determined than I that homosexuals were changing the shape of American culture. I have just taken down my copy of Michael's book, *Lovers* (Avon 1979), a remarkably sensitive and extended series of interviews and comments with a gay couple, in which Michael wrote: "Dear Dennis: I wish you would move to Manhattan—then we'd be able to continue this conversation unendingly and I'd learn something (and you, of course, would learn a lot)." One of the couple he interviewed, Philip Gefter, would go on to become a significant photography critic.

Looking back over thirty years to writing that book suggests that the path to breaking down the massive silences around homosexuality which allowed it to be only viewed as pathology was already far advanced before the hiatus of the AIDS epidemic. That this was happening as mainstream politics moved to the right, symbolised in Reagan's election in 1980, and the rise of the Moral Majority, reminds us that politics rarely move in a straight line. The references in *Homosexualization* to marriage seem to assume it is a dying institution, and indeed claimed we were better off without it: "The absence of gay marriage means that it is easier for homosexuals to develop other ways of living than in conventional coupledom; there has been considerable discussion, in the new gay writings, of the advantages and disadvantages of a whole range of possible living and social arrangements." That discussion has now largely disappeared, and ironically my book now lives on as a source for certain right-wing attacks on alleged homosexual conspiracies.

While working on the book I spent a few days in Orlando as a speaker at the Sixth Annual Florida Conference for Lesbians and Gay Men. At that stage Orlando boasted "the largest gay entertainment complex in the world", known, fittingly, as Parliament House, a mix of resort, motel and disco. I was struck by the overlap between leather and Christianity among the attendees, a reminder that the Metropolitan Community Church, founded by Troy Perry in 1968, is probably the largest continuing gay community institution in history, with over 40,000 members in twenty countries. But there were reminders, also, of the need for separate gay space:

2017

The conference cocktail party was in a downtown motel, over-decorated in plush pink, we delegates stuck away behind the dining room, where middle aged couples danced earnestly to musak-ed versions of Neil Diamond. We wanted to dance, and finally, bravely, four same sex couples took to the floor. The band dealt with the incursion politely by packing up their instruments and going home.

All authors seek fame, and sometimes we have brief moments of indulgence; mine came the week my book appeared as a window display in the windows of a large bookstore at one of the busiest intersections in the West Village. Thanks to a remarkable publicity man at St. Martin's, John Murphy, I did an abbreviated book tour, visiting gay bookstores, appearing on low rating radio programs and, in Los Angeles, on a morning talk show:

> The first feature will be four male strippers from Chippendale's, all of them tall, tanned, with blow-dried hair and perfect teeth, in short gorgeous. In turn they divest themselves of a business suit and tie, a Xorro cape, a bow tie and bib, a Flash Gordon outfit, stopping just at the point where one might expect to see the first outgrowths of pubic hair.
>
> I sip my coffee and wonder why none of them turn me on; is there a subtly different way of presenting oneself to a female audience that differs from stripping for men? When they leave the studios one, I decide, might be gay. In jeans and T-shirt he is suddenly sexy.
>
> They are followed in rapid succession by a supporting actor from *Best Little Whorehouse in Texas*, a local disc jockey, a woman who trains dogs, and the program's resident chef, who whips up alcoholic granitas for all of us. My granita is taken from me and I am placed on the commodious sofa, along with my hosts. Like nuns and policemen, talk show hosts come in pairs, usually a dumb man pretending to be smart, and a far

smarter woman pretending to be dumb. Here the man has red hair and cannot pronounce the title of my book; the woman looks like Farrah Fawcett.

The red-haired man kicked off the interview: "Why" he asked "Do some people stray from heterosexuality?", moving closer to Farah Fawcett as if he feared too close contact might lead to straying.

Prejudices die slowly: as late as 2014 Henry Makow, in a book called *Illuminati 3: Satanic Possession,* was quoting *Homosexualization* to illustrate homosexual-led rebellion "against God and the natural and moral order".

More fun was the small book-signing at the liquor store by the ferry wharf on Fire Island, which was a benefit for the newly formed Gay Men's Health Crisis. My notes tell me that we sold a few books, one to a man who bought it from his household's grocery money. But as that note reminds me, our world was spinning, and soon the progress I'd exulted in when writing *Homosexualization* would seem under a new and deadly attack. Already a slow panic was spreading amongst gay men, even amongst men who, as Roy Cohn claims in *Angels in America*, were *not* homosexual. I was slow to react, too caught up in the excitement of a new book, and the solipsistic world of the gay literati. A year after the first cases of what was then called GRID—'gay related immune deficiency'—were reported I wrote a piece in the *New York Native* about internal disputes within several national gay organisations in which there is no reference at all to the epidemic.

December 7: Melbourne

Towards 6.00 pm the House of Representatives filled up for the final vote on amending the Marriage Act. The voice vote for yes was overwhelming; there was a plaintive call for a division. Almost the entire Government and Opposition crowded together on one side of the House, enjoying the moment; a few disconsolate abstainers quietly slipped out of the chamber. The outburst of joy at the final tally was in part sheer relief.

Even members who had previously opposed change—and those who had carefully hidden their views throughout the long debates—seemed swept up in a moment of bipartisan celebration. Some in the gallery burst into song—I am too old to have learnt the lyrics of 'I am, you are, we are Australian'—and four of the cross-benchers unfurled a rainbow flag. It was a unique moment when normal politics gave way to a sense of shared nationhood.

The politicians are jockeying to take credit for the change. Even former Prime Minister Tony Abbott, who was inventive in his moves to derail it, now says he is looking forward to the wedding of his sister, a prominent campaigner for equal marriage. The backbench Liberals, who forced the party to move, albeit slowly, are jubilant: Tim Wilson, the smooth-faced member from Melbourne's bayside, used the final Parliamentary debate to propose to his boyfriend. The anomaly amidst the Liberal MPs was northern Queenslander Warren Entsch, former fitter and welder, and crocodile farmer, whose passion for the issue outflanked even his own gay colleagues. I met Entsch in 2011, when I was asked to speak at the University of Central Queensland in Rockhampton, after reports had suggested it was the most homophobic part of Australia. (I doubted that at the time; in the marriage poll 54% of respondents in the electorate of Capricornia voted yes.) Entsch flew down from Cairns to chair the event, and afterwards we had dinner in the Vice Chancellor's residence.

Warren Entsch struck me as one of those Liberal politicians who are capable of enormous empathy for people who are victimised—at dinner, he spoke movingly of encounters with young Aboriginal and gay people—without linking those stories to larger structural inequalities. My memory is that neither he nor I saw marriage equality as a central concern.

Meanwhile the new face of the queer movement is on show at the Pride in Practice Conference a few days earlier in the downtown Sheraton. About 150 people are here to embrace business support for 'LGBTI people', predominantly young, professional, well dressed. There are many speeches, but I keep waiting for someone to use the pronoun 'we', to identify *as* rather than *with* queers. A few of those in the final panel are openly gay, but even they speak in the polite third person. Here corporations are our allies, leading the way towards greater acceptance, a long march from the anti-capitalist rhetoric of early gay liberation. The gap between the community activists at the Loop Bar last month and the pragmatic corporates at the post-meeting reception is large, though not large enough, one suspects, to rule out contact in after-hours hook-ups.

My Facebook feed is filled with people saying they finally feel recognised as equal within Australia. The decision is primarily symbolic, with less practical effect than previous legal changes, such as the decriminalisation of homosexual behaviour and the inclusion of sexuality and gender orientation in a swag of anti-discrimination protections. But symbolic victories are important. The following day riots broke out across the Middle East in response to President Trump's decision to recognise Jerusalem as the capital of Israel. Like the marriage decision a largely symbolic gesture carried within it the possibility of enormous change, and the capacity to bring people out onto the streets.

There is an element of kitsch to the whole marriage celebration, as in the "high quality giclée prints" commissioned by Fairfax Media—*Australia says I do*—or gay Olympian diver Matthew Mitcham re-inventing himself as "ambassador for a new line of engagement rings for same-sex couples". (I admire Mitcham because he came out when he had everything to lose, insisting that he would continue his diving career as an openly gay man.) But this is a bittersweet moment for those of us, like me, who are not in long term partnerships. Hard to join in the celebrations wholeheartedly when they remind one of loss and ageing.

December 13: Melbourne

Go for a quick swim at the Fitzroy Pool. If Sydney is known for its beaches, Melbourne expresses itself through its pools. The old Olympic Pool became a footnote in history in the 1956 Olympic Games when a water polo game between Hungary and Russia turned, literally, bloody, in the aftermath of Soviet repression of the Hungarian uprising. The first chapter of Helen Garner's *Monkey Grip* is named 'Aqua Profonda', after the sign that dominates the deep end of the Fitzroy Pool, as Sophie Cunningham reminds us in her book *Melbourne*. The Coburg pool featured in the television version of Christos Tsiolkas's *The Slap*, and his novel *Barracuda* features a succession of Melbourne pools. The Beaurepaire Pool on the University of Melbourne campus is lined by murals and mosaics by the artist Leonard French. There are bayside pools, council pools dotted across the city, a major Aquatic Centre for competition and the old City Baths, housed in a brick Edwardian Baroque building on the edge of the city. Not surprisingly it was a meeting ground for homosexual men through most of its history, though now largely supplanted by gay saunas and the internet. The City Baths still houses a mikvah: a pool used for ritual immersion in Judaism, a small and very deep pool hidden away in a small room.

Every pool has its distinctive clientele: the Fitzroy and Collingwood pools, both owned by the City of Yarra, are strikingly different. Fitzroy has a full-size outdoor pool, which attracts the young and the beautiful, as intent on bronzing their bodies as on swimming. Collingwood has a smaller indoor pool, much used by the newer immigrant populations from the concrete housing projects down the road. Swimming pools, like tennis courts, are part of the civic richness of Australia, spaces where we learn to become Australian in ways unrelated to jingoism. As a child in Hobart we were taken for swimming lessons to the oddly named Amateur House, a grim now abandoned red brick building, where I failed to make the school team because I never mastered the art of diving.

December 16: Melbourne

Hanukkah with the Langer family. This is the festival commemorating the rededication of the Second Temple in Jerusalem at the time of the Maccabean Revolt against the Seleucid Empire, but we struggle to recall who exactly were the Maccabeans. "Zealots" suggests Beryl; perhaps, I wonder, the spiritual ancestors of Benjamin Netanyahu. Beryl, John and Zev sing a verse of the appropriate song, but the evening centres on the latkes, potato cakes drenched in oil to celebrate the miracle of the oil that lasted for eight days in the temple, perhaps a forecast of the later miracle of the loaves and fishes.

The Langers are in some ways my de facto family in Melbourne. In the 1960s Beryl won a scholarship to do a doctorate at the University of Toronto, where she met John and converted to Judaism to marry him; John followed her back to Melbourne where she and I were colleagues. Over thirty years we've forged a friendship that's grown through some tough times: as a teenager their elder son Zev was seriously ill and could have died. Anthony did die. At various points Zev and his brother Sam have house sat for me, now Zev and his girlfriend, Maya, live next door, and look after my cat when I am away. John, also a retired academic, is an environmental activist; Beryl has become a stalwart volunteer for the Greens, and is usually forbearing about my ambivalent relationship to the Labor Party.

I've had many Passover dinners at the Langers', both before and after Anthony's death, where attempts to follow the service, which is elaborate and involves various moments of symbolic food, compete with a general sense of irreverence. There have been other Seders in my life, and in different cities. At Harvard we were invited by a graduate student couple who were vegetarian and replaced the traditional Ashkenazi chicken with nut cutlets. A few years ago I had Seder with Masha Gessen and her family in New York, where the ritual of hiding the afikomen, a piece of matzo which the youngest child is sent to retrieve, led to dinner winding on for several jubilant hours.

I first met Masha in the early 1980s when she interviewed me for the gay journal *The Advocate*; our friendship resumed when she came to Melbourne in 2014 to attend the Melbourne Writers Festival. By then Masha was established as an extraordinary writer, whose books on post-Soviet Russia are already classics. (My favourite is *The Future is History*, 2017.) She has a ferocious appetite for work, constantly flying across the world to speak, while looking after three children and maintaining a constant flow of analysis of Russian, American, queer politics. I picture her sitting with me in a café in Harlem, writing in a notebook. She was writing when I arrived, she continued as soon as I left, in-between I had her full attention.

December 18: Melbourne

My friend Penny Andrews is in town. Penny is South African, 'coloured' under the old apartheid strictures, who'd been a close colleague when I first was at La Trobe in the late 1980s. She left to move to New York, and over the years built a career in leading US law schools, before returning to head the Law School at the University of Cape Town. "So", I ask her, "Are you permanently in South Africa?", knowing that Penny is unlikely to settle anywhere for long. She will move back to New York at the end of next year.

There are moments when one is privileged to encounter history through its actors, and Penny was central to two of these. The first was a dinner with Edwin Cameron in Durban on the eve of the International AIDS Conference. Edwin is a senior judge, an openly HIV positive gay man, and one of the generation who fought apartheid, working with the African National Congress during the years when they were struggling to overthrow the system. Nelson Mandela called him a hero; he is also one of the most generous and gentle people I have known in the testosterone heavy world of HIV activism. (He has written of his own experiences living—and coming close to dying—with HIV in his book *Witness to AIDS*.) Few people of his eminence have succeeded as well as Edwin in escaping increasing self-importance and pomposity.

This was still South Africa's time of hope. Mandela had stepped down as President a year earlier to be replaced by Thabo Mbeki. There had been jubilation at the peaceful transition, but already the full extent of Mbeki's weird and dangerous denialism of HIV was becoming evident. Mbeki claimed there was no evidence that HIV was the cause of AIDS, and promoted increasingly dubious 'cures', preventing the uptake of anti-retrovirals which could have saved thousands of lives. At the Conference Mandela didn't directly rebuke his successor but spoke instead of the suffering and the dying and the need for urgent action. It was clear he was troubled by Mbeki but was not yet ready to demand he retract his denialism.

Edwin spoke passionately of the implications of Presidential denial at the Conference, but at dinner he and Penny spoke of politics, national and legal, with an intensity that we never broach in Australia. A sense of real danger with which opponents of apartheid had lived, and the realities of the violence imposed by racism, made politics literally matters of life and death. Driving through the cities of South Africa one sees the startling inequality that is the legacy of apartheid and begets, inevitably, the consequent high rate of crime and violence.

A decade later Penny organised a dinner in Harlem, at one of the chic restaurants along Lennox Avenue, a world away from the Harlem familiar to me through Baldwin's novels. Two people at that dinner, older than me, reminisced about childhood travel in the South, when awareness of being black curtailed every stop. Travelling through segregated South Carolina and Alabama, a wrong move could literally threaten one's life; I heard the visceral fears, the tensions in the shoulders when driving into the next small town, the bladders bursting because there were no 'coloured' toilets available. Thanks to the movie we know that African Americans relied on *The Negro Motorist Green Book* to remain safe when driving in the old Confederacy.

One of those at dinner was Samuel Delaney, whose writings straddle fantasy, mythology and homosex, having been one of the first African-American writers of science fiction (*Dhalgren*; *Return to Nevèrÿon*) as well as one of the first genre writers to seriously up-end gender and sexual assumptions in prose that is both erotic and deeply literate. He walked me to the nearest subway, but we took different lines. When I check with him many years later Samuel has no memory of the evening, though he reminds me that he grew up only a few blocks away, on Seventh Avenue between 132nd and 133rd.

He does, however, remember that we met again a few days later at the Lambda Awards, the Oscar type ceremony for 'published works which celebrate or explore LGBT themes'. One of my books would be a nominee four years later, but these events are more fun when one has no stake in winning. Today various queer awards flourish, reminding us that as minorities make it they take on the available models for worldly success.

I am currently reading former Foreign Minister Gareth Evans' *Incorrigible Optimist* and am struck by how closely our early lives as student politicians overlapped: he, too, met Kirby and Wilenski as a young and impressionable undergraduate. Had I not been gay would I, like Gareth, have worked my way through the Labor Party? Maybe finally won preselection, or even office? Several others of our contemporaries were part of the remarkable group who constituted the Hawke/ Keating governments (1983–96); Gareth mentions Gordon Bilney, who as minister for Development Cooperation helped make some of the first grants to emerging AIDS community organisations in Asia.

Oddly the Foreign Minister with whom I had most contact was Liberal Alexander Downer. Because his term coincided with the large regional AIDS Conference in Melbourne in 2001 there were several meetings with him, which revealed him capable of being thoughtful in private and extraordinarily rude in public. Like him, Gareth is opinionated, impatient and loathe to suffer contradiction. But what stands out in Gareth's tenure as foreign minister is a strong commitment to international justice, which went far beyond the immediate interests of the government.

I benefitted from Gareth's innovations when I was awarded an Evans Grawemeyer Fellowship in 1996, funded by an award he'd been given for Ideas Improving World Order, which helped me apply for a short-term fellowship at the University of Chicago. In Chicago I was loosely attached to Arjun Appadurai's Globalization Project. Arjun was famous as a post-colonial scholar and author of key works on globalisation, but I had very little contact with him, a common experience for visitors to elite American Universities. The best part of what felt a very long six weeks living on campus was the ongoing discussion around sexuality and globalisation which in turn led to my signing a book project with Douglas Mitchell at the University of Chicago Press. The book, which became *Global Sex*, grew out of a presentation I made to a ferocious queer seminar which was less grounded in practical politics than I'd have liked: "But why" I asked a prominent cultural theorist, "Do you speak of futurity when you mean the future?" I have since learnt that the word is both a racing term, and the title of a book by Philip K Dick.

Writing *Global Sex* was fun, exploring as it did the apparently boundless possibilities we felt at the end of last century, after the end of the Cold War and the rapidly emerging technologies of communication. I ended the book with the comment that: "The interconnectedness of the world is both a threat and an opportunity." What I did not foresee was the rise of powerful forces which would seek to reverse the possibilities of interconnectedness, and the strength of religious and nationalistic chauvinisms which are so sadly evident across the Middle East, in Myanmar, in much of Europe. In the late 1990s it was easy to believe that acceptance of sexual diversity was growing across the world, even if I began the book by pointing to the way in which the Deputy Prime Minister of Malaysia Anwar Ibrahim's career was destroyed by accusations of sodomy. This year saw images of men being flogged, tortured, thrown off rooftops for the 'crime' of having sex with each other.

Several promotion events for the book were fun as well; a glossy Italian magazine decided to do a story based on the book, and I was driven around Manhattan for a day scouting images to illustrate the story, none of which appeared in the final edition.[27] In Mexico my imaginative publishers organised a discussion in a cultural centre in Roma, the fashionable quarter of Mexico City now known through Alfonso Cuarón's film of that name. A distinguished panel of writers, including Carlos Monsivais, spoke at length; I was given bulky earphones to link me to a translator who was squeezed into a makeshift booth at the back. The discussion was long, erudite and stimulating, but I felt infantilised by my total inability to speak Spanish, even, in some cases, to follow the arguments in English translation. One of the panel, film critic Carlos Bonfil, took me to the Zona Rosa, the gay

---

27 'Eros senza frontier', *L'Espresso*, August 16 2001, pp.80–84.

district of Mexico City, surprising for its openness (read the entry in Wikipedia for a flavour of voyeuristic disapproval of the area.). As in many cities outside the rich world Mexico combines the recognisable signs of contemporary gay culture with a range of traditional expressions of sexuality, unsuited to the language of Western taxonomies.

Global Sex is the only one of my books that lent itself to a movie, and I still have a folder of photographs I took as part of a project that never went beyond the initial rights: pictures of a Tokyo love hotel; a Calvin Klein billboard; a huge roadside picture of a heterosexual couple in bed, advertising 'Horny Goat Weed Tonight!'. I wrote a treatment, pivoting the camera from a traditional wedding in Manila to a beach party in Rio, but the project died, as do so many, and I retreated to academic life.

It was some years after writing *Global Sex* that I started thinking seriously about concepts of human security. I was drawn to the concept by a recognition of the dangers an unchecked AIDS epidemic could mean for social and political cohesion and started writing about the idea in the early 2000s. That decade saw the peak of global commitment to reversing the epidemic, with President George W Bush and Prime Minister Tony Blair taking a lead. I was enthused by the idea that we could envision security as encompassing more than guns and bombs, that *human* security placed an emphasis on the threats to our very survival posed by climate change, environmental degradation, crises of food and water supplies and, yes, epidemic diseases.

December 25: Sydney

Back in Sydney for family Xmas. Last Friday my sister, Vivien, took me to a party at the home of Wendy Bacon and Chris Nash, both of whom I'd known when I lived in Sydney in the 1970s. I first met Wendy when she was arrested for publishing an obscene poem in the student newspaper *Tharunka*; nearly fifty years later she was arrested again, for protesting the massive West Connex road project which will cut through much of the inner city. Pictures of the young Wendy wearing a nun's habit embossed with the words: 'I have been fucked by God's steel prick', became emblematic of the radical mood of the early seventies.

Wendy came to Sydney at the tail end of the Push and is a link between the self-indulgent anarchism of that group—some of whom boasted to me that they refused to vote for Whitlam in 1972—and a new activism, ready to risk jail. Few people have so single-mindedly retained their commitment to direct action; Wendy, now a matronly figure, with silver hair and a deep laugh, is still standing on picket lines. The arrests over West Connex have so far not resulted in any convictions, but she and Chris speak of the urban destruction caused by progress, with passion.

One of the few consolations of ageing is the reunion with people who have shared histories, even as these are increasingly shadowed by awareness of those who haven't survived, or those who are surviving in pain and difficulty. Wendy and I spoke together at a forum on sexual liberation at Sydney University in 1971, and we are yoked together in several of the books earnest young scholars are now producing about the sixties. I taught Chris at Sydney University, in a free-wheeling seminar with my colleague Terry Irving, when we were inspired by the New Left and the possibilities of radical change. Relations between lecturers and students were far looser than today; we hung out in pubs together, and one of Chris's classmates came to my office to give me a few joints, carefully rolled in red and white Tally Ho papers.

There's always the temptation of nostalgia in visiting Sydney, and constant surprise when the landmarks of my time as a young academic have given way to concrete and glass apartment blocks and hipster cafes. The physicality of Sydney remains the only real impediment to constant rebuilding, as the brutality of progress obliterates the older city, corner pubs becoming chic restaurants, old warehouses mutating into studio apartments, seeming permanent roadworks restoring tram lines that had once stretched across the Harbour and into the crevices of beachside suburbs from La Perouse to Narrabeen.

Garry Wotherspoon, whose *City of the Plain* (1991) was one of the first urban gay histories written, is talking about a new project, the biography of a man who lived across the camp and gang worlds of Sydney in the middle of last century. He tells me the story of parties, where men, naked but for face masks, have sex all over the house—"Please" says an earnest young man seated behind us, gesturing to his children who are well out of ear shot "Be careful." We lower our voices.

Christmas Day at my sister's is the usual warm chaotic too-much-food day, with small children running around and interrupting any serious conversation: I go back to Melbourne feeling tired and blessed.

2018

January 1: Melbourne

I slept through New Year's Eve. Not even the fireworks—Melbourne's biggest! most costly ever! as they are every year—woke me. But I realise I have never much liked New Year's Eve, with its crowds and its compulsory jollity.

I remember best one New Year's Eve from almost fifty years ago: 1970 in San Francisco, where I was spending a week with Reinhard Hassert. We ate on Market Street, at a restaurant which has since become a karaoke bar, went to several now lost bars on Polk Street, then San Francisco's gay strip, where men danced together, still a novelty. That felt exciting and frightening and liberating: men and men, women and women, a few transsexuals, the term we used then, claiming those few precious spaces in the small strip half way between Market and Russian Hill.

Midnight saw us at a party organised by the Society for Individual Rights (SIR), a precursor to gay liberation, whose New Year's Eve party several years before had been raided by the police. We knew nothing of this history that evening; when I wrote *Homosexual* I was more dismissive of SIR than I should have been. Before the Stonewall riots of 1969, regarded as the symbolic birth of gay liberation, there was already emerging a new assertion of rights in California that would explode over the coming decades.

In Sydney in the 1970s it was rather different: my colleague Lex Watson lived in a cottage on the edge of Balmain with an untidy garden that lapped the harbour, and he held large parties to watch the fireworks. Lex was not only a colleague, he was a central figure for four decades in the gay movement, particularly in the New South Wales campaign to decriminalise homosexual behaviour, which only happened in 1984, and in the early years of the AIDS crisis. His academic career came second; today someone as permanently politically engaged as was Lex would find it far harder to survive in academia. Just before his death of cancer in 2014 he was made a member of the Order of Australia, a recognition that he was probably the most significant gay activist of his generation. Lex was an avid fan of Wagner and, perhaps not surprisingly, attracted to the leather scene. As he aged he became more reclusive and an addictive hoarder, dying of cancer in 2014, leaving his house dirty and crammed with old newspapers.

Lex's parties gradually faded away as the commercial growth of Oxford Street lured more people, and New Year's Eve became the site for major public rather than private celebrations. Since then it's often been an evening to avoid; it brought out black demons for Anthony, who would sit, brooding and drinking red wine, on the back porch, and had to be coaxed across the road from where we might see the tips of the CBD fireworks. Perhaps not going out on New Year's Eve goes back to the end of 1992, when we slept through a panicked stampede not far from our hotel in Hong Kong. The stampede killed twenty-one people; the next day we walked up the steep hill to Lang Kwai Fong, where mourners were covering the debris from the previous night with white flowers.

January 3: Melbourne

Melbourne is absurdly languid today. I finish a review for an academic journal, torn between wanting to be supportive of a younger scholar and irritation at the over-theorisation. I look back at the novel I've been trying to write for well over a year and realise that I reveal more of myself in fiction than I do writing this journal. "There is nothing more calculated to conceal than artful disclosure": I put this in quote marks, though I am not sure if anyone has actually said it. Writing memoir is rather like going to one's doctor: one tries to tell everything that is relevant, and one omits the embarrassing detail that is most important. I suspect writing becomes harder as one ages, and truculent self-confidence gives way to greater recognition of one's limitations.

2018

It's a time for memoirs: my tables seem to overflow with them: Bill Hayes on Oliver Sacks; Mathieu Lindon on Michel Foucault; Armistead Maupin on himself, Richard Flanagan's autobiographical novel, *First Person*. Part of their fascination is where their stories intersect with my own life, as in the old Hobart Library on Argyle Street, where Flanagan apparently held a tenuous part time job, too young to have stamped out books for my parents. Maupin's autobiography reminds me of his home, nestled on San Francisco's Filbert Steps, rising up the improbably steep hill towards Coit Tower, a concrete phallic symbol sometimes described as resembling a fire hose nozzle, a memorial to a rich woman's fantasy.

I met Armistead Maupin soon after the *San Francisco Chronicle* started serialising his *Tales of the City*, and he was generous and sociable, hosting several joyous dinners in restaurants in North Beach, the Bohemian enclave below the Steps. Like Edmund White he combines an ability to write hard and well with an unerring eye for networking with the rich and famous. Reading Armistead's memoir, I realise I liked him better before he became a celebrity.

In those early days of a movement there is a presumed intimacy among writers/activists; it is one of the blessings that fades with success and corporatisation. I am re-living that time through Armistead's discovery of sex and politics, of the growth of San Francisco's sense of itself as the gay capital of the world. Back in Sydney one of the larger bars on Oxford Street had a large mural of San Francisco behind the upstairs bar, and young queers fantasised about moving there as earlier generations had longed for London and Paris.

January 4: Melbourne

The first week of January is perfect for catching up with people who haven't escaped to the beach. I drive through empty streets to have lunch with Colin Batrouney, who is director of health promotion for the Victorian AIDS Council, and author of several novels. I've known Colin since he played the part of Louis in the first Australian production of *Angels in America* in 1993. Ours is that relationship between friend and acquaintance for which English lacks a word. He was already both an AIDS activist and an established actor when he came to *Angels*; he's been a consistent part of the response to HIV now for quarter of a century.

Colin muses on the long-term impact of the epidemic: he wonders whether those of us who lost many of our peers have ever been able to sufficiently grieve. As we grow older many of those who should be ageing alongside us are no longer there. Our worlds have thinned out and younger men—for in Australia the death toll was almost entirely male: haemophiliacs and homosexuals—are now growing up without the shadow of AIDS.

January 10: Melbourne

Last night there were television images of the first same-sex weddings to take place since the new legislation came into place: two sets of women, in both cases almost caricatures of 'butch/femme: one woman in tuxedo and bow tie, the other in flowing chintz. The male couple, on the contrary, looked very similar, accentuated by matching white suits. All three pairs could have walked off the set of a 1970s British TV drama.

Have a very relaxed coffee with Andrew Giles, his two kids sitting next to us and immersed in playing games on their iPad. Andrew is a federal Labor MP, almost certainly a future minister, and an important voice for asylum seekers within the party. I'd met him several years ago—his electorate borders on the La Trobe campus—and he was an eager contributor to the anthology on the choice between Labor and the Greens in the 2016 election. My local shopping strip, Queens Parade, sits on the border between the one federal Greens seat (Melbourne, held by Adam Bandt) and the seat most likely to go Green (Batman), where yet another by-election looms as the citizenship of the current federal member comes under review. A dog comes by and Andrew's daughter, startled, throws herself into my arms. A telephone call from a senior Labor figure interrupts our conversation. Our discussion touched on electoral politics; more interesting was Andrew's interest in loneliness as a growing social phenomenon, and what the state might do to address it.

Having lost a life partner I'm very aware of the traps of loneliness, which will face most of us as we age. I'm battered by constant images of couples in advertisements for retirement cruises and villages, yet as we grow older we are increasingly unlikely to be happily coupled, due to illness and death. Britain already has a minister for loneliness, but despite reading several interviews with her I remain somewhat bemused by what she might achieve. The answer in part is to de-romanticise the idea of the perfect partner, able to fulfil all one's needs, but this is hardly within the remit of government.

Talking with Andrew Giles reminds me that despite the American influences on our political language the shape of our parties remains refreshingly different, even as the ideological gap between Democrats and Republicans now seems greater than that between Labor and Liberal. The Parliamentary system and the strength of the trade union movement have shaped our politics, as has compulsory voting.[28] But as membership of the major parties declines, they are less able to speak for large numbers of voters who increasingly seek alternatives. Exact figures are very hard to find, but none of Australia's parties have a membership as large as that of the most popular AFL teams. Increasingly, politicians are those who have worked their way up through the party machinery, often with little experience or knowledge outside their immediate political base. This in turn creates greater cynicism among voters, who are exposed to endless stories of corruption, self-interest and endless point-scoring. The tendency of politicians on both sides to constantly denigrate and belittle their opponents is a major contributor to the corrosion of liberal democracy.

I've been a short-lived member of the Labor Party at several times in my life, but in general have felt it easier to comment on politics by staying away from formal membership. Two years ago I attended the Labor National Conference on behalf of the university-based on-line site, *The Conversation*. Their chief political correspondent is

---

28 Judith Brett, *From Secret Ballot to Democracy Sausage*, Text, 2019.

the redoubtable Michelle Grattan, one of the doyens of the Canberra Press Gallery, whom I've known since we were junior academics at Monash University; I like to say I was there as Michelle's handbag. The Conference suggested a more vibrant and participatory party than media reports suggest, even if hard lobbying brought several nominal left-wing unions behind Bill Shorten's hard line on asylum seekers. Over the weekend several thousand people passed in and out of the conference. They attended the open discussions organised through the Labor Fringe, taking materials from the twenty or so stalls carrying everything from EMILY's List tea towels illustrating Julia Gillard's misogyny speech, to yoyos and free water from the health promotion booth. Here were rusted-on party veterans and union organisers alongside large groups of young supporters, many of them wearing the green T-shirts of Labor for Environment, the red of Labor for Refugees or the multi-colours of Rainbow Labor.

Maybe unrequited love captures my ambivalence about the Labor Party as well as it does my deeply conflicted views of the United States. Like so many of my generation I exulted in the election of Gough Whitlam in 1972, the first time in my memory that Australia had anything but a Liberal government. I knew Gough slightly, best in the awful period after his dismissal by the Governor-General and the double blow of the 1975 and 1977 elections, when he was resoundingly rebuffed by the electorate. Before the 1975 election I went to a dinner at the home of his wealthy supporters, whose North Shore neighbours politely picketed us as we arrived, and Margaret Whitlam promised a tennis date at the Lodge were Labor returned. Two years later Gough, weary after a second unsuccessful election campaign, arrived unannounced at my flat in Sydney, seemingly looking for companionship. I was surprised and overwhelmed, and not even sure why he was there; I think he felt my embarrassment and left quickly. Gough's self-confidence carried his party, and then his country, into new and splendid directions, but as he aged he increasingly became a parody of himself. "Difficult" as Gore Vidal observed of him "To tell the difference between vanity and overweening vanity."

2018

January 13: Melbourne

Last night was the opening event of *Better Together*, a national queer conference that's been pulled together to brainstorm what happens after marriage has been achieved. There are the necessary rhetorical flourishes which all conferences demand, and four international speakers, only one, a charismatic Filipina, not from the North Atlantic world. The people here are mainly in their twenties, equal numbers of women and men—one striking trans* woman catches my eye, dressed in a curvaceous white shift with a frangipani in her ear, she is the most elegant person in a room short on style.

The large floor of the Melbourne Town Hall this morning is full as the conference gets underway; I come in late, crouch at the back of the room. It has something of the feel of a revival meeting, with a heavy emphasis on individual experience. Over the weekend more than 600 people attend, and the conference drags on well into Saturday evening as every group demands that its hurts be heard. I'm back in the Town Hall Saturday morning to speak on a panel on global issues, but we merely skim the surface. Like much of contemporary politics this is a conference dominated by the confessional and the gestural: the highpoint is a reception at the Tennis Centre where Billy Jean King, in Melbourne for the fiftieth anniversary of her win at the Australian Open, demands that the Margaret Court Arena be renamed because of Court's consistent attacks on the queer community.

Words matter: but in the contemporary world it is easier to rally people around symbolic hurts rather than structural inequities. Does it matter that Court referred to trans* children as "the work of the devil?" Does it matter that Australia's national holiday commemorates the dispossession by British settlers of the Indigenous inhabitants? Does it matter that Donald Trump dismissed much of the world as consisting of "shithole countries"? Clearly yes: but how should we respond? Symbolic issues matter when they draw attention to structural inequalities, but they too easily become ends in themselves.

As individuals we care about our material circumstances; "the economy, stupid" was allegedly the advice that won Bill Clinton the

Presidency. Yes, people vote out of self-interest, though often less than politicians imagine. But collectively we are stirred to passion and sometimes violence by the symbolic. People are killed in the name of 'honour', not the fringe benefit tax.

January 19: Melbourne

A phone call asking me to be on a conservative radio chat show talking about an article I'd written on the limits of the 'LGBTIQ' acronym, then two hours later a further call to cancel. I suspect they finally read the article and decided it was too complex for their angry, blue rinse, denture-wearing, duck shooting, church going, respectable, suburban, Abbott-loving *deplorable* listenership: I'm tempted into that list of predictable stereotypes by Salman Rushdie, whose latest novel, *The Golden House*, I'm currently reading. It's a *tour de force* spurred by anger at the world and a frantic desire to remain relevant, with its share of intrigue, violence, confusion, rich with erudition and commentary, boasting its knowledge of Greek myths and popular cinema.

When I embarked on the novel—and it demands work; thus embarkation—I had no idea that it would raise issues of sexual and gender identity. Rushdie's sense of the dislocations of the modern world, the world that produced Donald Trump, here transmogrified into a character called the Joker, reveals itself most nakedly in the character of the youngest son of the Indian mogul Nero Golden, D(ionysius), who will kill himself because he cannot resolve his gender identity. Rushdie has clearly immersed himself in contemporary gender politics, and works hard to grasp how assumptions are changing, and biology proves less immutable than we once thought. But it's clear he feels what was once solid is collapsing, and it's Rushdie's voice we hear when D laments his failure "to enter the promised land which was barred to (him) by the limits of (his) perceptions."[29] This phrase recalls all those films where homosexual characters were allowed only if they died, literally or metaphorically (*Advise and Consent*; *The Fox*; *The Sergeant*; *The Killing of Sister George*).

---

29 Salman Rushdie, *The Golden House*, Random House, 2017, p.255.

2018

January 21: Melbourne

With Edward Hunter at the Triennial Exhibition at the National Gallery of Victoria. It's a massive show, not only in the downstairs viewing areas but with works nestled in amongst the halls of Victoriana, a set of massive replicas of human skulls sprawled beneath dignified family portraits. Lots of what's on show seems decorative, or technological wizardry, a fun fair for art-goers. But Ed has curated our visit, and we end up in a small screening room where there is a moving montage of videos taken by Irish artist Richard Mosse through long-range thermal imaging cameras, showing refugee flows from Syria, Afghanistan, Iraq, Libya, 'collateral damage' of several decades of the 'war against terror'. Brutality, violence, sweat, isolation, despair, all caught in a relentless monochrome, which renders both the refugees and their captors as alien others: the video runs for fifty minutes. Spectators silently watch on bean bags strewn across the floor

"And then what?" I ask. "Does it have any political effect?" Ed, ever optimistic, thinks it calls on people's empathy and he is probably right, but it's a matter of affect rather than effect, and what strikes me about our treatment of asylum seekers is how easily we look away. The Triennial speaks to global movements, inequalities, injustices, but does it reduce them to aesthetic spectacle?

January 23–24: Melbourne

Over a nostalgic dinner with Barbara Friday, Anne Mitchell and Andrea Goldsmith, we dive back into our childhoods, sharing memories of Enid Blyton's *Secret Seven*, the *Magic Faraway Tree*, especially the *Famous Five*, with the very butch tomboy, George. Blyton has faded in popularity, but her genteel racism and snobbery lives on, through authors like Elizabeth George—herself American—and television programs like *Midsomer Murders*, creating a sanitised image of England that is less and less accurate.

At the age of seven I had the best collection of Enid Blyton books in our street. So claims Barb, my neighbour when we lived for about a year on Brooker Avenue, a new road running parallel to the river from central Hobart. Not yet the highway it would become, our strip had been developed to provide homes for engineers working for the Hydro Electricity Commission. After my father's small home industry manufacturing light switches collapsed in the early 1950s, my parents moved to Tasmania, where my father took a job with the Hydro, and most of our neighbours in the street were British, lured to Tasmania by sunshine and engineering jobs. My father designed sub-stations and occasionally took me with him to visit projects being developed in the lush green interior of the state. In the 1950s dams and power stations seemed unproblematic, and we grew up believing that the future of Tasmania was entwined with cheap electricity that powered the manufacture of zinc and aluminium. The seven-storey yellow deco building where my father worked bestrode a major city intersection, and one of my earliest memories is the lighted crown atop which marked the coronation of Queen Elizabeth in 1953.

I didn't overlap with Greens leader Bob Brown, who moved to Hobart in 1972, the year my parents moved back to Sydney, where my father died the following year. Bob was central to the creation of the Greens, a charismatic figure with a stoic bravery combined with increasing skill in mainstream politics. The Right hated his access to Gillard during her post-2010 government; in fact, he caused her far less trouble than some within her own party. I'd met Bob briefly several times, and in late 2016 I spoke with him at an event at Fullers Bookstore, already a Hobart landmark when I was a kid. Brown sees the Greens as replacing Labor as the party of the left; I was politely sceptical. At dinner afterwards I re-met his partner, Paul Thomas, whom I'd encountered at an international gay gathering in Vienna thirty years earlier. Now they live on a farm near Sorrel, but Bob remains a passionate campaigner, committed to the vision that grew from blocking the damming of the Franklin River and, like Wendy Bacon, still willing to risk arrest.

Can the Greens break the stranglehold of the old politics and become a major political party, capable of winning government? Should they?

For this to happen they would need to move outside their largely inner-city bastions and win seats from both major parties. But the dilemma is that to appeal to a larger electorate means facing the same challenge from 'the left' that they pose to Labor now. The most brutal optimism about their future I've heard came from Jason Ball, the charismatic young footballer who challenged Liberal Minister Kelly O'Dwyer in one of Australia's richest electorates and won an impressive swing—but largely at the expense of Labor. "Your generation", said Jason in a matter of fact tone, "will die out, and the Greens will take over", but this seems as likely as our hopes for counter-cultural transformation forty years ago.

Barb and I went to different schools, and our paths didn't cross again until I met her through Anthony's colleague Anne Mitchell. They worked together to develop the first surveys of sexual behaviour and knowledge amongst school kids, and we encourage Anne to tell us stories of the first visits to schools, the Catholic teachers who embraced the study, the trek out to distant suburbs: I remember Anthony searching for Hoppers Crossing in the street directory, long before we accessed GPS on our phones. The research project uncovered large numbers of kids who feared for their safety because they were unsure or unable to speak freely about their sexuality and gender identities, and was the foundation for the Safe Schools Project, the subject of Benjamin Law's 2017 *Quarterly Essay*. In it he refers to Anne as "the 'loveable grandma' of the community".

Before they got together Anne and Barb were both married, and between them have many children and grandchildren, a choice that seemed impossible for gay men of my generation. Many men forced themselves into marriage because they desperately wanted children; women were more likely to discover the possibility of lesbian love long after marriage. Research suggests that female sexuality remains more fluid than male, but how far this is biological and how far socially conditioned is impossible to assert.

As Rushdie suggests, the idea of gender fluidity is the hottest issue now in sexual politics, as I'm reminded when I speak at an event called

Queers and Our Hidden Histories, part of the annual queer Midsumma Festival. I'm on stage with the curator of an extraordinary exhibition at the State Library, where five artists draw on the Lesbian and Gay Archives to explore questions of identity, and a younger performance artist who claims to be inspired by an allegedly 'gay' tortoise. I refrain from pointing out that 'gay' is an identity that hardly describes the sexual behaviour of reptiles, but how we refer to ourselves becomes the dominant question from the floor.

One older lesbian, a veteran of almost half a century of radical feminism, defines 'queer' as the umbrella, with many spokes, the different components of the 'LGBTI…' list. It's a lovely phrase, but it doesn't end the discussion. In the early days of the movement 'gay' was understood as a generic term for both women and men, and some lesbians still prefer to use the term; growing assertion of gender fluidity has made us increasingly aware of the limits and power of naming. I suggest that we can add so many categories that the term becomes meaningless, but I sense polite disagreement. Fear of offending now gives us terms like "LGBTIQ people with a cervix".

I've decided to tell the story of the first queer demonstration in Australia in October 1971, prompted rather oddly by a Liberal Party pre-selection for the safe Sydney seat of Berowra. Mobilised by Lex Watson, a group of us—women, men, straight, gay—picketed the party headquarters in downtown Sydney to oppose a right-wing conservative who was trying to unseat the then more liberal Attorney General, Tom Hughes. Balloons, placards, a big banner proclaiming we were part of the Campaign Against Moral Persecution (CAMP): we were almost completely ignored by the media, but there was a sense of excitement. For the first-time women stood in central Sydney with placards announcing 'Gay Is Good', a public coming out in a time when elaborate denial was part of the social fabric. Over the next few years small demonstrations became central to the growth of queer organising and spread quickly to other cities.

2018

January 28: Melbourne

It's the Pride March in St Kilda: and it's almost 37 degrees outside, so reluctantly I stay home. I've never been enthused about the idea of demonstrating pride by marching in a slow formation down Fitzroy Street, but I wanted to be part of the "No Pride in Detention" group this year. (Fitzroy Street is a central shopping street in one of the most liberal areas of Melbourne, close to the strip known for street sex workers. It is also the site of a proposed multi-storey LGBT Community Centre, funded in part by the state government.)

I decide it's time to cull my stamp collection. My father brought his with him when he fled Vienna in 1938, and I grew up sharing stamp collecting with him, so the collection now has accumulated over a century. Back in the early 1990s I wrote about stamps as political symbols, and *Paper Ambassadors* remains my only coffee table book, complete with colour plates. Letters today are far less common, and stamps have become commodities produced largely for collectors, but until the end of the last century they were common items for almost everyone in the literate world, and governments used them to promote official versions of good citizenship. Choosing illustrations was enormous fun: stamps from Czechoslovakia warning against smoking; the Miss World contest from Jamaica; even stamps commemorating the wedding of Charles and Diana from North Korea, presumably not available at local post offices in Pyongyang.

Many people helped me in writing *Paper Ambassadors*, including the Australian writer Donald Horne who'd noted a reference to stamps in a review I'd written of one of his books. In London I met Tony Benn, the British Labour politician who'd been Postmaster General in the mid-1960s and sought to modernise British stamps. He succeeded in shrinking the image of the Queen, which appears on every British stamp even today, and spoke of his success in showing a black face—on an issue honouring the Salvation Army—and commemorating poet Robert Burns, who was both an atheist and a republican. Today, when most Western countries have turned stamp production into purely commercial enterprises, Britain issues stamps depicting rock singers, television programs and children's books, although every Royal wedding produce its commemorative issues, as is also true in Australia. Our stamps have become increasingly bland and unadventurous, reflecting an increasingly outdated and parochial vision of Australia, as if designed by John Howard in his retirement. Not even Britain bothers, as does Australia Post, with an annual issue to mark the Queen's birthday.

I take down an old shoe box of philatelic envelopes, and decide many can go to Oxfam, where they are in turn sold off in bulk to a dealer. There are copious Australia Post covers, commemorating everything from the centenary of Broken Hill to the Perth Zoo, many of them addressed to 'meet market', the pre-web dating service run through the gay press. My favourite is a cover of 'endangered species' from the Cocos Islands, with the post code reading "Indian Ocean 6799". But some of the envelopes speak of history: one, from Vienna in 1938, has both German and Austrian stamps, the postal authorities not yet keeping up with the speed of the *Anschluss*. A cover, dated 1934, commemorates a delivery "leaving by air mail from New Zealand to Australia, via Melbourne to Papua & New Guinea", and there are stamps and postmarks from all three countries.

February 1: Melbourne

Meet up with novelist Christos Tsiolkas and political cartoonist Sam Wallman for a drink; three generations of gay men, linked by politics and friendship. Sam likes to hear stories of our pasts, and Christos and I reminisce about our first meeting, about the time he wrote *Loaded*, when we were introduced by a mutual friend, the mercurial Sasha Soldatow. Sasha was a writer, a performance artist, a translator, a prison activist, an anarchist, who died of liver failure in Sydney before his sixtieth birthday. He and I had a brief affair in the early, heady days of gay liberation, that turned sour; he idolised Christos, with whom he wrote the book *Jump Cuts*. *Loaded*, later filmed as *Head On*, relates a frenetic journey across Melbourne by a young Greek working-class gay man, motifs that reappear in many of Christos's works, even as fame and money lead him to reflect increasingly on his own very secure middle-class status.

Sam and I were both in the US during the Presidential elections; he and Christos supported Sanders, though they reluctantly concede that we can't know whether he might have beaten Trump. But they raise glasses to him, then to Corbyn: I don't join in. I am mystified by the appeal of grumpy old men to much younger leftists, but what I hear as recycled rhetoric they hear as a welcome antidote to bland neo-liberalism. Sam likes to embrace me as a fellow left-winger, but I'm more restrained in my political views than he guesses. In talking politics with these guys there's a natural slipping between the personal and the analytic, so we move from current debates about class to our experiences of monogamy. Both Sam and Christos have the art of asking deeply personal questions without being intrusive.

We're in the Laird, the inner-city gay pub once known as a centre for illicit gambling, now the best-known men-only queer space in Melbourne. In the late afternoon the small beer garden is almost empty, but as the evening gradually winds in it starts to fill up, as the pub is slowly taken over by fetishists: it's spit and polish night, where one section of the pub is reserved for men wearing at least "one major piece of leather or rubber/neoprene gear or FULL armed forces/emergency services uniform."

We're joined by Tony, a gay man who seems nonplussed by the rubber guys, and just wants people to hang with. We introduce ourselves; he offers to buy us drinks; suddenly he turns and stares, mouth open, at Christos. "Are you really Christos Tsiolkas?" he says, as star struck as a teenager brought face to face with a rock idol. Christos is too gentle to take offence, and soon the four of us are drinking together, even if, in my case, I barely get through one light beer. I've seen Christos morph from *enfant terrible* to established man of letters, and manage the transition far better than most others, maybe because he is so skilful at sublimating his anger into his writings. I've rarely liked any of his characters, much as I like the man who creates them. Christos's father was dying at the same time as Anthony, and Christos told me he had gone to a church and lit a candle for both of them, which touched me despite—because—neither of us are believers.

Christos has just finished a small book on Patrick White, which involved reading all his very long novels. White was a shadowy figure when I lived in Sydney in the 1970s, an early environmentalist and a patron of the Paris Theatre Company, briefly a crucible for new Australian plays. I regret never having met White; the closest I came was when he asked our mutual literary agent to show me a proof copy of *The Twyborn Affair*, before its publication at the end of 1979. Along with Virginia Woolf's *Orlando* and Vidal's *Myra Breckinridge* it is a reminder that gender fluidity has been central to our cultural heritage long before it took the political form it has today. For Christos, White's relationship with his Greek lover, Manoly Lascaris, is a key to his understanding of the immigrant experience, a constant theme in Christos's own writings. He and I are both children of immigrants, but Christos's identification with Greece is far stronger than mine with the complex chessboard of Eastern and Central Europe from which my parents both fled.

February 4: Melbourne

The Napier Street Temperance Hall was built in 1863, and became home to the YMCA, the South Melbourne Thistle Club, the South Melbourne Harmonic Society, the Emerald Hill branch of the Labor Party and friendly societies such as the Manchester Unity Independent Order of Oddfellows. Today it's a performing arts centre, and about sixty of us sit on high backed wire chairs to watch a performance by the Croatian dancer Bruno Isakovic. For forty minutes a naked Bruno silently stretches his body through a number of poses reminiscent of physique magazine covers from the 1960s, strangely sexless, like a table top dancer caught in slow motion. If he wore a jockstrap one would be tempted to stuff it with dollar notes; fully naked he stretches the limits between art and voyeurism.

I'm at *Deunded* because Bruno is the husband of an old friend, Zvonimir Dobrovic, an extraordinary arts entrepreneur who founded the ongoing festival Queer Zagreb. Zvonimir was entering his teens when Yugoslavia broke up, and Serb forces shelled coastal towns in the newly independent Croatia; the first Queer Zagreb took place in the shadow of the brutal civil wars, at a time when Croatia was making its first tentative moves to joining Western Europe. To be 'queer' in Zagreb was more than a fashion statement; police were stationed outside the opening party to protect us, although the group of demonstrators outside, waving anti-homosexual signs, seemed docile. I was more troubled by the smoke from Communist era cigarettes, which drove me out of the opening disco, half choking.

I was one of half a dozen 'Westerners' at the first gathering in 2003, and the gap between us and the ex-Yugoslavs was reflected in the very different ways each spoke of his experiences. That gap was captured by the New York performance artist David Drake, who sent up academic pretentiousness in a show called *Reinventing Vlad: When Romanian History Meets Western Pop Culture*. (David's family name was originally Drakula.) One distinguished American queer scholar spoke at length about the fashions at his gay gym in Boston, seemingly oblivious to the fact he was no longer in the United States. But as a charming young man from Belgrade told me: "Everything goes through America". Like all the locals, he was very aware of living through enormous transitions, seeking a sexual identity in societies where old structures were crumbling but in which a more inclusive liberal future was not assured. Now Croatia, like Slovenia, is part of the European Union, and Zvonko and Bruno's relationship is legally recognised.

February 8: Melbourne

Sexual harassment is in the news on a daily basis. The Lord Mayor of Melbourne has had to resign, as has a member of Donald Trump's staff. The front pages show pictures of the clearly pregnant mistress of Barnaby Joyce, leader of the National Party and Deputy Prime Minister and a fervent spokesman for 'the sanctity of marriage'. The storm of revelations that began late last year with multiple complaints against Harvey Weinstein have escalated, and every day brings new revelations of rape, harassment, gendered violence (often without any recognition of how men are sometimes the victims, as in mass rapes in the former Yugoslavia). Some feminists of my generation worry about a new witch hunt, the tendency to conflate rape and violence with clumsy and offensive flirtation. Heterosexual men rush to proclaim their solidarity with the Me Too movement, and gay men largely watch on, torn between support for the women and fears of a moral panic.

Harassment is such an imprecise term. A few years ago I was wondering through Hyde Park in Sydney, trying to take snaps of the strolling ibises on my iPhone. Suddenly I was surrounded by a group of police officers, who accused me of photographing a young woman who'd been sunbathing on the lawns. Startled, I showed them my phone; then blurted out: "But I'm gay". The officer in charge grinned, slapped me on the back, and apologised.

As Masha Gessen warned, the current mood "serves to blur the boundaries between rape, nonviolent sexual coercion, and bad, fumbling, drunken sex. The effect is both to criminalize bad sex and trivialize rape".[30] Sex panics have usually targeted the socially powerless—sex workers, pederasts, homosexuals. Today we are living through attacks on powerful celebrities, even as the Molester in Chief, the President of the United States, seems so unscathed by his own history that he can tweet sympathy for staff who've resigned because of evidence of wife abuse.

Postscript: Feb 16: The moral panics continue, having swept up both Oxfam and the Australian government. It appears some Oxfam humanitarian workers used their positions to demand sexual favours. But is paying sex workers always bad? Yes, prostitution is illegal—though widespread—in Haiti, but what about in countries where it is not? And should we prohibit all forms of transactional sex, without any recognition that sex is often parlayed in complex exchange of favours, not always monetary, in which the power dynamics are not as simple as a blanket prohibition suggests.

---

30   Masha Gessen, *New Yorker*, November 14 2017.

The air of old-fashioned moralism that surrounds every revelation of sex outside heterosexual marriage is reinforced when Prime Minister Turnbull, having publicly rebuked his Deputy, Barnaby Joyce, decrees that no minister in his government can have sexual relationship with a staffer. Joyce has now gone to the backbench.

February 11: Melbourne

Tommy Murphy's play *Strangers in Between* was first produced in Sydney in 2005 and is now enjoying a series of revivals. It's a contemporary coming out story, written when Murphy himself was only twenty-six, and one that could very easily slide into cliché: the young boy from the country, the older queen, the tentative happy ending that echoes Armistead Maupin's "logical family" (the reference is there in the program notes). But it's cleverly written, with unexpected twists, and the three actors last night were perfectly cast: the puppy-like Wil King, the charming Guy Simon, the veteran star, Simon Burke. Guy is staying with neighbours, and we all go off for a drink, a rooftop bar where we have to yell to be heard over the too loud music.

The play is moving to Sydney next week and Wil, who still lives with his parents in Melbourne, tells me how much he likes Sydney. "Yes" I say "That's where we used to all go to be gay." We agree that Sydney remains gay, but Melbourne is probably queerer. Simon is familiar to me from decades of stage and film—I vaguely recall his debut in the 1976 film *The Devil's Playground*, with its bleak portrayal of Catholic sexual repression, revisited today in the aftermath of the Royal Commission into Child Sexual Abuse. We've met before—oddly, I can visualise the flat where we were both at a party together, many decades ago, but not its owner—and we bond over mutual friends and memories.

Enid Blyton is still being read: there's a line in a poem by Brigitte Lewis, several generations younger than us, which refers to "moon face, fanny and dick, in the treehouse, I always wished existed." It's part of an anthology, *Bent Street: 2017* (Clouds of Magellan), which is being launched today at the very queer Hares and Hyenas bookshop. Rowland Thomson and Crusader Hillis have kept this bookstore alive for twenty-five years, making it a centre for performances and events for every shade of the queer community. Over the years hundreds of people have appeared on the tiny stage, backed by loud red chintz wallpaper, and this afternoon Greens MP Adam Bandt is speaking. He claims there's a new emphasis on quality in political life, in part a result of the marriage campaign, and hails Bernie Sanders and Jeremy Corbyn. But, I feel like shouting, they both lost.

I first met Adam during the 2010 election campaign, when he snatched a seat that had been Labor over a century and he played a pivotal role in maintaining Julia Gillard's precarious parliamentary majority. He is smart, relentless optimistic, a little geeky with a very quick political mind, more at home with the Africans in the Flemington housing blocks than the trees of Tasmania's Tarkine Wilderness. The right-wing press likes to paint Adam and his colleagues as tribunes of the inner-city latte sipping vegan elites, but his electorate has more public housing than any other in Australia.

February 21: Melbourne

The *New York Times* reports that 160 political scientists have ranked all US Presidents and placed Trump at the very bottom of the list. Even those respondents who identified as Republicans put him behind all but four mid-nineteenth century Presidents, Franklin Pierce, James Buchanan, Andrew Johnson and W.H. Harrison, who died after a month in office.

The poll was conducted just before the mass shooting at a school in greater Miami, one of a growing number of such mass shootings— Columbine, Las Vegas, Orlando—in the United States. In the following days the Florida state assembly would refuse to debate tighter restrictions on assault weapons but proclaimed pornography a threat to public health. Even President Trump asked for a ban on 'bump stocks', but within a week was floating the idea of arming teachers to forestall further shootings. The students at the Parklands High School have become symbols of resistance to the craziness of American gun laws, but nothing seems able to shake the gun culture.

2018

The lead story on the news tonight is the continuing bombardment by government forces of the Syrian district of Eastern Ghouta. Syria joins the long list of countries—Iraq, Afghanistan, Sudan, Congo, the former Yugoslavia, Rwanda, Myanmar—where civil strife has killed and exiled hundreds of thousands of people since the end of the Cold War.

The images from Ghouta stayed with me at *East West Street*, the theatrical narration of Philippe Sands' book on the origins of the concepts of 'crimes against humanity' and 'genocide' through the work of two Jews, both born in the same town in Poland, and both from families largely wiped out by the Holocaust. Sands anchors the story around the trial, and eventual hanging, of Hans Frank, Governor of German occupied Poland, but he brings it into the present, with the slow development of international law as a means of holding at least a small number of tyrants to justice.

Looking back, I realise how little I knew about the Holocaust as I was growing up. Many of my mother's family in Poland were wiped out; those few who survived were shadowy presences in conversations between her and my grandmother. But my Jewish heritage was an almost invisible presence in the very Anglo world of Hobart in my youth. A highlight was the August holidays, when my mother, sister and I stayed with my grandmother is Melbourne. Nana lived in a three-story brick apartment building in East St Kilda, filled with souvenirs of an emigrant history, and large oil paintings that were gradually sold off as money problems increased. The apartment block still stands, now industrial grey and pink rather than the dirty cream of my childhood, and trains rumble in the distance through Balaclava Station, this part of Melbourne having been laid out with names from the Crimean War: Alma, Inkerman, Odessa, Wellington. It was then the heart of Jewish Melbourne, and when my grandmother went shopping she spoke Russian or Polish everywhere except the pharmacy. Now, maybe sixty years later, the Balaclava shopping strip is lined with chic cafes, discount shops, take away sushi; but alongside one of the cafes is the old wall sign for 'Weislitzer Kosher Butcher', and the pharmacist has signs in Russian, promising both Russian speaking staff and "Russian remedies". Across the road an old Russian woman sells gefilte fish and tzimmes in the Balaclava Deli. From her accent I imagine she would have been a child in Russia when my grandmother bought fish on the same street.

My Patkin grandfather was active in Jewish organisations from his arrival in Melbourne in 1927, and became an ardent Zionist after the War, publicly clashing with Sir Isaac Isaacs, first Australian-born Governor-General, about the creation of Israel. With his nephew, Benzion, he was instrumental in the founding of Mount Scopus College, which opened the year he died. We were living in Melbourne at the time; my parents were determined that I would not be sent to a religious Jewish school but moving to Hobart resolved that battle. As a boy, in my grandmother's flat, with its heavy blue drapes and the old silver samovar, I read scraps of Jewish history and legend, but my grandfather died when I was six, and I was never taken to a synagogue.

As a Jew one is automatically assumed to be a supporter of Israel, by Jews and non-Jews alike. Under the law of return I could claim Israeli citizenship, which is denied to Palestinians who were expelled or live in the occupied territories, and this anomaly makes me deeply uncomfortable. The Jewish Passover service ends with the phrase 'Next year in Jerusalem', and in the aftermath of the 2014 war in Gaza I wrote a piece explaining my unwillingness to say these words. This led to an angry rebuke from Labor MP Michael Danby, who was the most stridently pro-Israeli politician in a party which was slowly questioning Australia's automatic support for whatever position the current Israeli government adopted.

I visited Israel in the late 1970s, and it felt a foreign country, more like my images of Lebanon than the sort of extended East St. Kilda I'd imagined from my childhood. Exchanging money in a bank the teller looked at my passport, then my face, and asked in that peculiarly assertive tone of Israelis: "So when are you making aliyah" (i.e. moving to Israel). The question annoyed me.

It's not always easy to balance opposition to Israel's policies with an awareness of anti-Semitism. Nine years ago I took part in a public reading of Caryl Churchill's play *Seven Jewish Children: A Play for Gaza*. She wrote the play in response to the 2008–9 Gaza war, and it was attacked as anti-Semitic in much of the conservative press. The reading took place at the Victorian State Library in front of a packed audience, and I stood with one of my co-readers, a Palestinian Australian, as the audience filed in. "Look at all the respectable Anglos", he said to me, "Come to watch us Semites perform". One of my co-performers was actress Miriam Margolyes; another was an Anglo academic who struck me as the only one of us who might cross the line between opposition to Israeli policy and anti-Semitism. But the English seem to have specialised in genteel anti-Semitism; it imbues the novels of Christie and creeps through in Isherwood's diaries.

February 23: Melbourne

When I grew up in Hobart it was embarrassingly exotic to have parents who spoke with foreign accents. My mother, who came here when she was eleven, was most comfortable speaking English. My father, who came as an adult, was determined to fully master the language. He joined the public speaking group Rostrum, where he was complimented for speaking so well for someone whose "native language was Austrian". My mother had a romance with French—it's not accidental that both Vivien and I have names that could pass for French—which I inherited, even though I dropped out of French after first year University, defeated by the novels of Balzac and Stendhal.

Last week I met with a potential French tutor and, fired by our discussion, went in search of current French magazines. We'd discussed reading *Nouvel Observateur* or *Canard Enchaine*, maybe *Charlie Hebdo*; I'd joked that I'd buy *Paris Match* and read about the British Royals in French. Yes, many of these are accessible on line, but I wanted the texture, the different feel of each revue's choice of format and paper, the ability to tear out pages and underline difficult passages.

One used to be able to find at least some of these publications in Melbourne. Now, in a much larger city, with a bigger francophone population, the newsagents where one could browse through several hundred magazines from across the world are largely gone. In one, a chic if narrow shop on Elizabeth Street, there is a selection of fashion and design revues, heavy with glossy paper and detachable perfume samples, but none of the weekly magazines that chart current developments in France.

As one ages one becomes increasingly nostalgic for what has passed, and increasingly ready to assume things in general are becoming worse. We remember how those older than us lamented what now seems quotidian: men with long hair and ear-studs, swearing on television, weekend shopping. But not everything that passes is a cause for rejoicing, and the huge strides of electronic media do not necessarily compensate for the decline of print culture.

February 25: Melbourne

About eighty of us gathered in a wine bar on the less fashionable end of Melbourne's inner north to meet the Greens candidate for the forthcoming Batman by-election. It's a polite group, probably equal numbers of women and men, ranging from students to retirees. No one here looks like the crazed tree-hugging hippies of right-wing imagination; the dress code seems largely understated but neat, as if no-one wants to stand out too much. The young ministerial staffers seem very much like their counterparts in the Labor Party.

I talk to a woman, dressed in off-white, whom I have never met, but for some reason she tells me the story of her family, almost all wiped out by the Holocaust and its afterlife, and how she joined a synagogue, so she wouldn't sit alone at home through Jewish holidays. Greens leader Richard Di Natale gives a stirring speech about Greens leadership on issues including asylum seekers, coal mining, housing, equal marriage and political corruption; I chat briefly to the first Greens state member in Queensland, and greet Alex Bhathal, who, if she wins Batman, will become the first Sikh in an Australian

Parliament. I know the contours of this electorate, which stretches from my home to La Trobe's Bundoora campus. It's existed as a federal electorate for over a century, and with rare exceptions been held by the Labor Party. Bhathal has run for the seat several times, and the Greens vote has risen to the point where Labor relied on Liberal Party preferences to win in 2016. Driving through Batman one sees the growth of a new Australian suburbia, with town houses and apartment blocks. There are long established Greek and Italian communities, but Chinese, Arabic and Hindi speakers are increasingly present. This is hardly the thicket of rich hippies whom the media depict as the core constituency of the Greens.

I've supported Alex Bhathal in previous elections, once hosting an afternoon tea for her at a local café, and she is well liked. But some of my friends who'd voted for her are attracted to the Labor candidate, Ged Kearney, a former nurse and union leader. She and Bhathal would agree on most issues in private, but party politics require them to accentuate difference, and, in the case of Labor, to offer some judicious pork-barrelling. Kearney offers us a tram line extension and an LGBTIQ health centre; Bhathal speaks of ending coal mining and off-shore detention of asylum seekers.

March 2–4: Sydney

Yesterday I flew to Sydney to take part in the fortieth anniversary of Gay and Lesbian Mardi Gras.

Mardi Gras has become Australia's queer foundation myth, growing out of a street march in winter 1978 which led to a very ugly confrontation between cops and marchers, and a spurt in lesbian and gay activism. The march began as part of a Gay Solidarity event, marking the anniversary of Stonewall riots, and drew people from the bars along Oxford Street, many of them drifting into their first queer demonstration. Mardi Gras could not have happened without the earlier gay movement, nor the growth of a commercial scene, then flourishing on Oxford Street between Paddington and the city. Within a couple of years, the decision was made to move the festival to the end of Sydney's summer, rather than commemorating Stonewall in New York, and it's now the largest night-time event in Australia, a mega commercial business riffing off a huge street party. Tourist groups fly in from southeast Asia to watch a parade they are unlikely to see back home.

I was at the first Mardi Gras; stood with a friend watching the police lay into protestors on Darlinghurst Road and fleeing before they could reach us. My diary reminds me that the following week was full of phone calls, appeals for funds, and several media appearances, but I was not traumatised as were some of those arrested. Mardi Gras survived internal political and financial tensions, demands to ban it from right wing fundamentalists during the early days of AIDS, and has become the central event of Australian queer life, taking over the inner east of Sydney for most of Saturday and broadcast on national television. Last weekend the ABC showed a telemovie about the invention of Mardi Gras, powerful if historically somewhat selective.

This evening there is a reunion at the Australian Museum; I line up for security and am given a nametag bearing the words: '40 Years Out and Proud'. On the top floor more than a hundred people gather, more women than men, evidence of the toll of AIDS in the 1990s remarks Meredith Burgmann. Meredith was one of a few left activists who'd been involved in a civil liberties demonstration that morning, and then rallied to support those arrested. She would go on to become a senior Labor politician and President of the Australian Council for International Development. Some years ago she encouraged me to request my ASIO files for a book she edited, *Dirty Secrets*, in which twenty-eight Australians recount what we were able to gleam from our secret service files. In my case they were deeply disappointing, consisting largely of reprints of articles that were freely available at the time. Some of the files are redacted and may well contain more prurient information than those I could access, but my sad conclusion was that ASIO officials spent considerable time at Xerox machines copying anything that seemed vaguely left wing[31]. No material for blackmail here.

---

31   Meredith Burgmann, *Dirty Secrets: Our ASIO Files*, NewSouth, 2014.

2018

Some of the people at the reception are people whose pictures I'd seen that afternoon at the pop-up Museum of Love and Protest, a two-storey exhibition of Mardi Gras memories, housed in the convict era dark sandstone Darlinghurst jail, across the road from the police station where the arrested protestors were held in 1978. But most are unknown to me, a reminder that Mardi Gras involved large numbers of people who had had little contact with the early gay movement. Of the people I knew in the heady days of Sydney gay liberation I spot only one in the photographs, but the naïve radicalism of early gay liberation had largely played itself out by the mid-1970s, when religious and sporting clubs were creating new possibilities for queer organising. The very success of the movement meant it inevitably became more mainstream, more suburban, more conventional.

By early Saturday afternoon spectators have begun staking out vantage spots on Oxford Street, patiently waiting on milk crates as police move to set up road barriers. We are told to gather by 6, to wear black tops, as we will be issued commemorative pink ribands, and I realise that in my haste to pack I'm wearing a dark olive t-shirt. Already the surrounds of Hyde Park are full of people, noise and music; we need passes to move across the Park to take up our places alongside the bus that carries some of the veterans. Ahead of us are dykes on bikes and the First Nations float; a stream of fit young people wearing colourful headgear stream past, apparently part of the ANZ Bank presence. I yell greetings to Alex Greenwich, one of the leaders of the marriage campaign and independent member for the state electorate that claims the highest number of openly gay voters in the country. I'd like to talk with him, but I settle for a few quick selfies: in the tumult of the crowd there are intimacies, revelations, gossip, but I hear very little of what's said, half deaf from a cold and the relentless disco blare from the waiting trucks.

At last: we set off up Oxford Street, which is lined ten-deep with spectators, cheering, clapping, photographing. Some of the 78ers are on the double decker bus, rather like a pensioners' trip to the seaside, but walking is calmer; I talk with a number of people—Meredith

Burgmann, Wendy Bacon, Kell Boston—and take a picture of photographer William Yang, who's chronicled gay Sydney for four decades, as he photographs me from the side of the road. (In William's photograph I appear somewhat haggard, as befits a veteran on a long march.) There's an odd sensation of having been turned into talismans, simultaneously memorialised and passed by, as successive generations reinvent themselves in ways we couldn't have imagined. The crowds remain thick for several kilometres; I want to leave the march and realise it's almost impossible to penetrate the crowds. The march peters out several kilometres past Taylor Square, where there are stands for us to watch the rest of the parade, but I'm sore and tired and start back for my hotel, which requires a long detour through the grubby, crowded backstreets of Darlinghurst, littered with drink cans, discarded wrappers, the odd lonely milk crate, even a scarlet stiletto heel, detached in a gutter. I need to show my Mardi Gras wristbands to approach the hotel.

Today's generation of activists are more generous than ours in acknowledging the past, as if they have learnt from Indigenous practices of recognising tribal elders. Unlike gay activists in some of Europe and the United States, my generation had no elders to acknowledge, although we were shaped by the various currents of leftist thought that flourished in the latter years of the Vietnam War. (Many of those who created Mardi Gras came out of the Communist Party). We saw our struggle as part of a broader movement for radical change; breaking that link allowed for the growth of what we now call the LGBTI movement, but it also led to all the excesses of single-issue politics. I was always more cautious than my rhetoric; at a writers festival some years ago a surprisingly aggressive David Marr attacked me for claiming sexual liberation required the downfall of capitalism, but if I'd written that I suspect I never believed the downfall was either desirable or likely.

The liberationist Terry Bell, then part of a short-lived infatuation with the French Marxist Althusser, once accused me of being a wishy washy liberal. I preferred to call myself a democratic socialist, but my politics have been drearily consistent over half a century. I share the nostalgia of many in my generation for Whitlam's vision of a more equitable society, managed by a strong state, but today the proponents of state power see it as protecting the powerful rather than the most vulnerable. Ferreting through old papers I find one of the first political articles I ever wrote: it was called 'Labor in the Age of Whitlam', and written shortly after he replaced Arthur Calwell and went on to win the 1972 election. It's a mark of how slowly politics change that back in 1968 I wrote of the dilemma facing Labor being "how to attract new types of supporters without alienating the traditional working-class voter."[32]

That article appeared in *Outlook: an independent socialist journal*, whose editor, Helen G Palmer, was among a group of Australian intellectuals expelled from the Communist Party after the tumult of 1956. In my naivety I doubt that I saw it as anything other than a leftist journal that would publish a young academic. I already thought of myself as 'new left', without any real comprehension of what the new owed to the old; looking back I recognise the influence of several former Communist Party members, such as the historians Ian Turner and Rex Mortimer, on my thinking.

But even in the 1980s, the era of Thatcher and Reagan, it was still possible to think of oneself as a socialist. I first met Julia Gillard through the Socialist Forum, an earnest group which straddled ex-Communists and Labor hopefuls. Julia was even less of a Marxist than I, although her association with the Forum, which discreetly died before she entered Parliament, was thrown at her during her prime ministership. I remember little of her presence in the Forum, other than the image of her diligently working the Gestetner Machine as the group laboriously debated our differences with the Hawke government.

Like most of the people who've worked with her, I always found Julia smart, witty and likeable; highly ambitious, as the best politicians must be, with a capacity for detail and an infectious laugh, that television distorted into an ocker whine. When she was still a backbencher she came to our place for dinner, and there was a fierce argument with

---

32   *Outlook*, December 1968.

Judy Brett about Labor's support for private schools. I visited her at her electorate office in the outer western suburbs of Melbourne just before the 2004 election and was impressed by her calm as she seemed on track to become a senior government minister (she was then shadow minister for health). "How do you sleep?" I asked her, shaken by the campaign itinerary that would criss-cross the country for the next several months. "I can sleep wherever I am," she replied calmly. Some years later we met for lunch at a café in Williamstown, where she said nothing to indicate she and Rudd were about to challenge Kim Beazley for leadership of the party. One can imagine a Shakespearean play about their victory, her subsequent deposal of Rudd with the aid of a group of mean-spirited courtiers, and the short-lived revenge of Rudd but Julia herself is one of the most unpretentious senior politicians I've ever known.

The day after Mardi Gras, Oxford Street looks empty and tired, though the worst of the mess has been cleared away. I visit my nephew and his family in the morning, am fed fortifying tea with honey, lemon and whisky, then go collapse with my cold. It feels like the ultimate revenge of Fred Nile, the fundamentalist Christian minister politician who has consistently prayed for rain to wash out Mardi Gras through most of its four decades.

March 5: Adelaide

Flew from Sydney to Adelaide, further cementing my cold. After Sydney and Melbourne, Adelaide feels spacious, still growing into Colonel Light's 1837 plans for a convict-free settlement. Below the monuments to civic virtue which edge North Terrace, on the edge of the inevitable Rundle shopping mall, lies Hindley Street, perhaps the saddest city street in Australia, lined with massage parlours and cheap food joints, a few shops boarded up, patiently waiting to be transformed into inner city apartments. But unique to Hindley Street are the outside bars where people sit smoking through sheesha pipes, with an occasional illicit hint of marijuana wafting through the ubiquitous odours of fast food.

2018

I first visited Adelaide at the end of winter 1972 and spoke at the foundation meeting of gay liberation at the University of Adelaide. A few months earlier a university lecturer, George Duncan, had been drowned, presumably by police, while cruising on the banks of the Torrens. Almost twenty years later an inquiry found that there was insufficient evidence to charge any of the officers present that night. Don Dunstan was already premier and convinced of the need to remove the criminal restrictions on homosexuality, for both personal and philosophical reasons. Three years later South Australia became the first jurisdiction in Australia to decriminalise homosexual behaviour. That this story has been largely forgotten in favour of the first Mardi Gras six years later underlines the dominance of Sydney in creating Australian mythology.

The last time I met Dunstan he had been forced out of South Australian politics and lived morosely in Melbourne, but during his premiership there was a sense that South Australia was an exciting centre of cultural and intellectual life. My diary for the time is full of names of people who would leave Adelaide over the next few years, including Jill Matthews, now an emeritus professor at the ANU, then an energetic, thin, red-haired woman who leapt on a table in the University refectory and called on everyone not willing to come out to leave the room.

This time I'm at the Adelaide Festival with Andrea Goldsmith for a performance of Brett Dean's new opera *Hamlet*, which brings out the Oedipal undertones of the tragedy very movingly. The festival includes Writers Week, still the most accessible major literary festival in Australia. Adelaide pioneered the idea in Australia, almost fifty years ago, and now there are festivals in dozens of country towns and outer suburbs. I was a guest of the festival in 1990 along with two remarkable New Zealand writers, Witi Ihimaera and Stevan Eldred-Grigg. With Lisa Alther and Armistead Maupin I suppose we made up the unofficial gaggle of queer writers, though Witi was not yet publicly out. He is best known for his novels exploring Maori life (*Tangi*; *Whale Rider* etc.), but a few years later he wrote a coming out novel set in an Auckland sauna, *Nights in the Gardens of Spain*, in which the main character is deliberately not Maori, rather as Baldwin created white characters in his early homosexual novel, *Giovanni's Room*. In Adelaide the invited writers stayed for several nights in a motel south of the city, and were taken on an expedition to a sanctuary, where kangaroos tried to snatch away our lunches. That evening we were served kangaroo steaks: the visiting Americans were horrified. The Australians ate the steaks stoically.

Writers Week still unfolds in tents on the laws sloping down between Government House and the Torrens; on a Tuesday morning the audience is, not surprisingly, leaning towards the elderly, who sit attentively as British writer Allan Hollinghurst talks about gay love across generations. The seemingly ultra-respectable audiences at Writers Fests are almost unshockable. I've read most of Hollinghurst's novels; my discovery at the Fest is the American Thomas Mullen, who speaks with passion about his novel *Darktown*, a thriller set in the vicious segregation of Atlanta in 1948. Impressed I walk into the book tent and buy a copy.

Thomas Mullen was born in 1974, a decade after the Civil Rights Movement forced the end of the most overt legal segregation in the United States, but as he reminds us, racism remains basic to understanding the United States. I had an African American friend in Chicago, a quiet history graduate student, who jogged, and never ran too close to a white woman in case he was accused of threatening her. Hyde Park, Chicago, home of the University, felt as segregated as Johannesburg, the University an oasis of white privilege surrounded by African American suburbia. At one point I was invited to a cocktail party hosted by one of the University's most prestigious academics, where an equally prestigious academic lectured me on the iniquities of racism at the University. Looking round the room it seemed that the only African-Americans there were serving the drinks.

Leaving Adelaide, I see Tony Abbott standing in line waiting to go through the same security barriers that face me. There's something very comforting about knowing that a former Prime Minister is treated like everyone else. I think of this the following weekend when I go to vote in the Batman by-election, and swap banter with one of the Labor poll workers, the state Minister for Planning. Labor held the seat with a swing to them, most notably in the southern, and most progressive, end of the electorate. One of the women with whom I play tennis, who works with young Syrian refugees, told me she switched her vote to Kearney because she would try to change Labor's policies on asylum seekers.

March 22: Melbourne

"Out of despair comes courage", says the young Syrian refugee who is hoping to be chosen as Mr. Gay Syria. He's a central character in a documentary about the lives of a group of gay Syrian refugees caught between Istanbul and Berlin, grasping at the dangers and the exuberance of making a statement through the Mr Gay World pageant. I'm seeing it at the Melbourne Queer Film Festival, in a packed cinema. The audience, overwhelmingly male, ranging across three generations in age, are visibly shaken by the reminder of how tenuous life is for so many queers outside the enclaves of western liberalism.

The Queer Film Festival here has entered into comfortable middle age, but even as more of the films are available to download—sometimes months before the festival—people come as much for the experience of seeing a film with others as for the films themselves. There are perhaps a hundred or so such festivals across the world, some of them in cities—Minsk, Kampala, Yangoon—where resistance to queer expression is strong. Three years ago I was a guest at Kashish, the Queer Film Festival in Mumbai, held in the Liberty Cinema, a well-preserved dowager from 1947, flying a rainbow flag just down the road from Mumbai's main hospital. That year the festival featured Australian film, and Saturday night's major attraction was the first Indian cinema screening of *The Adventures of Priscilla, Queen of the Desert*. The three drag queens on stage during the opening ceremony could have walked straight off the set of *Priscilla*; watching them was like going back thirty years to the drag bars of Oxford Street. But social change is never linear; while there were echoes of the past, the opening of Kashish was taking place in a very different time and place. The references might seem familiar, even hackneyed; their meaning for the audience was very different than it was for me.

Because the language of the festival was predominantly English, and the various formal discussions were led by cosmopolitan Indians at home in several languages, the rhetoric and the reality were strangely disconnected. Several locals complained to me that Westerners come to Mumbai looking for bars, saunas and pink businesses, and complain at their absence. But these same locals use a global language to describe themselves; they are very aware of the latest international developments, and I heard frequent references to the Irish vote for same-sex marriage in 2015. The impact of the internet means that men seeking sex with other men now use their smart phones much as their counterparts would in Sydney or San Francisco. But there were also unmistakable Indian references, as in the story of the marriage advertisement posted in a local paper, seeking a "well-placed, animal-loving, vegetarian GROOM for my son ..." The woman who placed this post is the mother of a gay rights activist, and the advertisement caused some consternation.

There was very little drag in *Mr Gay Syria*, but there were echoes of the mixture of bravado and subterfuge which emerges in sometimes surprisingly similar ways in very different environments. The film included shots from the police breaking up a Gay Pride march in Istanbul, a stark reminder that persecution because of sexual and gender expression continues and in many places is getting worse.

March 24: Melbourne

The second 'adult in the room' (National Security Advisor, HR McMaster) is to go. He will be replaced by John Bolton, perhaps the nastiest of George W Bush's team of hawks, whose instincts might be termed imperial isolationism. The United States will continue to exert pressure across the world, but in more unpredictable and unilateral ways than in the past. The combination of Presidential self-interest and ideological fervour wielded by the world's most powerful state is a frightening prospect.

When I first moved to Melbourne I bought a nineteenth century weatherboard cottage opposite a park in Clifton Hill, just north of Collingwood. Already the old working class were leaving the area, and over the past decade there's been an explosion of development, as inner-city gentrification ruthlessly converts old warehouses and hotels to apartment complexes. Where every block had its pub, now there are angular steel cafes, where I am given "a chilled, smoky piece of zucchini with ricotta and mint", to tide me over while I wait for a friend. The area is full of hipsters and young mothers with designer prams. Is it because I am ageing, or are the young more beautiful than we were? Certainly bodies have changed, and become more extreme, either gym-toned or tending to the obese.

The gym culture took off seriously in the 1980s, pioneered by gay men, terrified by the new spectre of AIDS. I sat in a cafe watching men go into the gym on Sixth Avenue across from the Christopher Street subway, thinking that Freud would see this new preoccupation with perfecting the body as a clear example of sexual repression. Like gay bars, gyms moved from being slightly disreputable and hidden from the street to mall-like glass-fronted spaces, as a new narcissism became part of middle-class urban life.

April 6: San Francisco

When Market Street was laid out at the beginning of the California Gold Rush a mob rioted, apparently seeing the thoroughfare as an assault on landowners. It became the major spur of the city, carrying streetcars and trolley buses and straddling both the city and Bay Area rail systems. Today it's a symbol of the enormous disparities of contemporary American life: as expensive condos erupt along the four-mile stretch from downtown to the Castro the number of homeless along the street seem to grow, many of them intellectually or physically disabled.

I'm staying near the base of Powell Street to attend a conference of the International Studies Association, which sprawls across two massive Hilton Hotels, with almost 6000 attendees. They throng the foyers and long corridors of the main hotel, a monument to brutalist architecture of the 1960s. The meeting rooms are small and claustrophobic, the rooftop bar opens up to views across the whole of the Bay area. The Beatles stayed here and the hotel is featured in the film *Petulia*, an appropriately unpleasant story.

Academic conferences have their own anxious rhythm, as people run from session to session, set up meetings, woo publishers, test out the job market, try to summarise complex papers in ten-minute soundbites. I'm here for a workshop on the polarisation of queer rights within international politics and enjoy the chance to spend time with people working in the field, some of whom I already know, all of whom are allies. I've been thinking about these concepts for some years, spurred on by my friend and colleague Jonathan Symons. I first met Jon when he had just finished his doctorate in international relations and came to teach at La Trobe. In his thesis he'd explored the international polarisation that existed around the hunting of whales, as countries including Australia sought to ban commercial whaling while others, Japan and Norway, claimed whale meat as an essential part of the traditional diet. "I wonder", mused Jon, "if the same polarisation is true of international attitudes to sexuality." Out of that first discussion developed a collegial friendship which led to our book *Queer Wars: The New Global Polarization over Gay Rights*.

Writing with Jon was remarkably easy; we shared drafts, rewrote each other's words, to a point where I was no longer sure which were his and which mine. Before the book we co-wrote an academic article rehearsing some of the arguments; the reviewers for the journal we submitted this to seemed more concerned with theoretical niceties than the fact that people were being killed because of their sexuality.[33]

As Andrea Cornwall noted at our workshop, the ideas were often reminiscent of the 1970s, but the context is very different. Later in the

---

33 Jonathan Symons and Dennis Altman, 'International norm polarization: sexuality as a subject of human rights protection', *International Theory* 7:1, March 2015, pp.61–95.

week I meet Juan Carlos Valarezo Sanchez, an Ecuadorian political scientist who explains his country's policy of supporting women's rights in its international relations, or, in academic language, transversalising gender. The best meetings I have are outside the conference, when I catch up with a couple of prominent queer activists who manage global networks responding to the realities that we'd been discussing in the workshop. Julie Dorf asks me to meet her at Boba Guys, a milk tea shop where teas are brewed in multiple beakers, rather like the chemistry lab at Hogwarts, and the barista talks us through the process as if it were, in fact, a chemistry demonstration. Julie was a founder of the International Gay and Lesbian Human Rights Commission, the first American based organisation to take international queer issues seriously, and is now an energetic philanthropist, who briefs me on some current projects in between necessary gossip. The anthropologist Niko Besnier wrote a book on "gossip and the everyday production of politics", and gossip is often the glue that holds social movements together.

Travelling between Union Square and the Castro I'm constantly reminded that everything here is gaudier, more extreme than in Australia. On the corner of Market and 18th Street a young man stretches out his arm on which perch two macaws; down the street two middle aged men are lounged against the wall, naked but for home-made cod pieces. Around the Powell Street Station homeless women push multiple trolley past the Crazy Horse Gentlemen's Club and the Academy of Bartending and Mixology, and there's a sense of casual wariness as people hustle drugs and sex, always wary of a sudden shift in mood.

April 13: Los Angeles

West Hollywood is searing blue skies and perfect bodies, even as gym-bulked shoulders support faces disproportionately small for the bodies that carry them.

So how has America changed since Trump's election?

I'm back with three old comrades: Jeff O'Malley; Sofia Gruskin; Anthony Chase (I was last with Sofia and Anthony the week of the

2016 elections). We're sitting on the deck at Lukshon, a contemporary Asian restaurant in a carefully tended deco building in Culver City, once the home of Helms Bakery, official bakers for both the 1932 Los Angeles and 1936 Berlin Olympics.

All three of my friends are foodies, and we munch on tea leaf salad and sea urchin arancini as they ponder the question. Jeff's husband, Patrick, is Jamaican, and they live in Harlem; "Black Americans", says Jeff, "are much angrier." With reason. Trump has reversed decades of painful progress, creating an Administration which is perhaps the most overtly racist since Woodrow Wilson's a century ago. "It's much harder for my students," says Sofia. "Many of our basic assumptions are under fire, and I don't know how to reassure them." A few months later my friend Phillip Ayoub is far more emphatic: "Trump", he said, "has made it possible for people to express prejudices of which they previously might have been ashamed." Sadly, the Trump effect is happening across the world. What used to be angry expostulations that might be shared with a friend or two are now tweeted instantly across the world, and the result is a steady decline of civility, which crosses over between public and private life.

Prime Minister Paul Keating observed that when you change the government the country changes. But it is equally true that governments reflect the changes that have already occurred. Only a minority of American elected Trump; under 60% of those eligible to vote did so. A nation is far more than its government, but it is hard not to feel bitter about the millions of Americans who stayed away, especially given the obstacles facing some who did seek to vote.

April 17: Melbourne

In jet-lag haze I drive to the New International Bookshop to take part in a discussion on the future of the Greens. The Bookshop is in the basement of the Trades Hall, a grand Victorian building that is the oldest functioning union building in the world. Outside a small group of sex workers and supporters picket the event because one of the speakers, Kathleen Maltzahn, a Greens candidate in the forthcoming state elections, is a vocal supporter of the Swedish model of criminalising sex work by fining the buyers. (Were the United States to adopt this position the current President could well face prosecution.) During the evening the protestors will release a flock of red balloons into the store, symbol of the global sex work movement. The panel includes Greens MP Adam Bandt, who speaks passionately of the need for renewable energy, and a retired professor of Politics who, like me, belongs to the generation of much of the attendees. There are the predictable comments from the audience, some of whom had their hands up before they'd thought what to say; it feels rather like a throw-back to earnest leftist gatherings in the seventies. Upstairs a younger crowd are enjoying several shows as part of the Comedy Festival.

There is general agreement that neo-liberal economics have failed, but less clarity about what might replace them. For me the evening poses the central dilemma for the Greens: how can they build electoral support while pointing to the need to drastically alter our way of life in response to a global climate emergency? Adam wants stronger government and more equitable taxes, both of which I agree with. But can a democratic politician win votes by telling people that they need to cut back drastically on consumption, which means giving up much of what has been taken for granted? Can we imagine an Australian government limiting the right to buy a car, which is the practice in some Chinese cities? Or demanding a limit to how large houses can become?

April 23: Melbourne

Coming back from overseas one sees one's own country more clearly. What strikes me this time is the growth of Melbourne, which is exploding in all directions, a massive expanse of road works and building sites. The newspapers run daily stories on the dilemmas of growth: every week, it seems, new rail links are proposed, old buildings demolished. Along Dandenong Road, where I drive to deliver a book, it's impossible to find street numbers in the stretch of building sites. Over 2000 people a week are moving to Melbourne, which is becoming a megalopolis despite itself. The city has literally doubled in size in the thirty years I've lived here.

Increasingly we live in our local enclaves, because crossing the city becomes more and more challenging. I used to go to the bayside beaches; now I stick with the local pools. Back at the Fitzroy Baths there are perhaps fifty people lying in the autumnal sun, some of them reading books. I walk round trying to read the book covers; there are a surprising number from the past. One man is reading Vonnegut's *Cat's Cradle*, in an old Penguin orange edition; someone else is lost in Simone de Beauvoir. Why do some writers remain, while others seem forgotten? When I was at school George Bernard Shaw loomed large—we studied *Saint Joan* in our final year—today he has faded alongside the three volume romances of a century ago.

I'm dwelling on the past because a Facebook friend has asked me to post ten images of album covers which made a lasting impression on me; classical music wasn't exempt, but I don't identify it with the 33 revs LPs that I still treasure, even if never play. I begin with Lou Reed's *Transformer* and end with *Die Neue Marlene* (Dietrich); I have very early memories of my mother singing *In den Kasernen*; of seeing Dietrich perform at the very end of her career. I've deliberately included several Australian artists: there are images of Robyn Archer's album *Tonight Lola Blau* and of the Captain Matchbox Whoopee Band, on whose lead singer I had something of a crush.

Thinking of Dietrich takes me back to an extraordinary month with Anthony at the Rockefeller Foundation's villa on Lake Como. We were lucky to share our time with the American composer Daron Hagen and singer Gilda Lyons, and we created a pastiche of *In den Kasernen* for a farewell evening entertainment. Daron is among the few contemporary composers of opera whose work is performed at major houses; eight years ago I was in Seattle for the premiere of his opera *Amelia*, inspired by the life of aviatrix Amelia Earhart and haunted by memories of the long losing war in Vietnam. It's a powerful piece, with very moving ensemble pieces, and a reminder that opera can be political in the broad sense. But so too can musicals, and the line between, say, Verdi's *Nabucco* and Lin-Manuel Miranda's *Hamilton* is less than the keepers of high culture imagine.

May 3: *Melbourne*

Perhaps 100 people line up for Andre Aciman's signature. We've been in conversation at the Athenaeum Theatre, Melbourne's oldest, where up to 400 people listen as we discuss love, language, identity, music and the mix of remorse and regret that is so strong in his writing. Two older Jewish men on stage make for interesting chemistry; his background is Sephardic and mine Ashkenazi, both from multi-lingual families (but speaking very different languages), with similar tenuous relationships to our shared Jewishness.

Aciman is best known for his book *Call Me By Your Name*, which tells the story of a summer romance between a teenager and a young man, set in an idyllic Italian town. It was filmed last year, and the audience seems predominantly young women, attracted by the idea of romantic love that is the leitmotif of all his writings. When one young woman asks whether love of the sort he described was anything more than "a fairy-tale", I feel a wave of agreement quietly nod through the theatre. The most interesting question comes in halting English from an Italian who is upset that the book, though set in Italy, reduces the Italians to minor roles; I had a similar reaction to the way Aciman writes of Egyptians in his memoir *Out of Egypt*. But he is a writer whose preoccupations are those of personal relations, even where, as in his own life, these relations take place within huge historical events. All his novels are written in the first person, and they are all to some extent autobiographical. He is most thrown when someone asks how much of *Call Me…* was his own story. He assures us that he had never sought intercourse with a peach, neatly avoiding the larger question of how far the adolescent Elio was modelled on his own life.

May 4: Melbourne

From where I am seated there seems to be a vivid blue sky, rising above twisted white columns on which perch heroic statues of Roman warriors. I'm back in the Forum Theatre, this time for the annual dinner of the Human Rights Legal Centre.

There are perhaps 400 people grouped at tables in front of the stage, supporters who include most of the city's human rights advocates. The Centre has had a year of exciting successes, working with most of the country's big law firms on issues ranging from Aboriginal women in custody to protecting free speech in a case brought by former Greens leader Bob Brown. They are leading advocates for asylum seekers and played a major role in the marriage equality campaign.

That campaign is the focus of the evening, with an emotional Magda Szubanski as the featured, and strangely nervous, speaker. Magda, who is best known for playing the overweight sports-obsessed wallflower in the series *Kath and Kim*, and was twice voted Australia's most trusted personality, was one of several high-profile spokespeople during the campaign, but even Magda was upstaged by singer Paul Kelly, whose song 'Little Kings', now twenty years old, captured the fears of many of us.

We're exhorted from the stage to bid in the evening auction; I've spent a few minutes browsing through the offerings, tempted by the possibility of lunch with Deputy Labor Leader Tanya Plibersek—but which five people would I invite to join me?—and settle on a large ceramic platter, watching the bids on my mobile during the speeches. When the bidding reaches $230 I sign off, happy to have helped raise the price, and leave a larger donation as I slip out before the end of the evening.

May 18–19: Castlemaine

It's the opening event of Insert Self Here (ISH), an annual Queer Ideas, Activism and Arts Day, the brainchild of poet Terence Jaensch, in the old goldfields town of Castlemaine. We're in an old goods shed, cold and stark at night, with a film projecting onto the far wall. Men wander along night streets, into the darker patches of city parks, cast furtive looks at each other, hook up in quick pairs or occasional groups, for furtive sex. The film *Secret and Divine Signs* is a homage to cruising, no longer as central a part of the gay male experience. Although the film-maker is Australian the film is shot in New York, and there are moments of nostalgia as we catch glimpses of Fire Island, of the Rambles, a wooded hillock within Central Park once crowded with cruising men. The film ends with a clip from *Calamity Jane*, a striking moment of eye contact between two women.

Cruising for sex was a central part of gay male experience before commercial venues flourished, technology meant it became far easier to set up meetings on line, and gentrification wiped out many of the half-hidden places for casual encounters. Street cruising still happens, but it seems more common in societies where homosex remains furtive, and men are less likely to have homes to which they can take a possible partner. I've seen few places as cruisy as the shopping malls of southeast Asia, where men ride up and down escalators, and linger slowly before window displays, even as the mall guards ignore the sexual transactions enacted in front of them.

Most important, the possibilities of cruising on line have changed the contours of gay male life. These are not restricted to gay men, although my hunch is that sites like Grindr and Scruff are more overtly sexual than ones catering to heterosexual desires. Today there is a large world of potentially available men at the end of one's mobile, allowing one to meet people one might never otherwise encounter. Of course there are scams and lies; but so were there when we met in parks or bars. My sense is that people can be remarkably honest about their desires through the safety of an electronic exchange. Women I know who've used sites like Tinder complain that gay male sites are at least honest about wanting to hook up for sex, but gay men also use these sites to find companionship as much as sex.

"There's a dingo park beyond the new jail", one of the people who've braved the cold to watch the film, and drink post-performance wine, tells me. The jail he referred to replaced the original Castlemaine Gaol, built in 1861 and now an arts centre, preserving the old two-storey blocks of cells, all concrete and narrow passageways. We're here this morning to talk about queer pulp fiction, and one of my co-panellists, the delightful Nevo Zisin, conjures up a queer library, which allows for every variation of sexual and gender desires, much as Nevo tries to live their life.

I take us back seven decades, to the pulp Gore Vidal wrote in the early 1950s for money, and published under various nom-de-plumes, most notably Katherine Everard, named after the bathhouse in New York where Gore had met his partner Howard Austen. His three detective stories, written under the name Edgar Box, display his wit, his snobbishness, and a disappointing inability to carry off the absurd plots of which Agatha Christie was the master.

My talk matches perfectly the retro morning tea which has been assembled, complete with scones and asparagus rolls, tinned spears wrapped in crustless white bread. I take away a bag of soft sandwiches to carry me through the almost two-hour train trip back to the city, slightly slower than it would have been a century earlier.

June 3: Melbourne

There's a framed poster in my hall that commemorates the sixtieth anniversary of the reign of King Bhumipol of Thailand. In an ornate gilded state room fifty members of ruling royal families are seated around the King and Queen, including the reigning monarchs of Brunei, Japan, Lesotho, Spain and Sweden and a host of lesser royals, amongst whom stands a dyspeptic Prince Andrew and the Colonel Crown Prince of Tonga. I found this poster many years ago in a shop window in Bangkok, and bought it for a few hundred baht; now, a decade later, I'm suddenly fascinated by the persistence of monarchy in the modern world. The more I read the more appalled I am by the extravagance and panoply of most royals but, equally, genuinely curious about the deference that monarchies still command.

2018

I've been watching *The Crown*, the imagined reproduction of the reign of the second Elizabeth. She came to the throne when I was a child, and my earliest political memories are of an avuncular if awestruck Prime Minister Menzies escorting her through the endless routine of a Royal Visit. What is most striking, watching the episodes which straddle my school years, is the enormous weight of divorce around the Royals. Association with divorce unseated her uncle, kept her sister from marrying for many years and, if television is to be believed, threatened her own marriage. Now three of her four children have divorced and her grandson has recently announced an engagement to a woman he's been living with for some time.

Even convinced republicans re-live our lives through the milestones of the royal soap opera, and *The Crown* feels little different to series such as *West Wing* or *House of Cards*, both imagined political histories. Modern communications underline our ability to move between physical and electronic realities, until they collide and we realise that 'President Donald Trump' really is the President.

Two of my neighbours are here for a pizza dinner: Ashenafi Biru is Ethiopian and I ask him whether there is a movement to restore the monarchy in Ethiopia: Yes, of course, just as there is in Romania, Georgia and, most puzzling of all, Brazil, which established its own monarchy after breaking from Portugal and deposed their second Emperor a hundred and fifty years ago. As in the case of France and Ethiopia there are several claimants to the throne and apparently considerable support for restoration.

To even suggest there is a case for monarchies shocks most of my leftist friends, but Ashenafi is rather taken with the possibility, as a way of establishing a national symbol above politics. My sense is that monarchies combine celebrity with nostalgia for a greater past, embodied in the massive palaces that remain in once imperial capitals like Brussels and Vienna. At the same time there is a strong argument for separating effective and ceremonial power, as Walter Bagehot argued in the nineteenth century.

I voted enthusiastically for a republic in the referendum of 1999, in which the republican forces were split and John Howard's desire for continuity carried the day. Memorably the debate saw Malcolm Turnbull and Tony Abbott bitterly opposed, though Turnbull moderated his position considerably once he became Prime Minister. Today there is probably even less enthusiasm for a republic than there was then; I suspect there is little point raising the issue until the current Queen dies and Donald Trump is no longer in office. Yes, the Queen's head is on our coins, but the current system, where the Australian appointed Governor-General is effectively the head of state, is hardly of great concern, though allowing the Prime Minister sole control over the appointment is. Maybe like many Canadians we remain attached to the monarchy as a form of resistance to American hegemony.

June 8: Melbourne

It was a mistake to book a gourmet hotel on a Friday night; the small upstairs restaurant is packed with loud revellers, and the food is oversalted. We eat fast and walk down to the Brunswick Street strip, encase ourselves in a vegan ice cream parlour, where sugar and exotic fruits compensate for the lack of dairy. I'm with Bill O'Loughlin, a long-term survivor of HIV, whom I've been friends with since the early days of the epidemic.

Bill, like many gay men of his generation—as well as Tony Abbott—had a brief flirtation with the idea of priesthood, and after discovering he was HIV positive began a long career as a counsellor, advocate and consultant. He's one of those friends one sees too rarely and immediately warms to, someone with whom I share intimacies and gossip and political analysis. There's a constant movement in and out of the bar, bursts of cold air as people come in and out, even an Uber delivery man—"Who" asks Bill, with some scorn "sends out for gelato?"

At the beginning of the 1990s Bill and I were Vice Presidents of the Victorian AIDS Council, at a time, says Bill, when we were the same age as the young men getting infected. This was before working in 'the sector' became professionalised, and staff and volunteers hung out together in the local gay pub, where I now go occasionally with Christos Tsiolkas and Sam Wallman. Young men now work in HIV who weren't born when our contemporaries were dying, and for whom this is another career path.

I remember the long evenings at board meetings, the strange obsessions and feuds that develop in a crisis, the arguments over trivia—what colour should be used on a pamphlet; who deserved free tickets to a fundraiser—which could cloud the awful reality that our contemporaries were dying and medicine had as yet no answers. It was awful, but it had its moments of real community and some glamour: for a few years AIDS was chic, identified with Princess Diana and Elizabeth Taylor. Back in Melbourne there was a fundraising evening featuring the film *Strictly Ballroom*, and a party afterwards where, giddy as a teenager, I danced a few moments with actor Paul Mercurio.

One of the smartest moves of Minister Blewett was to tap Ita Buttrose to chair the National Advisory Committee on AIDS. Ita was then the best-known woman in Australia, editor of a number of major publications, a frequent figure on television, even the subject of a Cold Chisel song. At an early national AIDS conference I sat behind Ita, watching her carefully polish her nails during a discussion of anal intercourse. The epidemic unsettled silences around homosexuality, sex work, injecting, doctor-patient relations, in ways that will outlast the epidemic.

Bill and I talk about the strange new world of chats, meetings, half-formed couplings, that the web and its sex apps have made possible. Almost half a century after Gay Lib proclaimed that we should all come out, we are struck by the number of men on line who stress that they are *discreet*, by the oddity that men who are happy to post pictures of their genitalia won't show their faces. There is an ethnographic richness to sex apps: "Do you blast?" asks one young man, and I have to search an on-line dictionary to be sure what he's asking.

Dinner with Bill brings back memories of Scott O'Hara, a gay porn star of the 1980s who died in 1998, just as deaths from AIDS were declining. I'd met Scott in the heady mix of gay politics in San Francisco during the early Reagan years and loved the bravado and intelligence that fed his writings. I hardly knew him, but he stayed with me on a brief visit to Melbourne in 1989 and he came with me to Bill's birthday party. Bill remembers that: "By wonderful coincidence someone had given me some porn mags for my birthday and one featured him, so whilst he was in the kitchen those in the lounge were poring over him visually, Ian G— (enthusiastic wanker) wanted to ask him to perform in the back garden, and I heard he went on to Porter St and gave a performance on the raised decking beside the spa pool."

In the early 1990s Scott published the journal *Steam* which he claimed as "the intellectual review of public sex". Although Scott was too young to have lived through the early gay liberation years he reminded me of the men I'd known in New York in the early 1970s, ferocious in the pursuit of sex and freedom. He could be surprisingly gentle and intellectual, but his performative self was all cocksure, and built around the fantasies of the ever-ready stud.

June 12: Melbourne

"Keep your friends close and your enemies closer": maybe this explains the behaviour of Donald Trump, quarrelling with his G-7 partners then rushing to embrace Kim Jong-un in Singapore. It is bizarre to see him proclaiming his "excellent relationship" with a murderous thug, while attacking the Prime Minister of Canada as weak and a liar. Not only did Trump help legitimise this murderous thug, he was willing to travel half way around the world, allowing Kim the luxury of staying within his own time zone. But maybe Trump ignores jet lag, as he ignores most things that question his mastery of the world.

Lunch with Terence Jaench, who organised the queer fest I attended in Castlemaine last month. Terrence had spent some time living in New York and we reflected a little on why we both gave up the idea of settling in the United States. A lawyer I knew when I lived there in the early 1980s said he could get me a green card for a thousand dollars, but exciting as New York was it always felt temporary. Perhaps as a child of refugee parents I felt too strong an emotional tie to uproot myself from the country that had given them refuge.

Several prominent Australian writers, most notably Sumner Locke Elliott and Peter Carey, expatriated themselves to New York, but continued to write novels that reveal a deep nostalgia for Australia. I discovered Elliot's novels of Sydney in the 1930s many decades ago, and they became known through film (*Careful He Might Hear You*) and television adaptations (*Water Under the Bridge*; *Eden's Lost*). I'm not sure whether I knew from my early encounters with his books that he was gay, but I soon discovered that was a major factor in his migration to the US after World War II, and it became public with the publication of *Fairyland* in 1990, a year before his death. Wikipedia, a source always to be read with suspicion, claims "Elliott had affairs but never had any stable relationships", but he had a long-term partnership with the novelist Whitfield Cook, who wrote the screenplay for Hitchcock's *Strangers on a Train*. I flirted for a time at writing a biography of Elliott but reading through his papers at Boston University I realised that there was not enough about his life that interested me to surrender to it for the several years it takes to write a good biography. His best novels remain very readable and *Fairyland* is the best account we have of what it was like to be homosexual in Sydney in the inter-War period.

I regret not having met Elliott, to whom I'd written a fan letter: I was heading uptown to meet him at his East Side apartment when I was arrested for using slugs (fake coins) on the New York subway. I deserved to be arrested, though I am not sure I deserved to be held for several hours in a cell near the Times Square subway before being released. Some weeks later I appeared in court, where a lawyer friend spoke briefly to the magistrate, and succeeded in not having a conviction recorded (which might have debarred me from re-entering the United States). Ever since then I have been scrupulous in paying for public transport. After that incident I felt too embarrassed to seek out Elliott again.

Elliott never regretted his move to the United States; Peter Carey often muses on it ruefully and his writings constantly circle back to

Australia. A few years ago he told an interviewer that: "living far from his original home will always entail a small amount of sadness. 'Nostalgia is something we think of as fuzzy. But it's pain. Pain concerning the past. It's true about my country; about the past of my country; it's true about loss, death; time. All of those things. I'm not quite homesick now, but it's a sort of a ... the past is home.'" Perhaps when it came to it I couldn't face the pain of being an expatriate, the sense of being an outsider however successful one might be in one's adopted country. Unlike refugees, expatriates choose to exile themselves. I didn't want to become an American; I didn't want to live in a country where I would not be a full citizen. There are moments when I miss the sheer exuberance and scale of the United States, but these are increasingly outweighed by the pervasive violence and inequality that haunts so much of the country.

June 15: Melbourne

There's a book launch at Hares and Hyenas, for the autobiography of a remarkable medico, David Bradford, an important figure in venereology, HIV and Indigenous health in Australia. After working at the old STD Clinic in Melbourne, David left to co-found a medical practice in Carlton, where I was one of his first patients; we later sat on one of the early AIDS advisory committees. Sometime last year we had coffee on Brunswick Street, and I introduced him to Nathan Hollier at Monash University Publishing, so we now share a publisher.

There are perhaps a hundred people in the store, most of them people who'd worked with or been patients of David during the terrible decade when young men, predominantly haemophiliac and homosexual, were dying from AIDS. It's an evening for reminiscences, for grief but also for celebration. I talk briefly with Maureen O'Brien, one of the early workers at the Victorian AIDS Council, who gave me my first HIV test and was very nervous that she might have to give bad news to someone she knew as a friend. A group of us, now ageing gay men, recall the fright at finding any unexpected skin lesion or swollen gland, and the awful, protracted deaths of men younger than their doctors.

I'm thinking about this when I get home, and there's a phone call from Vlad Viski, a remarkable gay scholar/activist who's reached out to me from Bucharest. He wants to digitise an archive of letters written by Romanian homosexuals in the early 1990s, a period of social and political upheaval following the overthrow of the Ceausescu regime, and a place in which being gay was dangerous and largely hidden. We talk for a while and I'm struck by the sheer resourcefulness of young activists in difficult situations; Vlad has lived and studied in China, Israel and the United States, now he's a central figure in Romania's queer movement.

June 19: Melbourne

I first knew Sally Warhaft as a graduate student; for someone who hates the heat she perversely did field work in India, living in a fishing community near Mumbai. She was the first editor of the very successful *Monthly* magazine, until she fell out with its publisher and left rather abruptly. That was almost ten years ago, but the pain lingers, although Sally has since built a successful career as a journalist and commentator.

Tonight we are meeting in a favourite restaurant, a small unpretentious French bistro which cleverly offers few choices, all excellent. Most recently Sally was a candidate for the Lord Mayoralty of Melbourne, a by-election brought about after allegations of sexual harassment forced Mayor Robert Doyle to resign, one of the first local casualties of the Me Too movement. The City Council is governed by rules more like a remnant of nineteenth century rotten boroughs than I'd realised, in which non-resident property owners have a considerable share of the vote. Sally's run seemed strangely quixotic to me; she had no party backing and few resources. Early in the campaign she was approached by potential donors determined to stave off a possible Greens victory; in the end the Victorian establishment fell in behind Sally Capp, former executive director of the development lobbying group the Property Council of Victoria.

"Why run?" I ask her, and it seems to have been a sudden decision, born of the apparent sleaze surrounding Doyle and a commitment to electing a woman and someone less connected to big property interests than Capp. Sally had high recognition as a regular voice on the ABC and in the end polled a very respectable 9% of the vote, ahead of all the other Independents.

We talk American politics and Sally tells me the story of a visiting American who borrowed a house on the Great Ocean Road. Once settled in he went to the corner store and asked to buy a gun, unaware of Australia's laws. Despite occasional moves to retreat from it, John Howard's legacy of tough gun laws remain.

June 25: Sydney

A conference has been arranged at Sydney University to celebrate the fortieth anniversary of Mardi Gras, in case we'd forgotten. Over a hundred people spent two days in the sprawling University Business School at what was a mix of academic papers, community reports and considerable nostalgia.

In the early 1970s Sydney University was central to the emergence of what we then called the gay and lesbian movement. In this atmosphere much of the intellectual weight of the early gay movement was in the Merewether Building, an unremarkable brown brick structure opposite the main campus, which housed the Faculty of Economics. My colleagues in the Government Department, Lex Watson and Sue Wills, were presidents of CAMP, the first substantial queer organisation; Garry Wotherspoon was one floor above in Economic History, beginning to write the gay history of Sydney. Some of our students would become the leaders of the movement. The early 1970s saw the University bitterly divided over issues that today we would call culture wars. As opposition to the war in Vietnam increased, the new radicalism bled into other issues; both the Philosophy and the Economics departments split over fundamental questions about their disciplines.

The summer after that first demonstration in 1971 at Liberal Party headquarters I took part in what became the launch of Sydney Gay Liberation at a big public event on campus. Germaine Greer was in Sydney promoting her book *The Female Eunuch*, and our mutual friend

Liz Fell persuaded her to speak at a panel on sexual liberation, which also included Gillian Leahy from Sydney Women's Liberation. (All three women had close links to the Sydney Push.) I'd been in bed with mumps that month—I imagined the publicity were I to give Germaine mumps—but the evening felt a triumph. Germaine declared her support for gay liberation and I proclaimed that gay liberation had come to Australia, I hope with less pomposity than that phrase suggests.

There's an air of celebration about the fortieth Anniversary Conference, a recognition of how much has changed in forty years since that first Mardi Gras. But the triumphalism bothers me. The evening of my return to Melbourne I have a long rambling phone conversation with an old friend, now an Australian Ambassador in a country where homophobia is official government policy. Too much of the celebration in Australia is inward looking, unconcerned with the greater world, even while people fleeing persecution because of their sexuality are interned in our offshore detention camps.

June 29: Melbourne

I go into the city on a freezing cold day to speak in an airless ABC 'Tardis studio' with Geraldine Doogue. Geraldine is a legendary broadcaster, whom I've known vaguely over many years; today she's talking with me about the dominance of the Anglosphere on our imagination. The Anglosphere is an awkward term, beloved of former Prime Minister Abbott, that covers the rich English-speaking world. The word was coined by the science-fiction writer Neal Stephenson in his 1995 novel *The Diamond Age* and then picked up by a number of conservative commentators. But its influence is equally dominant on the left. We may be wary of Trump's America and a little bemused by the reappearance of Little Britain, but we still look unreflectively to the US and Britain for intellectual guidance.

Our conversation grew out of an article I'd written for *The Conversation* about our strange fixation on the North Atlantic, which was prompted by the ABC's flagship *Q and A* program during Sydney Writers' Festival last year. Four of the five writers on the panel worked and lived in New

York, and most of the questions were about American politics. The following week the program line up included a British Tory novelist, Stanley Johnson, whose real claim to fame seemed to be that he was Boris Johnson's father. Despite political rhetoric about Australia's relations with Asia both left and right seem obsessed with the Old World.

The interview over, we talk about the relentless war of attrition against the ABC and the recent vote at the Liberal Party national conference to sell it off, a motion no-one rose to speak against. I suggest that Geraldine should capitalise on the inbuilt deference of conservatives and invite a British peer on air to talk about the value of public broadcasting.

I've been in and out of ABC studios since I was a teenager in Hobart and took part in several school radio plays. When the ABC's 'youth station', Double J (later Triple J) started broadcasting in 1975 I became a semi-regular commentator, originally on politics, later, though probably quite unqualified, as a drama critic. The afternoon the Governor-General dismissed the Whitlam government a producer rang me, very agitated, asking me to come into the studios immediately. On the subsequent election day, a hot December Saturday, I was in the Canberra tally room with JJ announcers as Malcolm Fraser's Liberals won the largest majority to date in Australian history. The following year I occasionally took part in a Sunday evening program which tried to stretch the boundaries of radio: one evening I was massaged while on air, as Tina Jorgenson and I swapped banter with visiting film star Dennis Hopper, in Australia for the filming of *Mad Dog Morgan*.

I returned, though more decorously, to political commentary for a few years in Melbourne on the local ABC radio station, working with drive-time host Lindy Burns. I admired the skill with which she managed to weave our conversation into the constant interruptions of weather, traffic reports and listeners' phone calls, and liked the challenge to say something meaningful within those restraints. Most fun was when I sat with Lindy in the ABC box at the Australian Tennis Open and heard gossip about the players on court from a couple of retired professionals.

2018

July: Munich/Paris/Berlin/Amsterdam

On the last night of a month travelling in Europe I am at the National Theatre in Munich to see a disappointingly unimaginative staging of Verdi's opera *The Sicilian Vespers*. As this is a lengthy melodrama, with a crudely nationalistic and sexist libretto, it needs irony to make it effective for a contemporary audience, and irony may be too much to expect from an Opera House where many of Wagner's works were premiered.

We associate Munich with the rise of Hitler and perhaps with the assassination of Israeli athletes at the 1972 Olympic Games, but as capital of the nineteenth century kingdom of Bavaria it was the home of Ludwig II, reputed to be mad, probably homosexual and certainly camp. His portrait hangs in the lobby of the Deutsche Eiche, which combines a decent three-star hotel, a roof terrace favoured by young women with too much money, and a gay sauna, perhaps the largest in Europe. The hotel was a favourite hangout for film director Rainer Fassbinder, who filmed several sequences there, and boasts a long list of celebrity guests, mixing queer and social worlds with a particular German insouciance.

Although they have declined as gay meeting spaces in the United States, elsewhere saunas, or bathhouses as the Americans call them, remain central to gay life, and a sexual space that is hard to imagine in the heterosexual world. My first discovery of bathhouses was in New York, when I followed an intent young man across the Village to the St Marks Baths, then transitioning from its existence as a communal bathhouse for the men of the lower East Side to a sex venue. The first times I went there, I saw young and attractive men flaunting themselves in the basement pool and prowling the corridors of the first floor, while old Jewish men from the neighbourhood lay in the steam rooms on the ground floor, apparently oblivious to or unconcerned by the activities going on around them. It was at the Baths that I met the first man I ever spent a night with, a somewhat older man with a rather mysterious occupation, a small apartment in Queens, and stories of an affair with Tony Perkins, whom I vaguely knew from the film *Psycho*.

Gay saunas may well be the most interesting social space invented by homosexuals, allowing as they do for instant sexual gratification which can lead to lifelong intimacy (I met two of my partners in bathhouses). Like the equally famous Continental Baths where Bette Midler sang on Saturday nights to men grouped around the pool, the St Marks became a major gathering place, as much for socialising as for sex, and was closed down in the frenzied responses to AIDS in the mid-1980s. When I last visited Manhattan the building had been taken over by a Korean restaurant and a karaoke bar; I bought frozen yoghurt next door, alongside young mothers with expensive strollers.

The availability of instant sex with men whose name one might never know is only part of the attraction; saunas are also places of escape from the outside world, of physical, even mental relaxation in an atmosphere that is both erotic and affirming. The literary theorist Leo Bersani attacked me for suggesting that gay saunas were spaces of "Whitmanesque democracy", insisting that they are instead sites of "ruthlessly ranked, hierarchized, and competitive encounters".[34] But now, though I am a lot older and look it, I'd stick to my description: there *is* a wild democracy in the throng of naked bodies, the fluctuations of desire, the sudden moments of intimacy which may or may not be erotic. Some European saunas are frequented by young men seeking money: at the entrance to the Deutsche Eiche sauna there was a sign asking patrons to report anyone who "demanded for paying sex". At my suggestion the notice was amended to read "approaches you ..."

It's been a busy month, split between Paris, Berlin and Amsterdam, with a side trip to Nantes to see old friends Meaghan Morris and Andre Frankovits. Meaghan is about to head off to Cardiff, where she is a visiting professor in martial arts studies, but she and Andre spend some of the year in Nantes and took me on a river cruise up the Erdre, on the fringes of the Loire Valley. In Berlin my friend Anthea Caddy now has a five-month old baby and is living in Wedding, a poor immigrant neighbourhood on the verge of gentrification. I've

---

34   Leo Bersani, 'Is the Rectum a Grave?', *AIDS: Cultural Analysis/Cultural Activism* 43, 1987, p.206.

crossed Germany several times by train and experienced the realities of a persistent heatwave, which one would only wish upon the most stalwart climate change denialists.

In Berlin I buy a postcard of Hannah Arendt, who is remembered in a street name near the Jewish Memorial. I was a young and raw graduate student at Cornell University when Hannah Arendt visited for the semester, and a group of nervous graduate students in government enrolled in her subject, knowing only that she would teach it. Arendt was already famous for her writings (*Eichmann in Jerusalem* had appeared several years earlier) but she was also remarkably familiar, coming like my father from the German speaking Jewish intelligentsia. My memory of her conflates with the memories of my Viennese grandmother, half a generation older, but similar in style. At our first class Arendt decided that we would approach the intellectual history of the twentieth century through its novels—we read Andre Maurois and Thomas Mann's *Magic Mountain*—which influenced me when I started teaching. For many years the first assignment in my American politics classes was a review of a political novel, until it became clear this was too tempting a topic for plagiarism. Our classes ranged widely; she shared with us her growing opposition to the war in Vietnam, as did George Kahin, one of the greatest Western authorities on Indonesian politics. I had planned to learn Bahasa Indonesian and work under Kahin until I fell into my lifelong infatuation with the United States. While I was at Cornell the Menzies government committed troops to fight alongside Americans in Vietnam, and I sought Kahin's advice on how far I, as an Australian, could be active in the campus anti-war movement.

In Paris I have dinner with Antoine Idier, the biographer of writer Guy Hocquenghem. Guy was a charismatic and brilliant figure, whose book *le desir homosexuel* (1972) was a key text in the radical rethinking of sexuality that accompanied the gay liberation movements of the early 1970s. I came to know him during my time living in Paris in 1977, saw him move effortlessly from the hammams of working-class Arab Paris to the opera. I first met Antoine when he was writing his book—*Les vies de Guy Hocquenghem*. *Politique, sexualité, culture*—and I relished the experience of reminiscing about Guy with someone too young to have known him. My diary records a dinner in Paris at Guy's apartment in Montmartre where both Doug Ireland and Edmund White were present, along with the philosophers Gabriel Matzneff and Rene Scherer. At the time, as Antoine reminds me, Guy and Rene had just published a controversial book, *l'ame atomique*, which extolled a soul that was "libre, sensuelle, epicurienne". Looking back now it seems a lament for an age that was passing, as Guy would become infected with HIV and die four years later.

At a café in Les Halles I meet a friend, Guillaume Marche, who's involved in organising a conference to mark the fiftieth anniversary next year of the Stonewall rising. "Why Stonewall?" I ask—after all, FHAR, a revolutionary gay group in Paris, grew out of the events of May 1968, the year before—but the American mythology seems stronger than national memory. (The Paris Conference is linked to French scholars of the United States; it has already been attacked because the advisory committee is too white and too cis-gendered.) Crossing the Main River in Frankfurt I take a photo of a large banner promoting "Christopher Street Day"; a few days later I see posters for another "Christopher Street Day" in Berlin. There are such celebrations across Germany and Switzerland, even though both countries have homosexual movements which long predate the American gay liberation movement that the street celebrates. Only in the southern hemisphere, above all in the Mardi Gras of Brazil and Australia, is Stonewall, and the ensuing Pride marches, not taken as the exemplar.

Almost forty years ago I wrote an article for the American gay magazine *The Advocate* on "the Americanization of the French Homosexual", in which I described an evening at a disco, modelled on the gay discos of New York:

> The Wednesday before the Fourth of July Le Palace was decked out with stars and stripes and the light show used slides projected on the former cinema screen as a homage to the United States, the new Mecca for French homosexuals.

2018

The following night, a visiting U.S. naval band was welcomed to Le Palace, and the ecstatic audience sang along with their rendition of 'In the Navy'.

'In the Navy' was the song of the Village People, six male singers, each a stereotypical gay fantasy at the point where macho had become the defining style of a new post-Stonewall, pre-AIDS gay world, a long way away from the elegantly dressed and coiffed world of discreet homosexual clubs on the Rue St. Anne. Ironically the group was invented by a Frenchman, Jacques Morali, a reminder that cultural influences never flow only in one direction. The Village People were so omnipresent that I cited them in the opening paragraph of my book *The Homosexualization of America*, even though one editor claimed they would be forgotten before the book appeared.

Paris and Berlin were stops on the way to the International AIDS Conference in Amsterdam, where I gave an opening plenary to the pre-conference on social sciences and the humanities. I'd thought of calling my talk 'Why *Angels in America* Still Matters', stressing that creative responses to the epidemic offer an insight beyond the empirically produced data of conventional science. To perhaps a hundred earnest social scientists I speak of the ways in which those of us who come from the argumentative disciplines are wedged between the biomedical and community assumptions of 'evidence': the former denies any subjectivity, while increasingly the latter insists one can only speak from immediate experience, which is equally restrictive. The following day there's a larger and more colourful meeting of 'MPACT', a global forum for "gay men's health and rights", which meets in the splendid neo-renaissance building of the Royal Tropical Institute. Here are men from all parts of the world, although the formal presenters are disconcertingly first world, including Paul-Gilbert Colletaz from the Global Network of Sex Work Projects who makes the rhetoric of sex worker empowerment sound fresh. Looking around the men in the room I'm struck by how well-groomed and buffed is this generation of activists; mine was scruffier, far less likely to work out or use hair products.

The Conference, more like a trade fair than an academic gathering, sprawls across the vast Amsterdam Conference Centre, and extends into the city, as when sex worker activists, waving red umbrellas, march into the centre to demand recognition, an easy demand in a city where one can see scantily clad women standing against open windows touting for company. There is celebrity here, in the appearance of Elton John and Prince Harry, there is optimism about biomedical advances balanced against declining resources, there is anger, as small groups of protestors march through the pharmaceutical displays calling for cheaper drugs. On the first evening there is a reception for the Australian contingent and Tasmanian Senator Lisa Singh and I go for a drink with a group of sex worker activists, something it's hard to imagine an American Senator doing, at least in public. Singh was placed in an unwinnable position on the Labor ticket for the last Senate election and ran an extraordinary campaign to leapfrog to victory.

The next day I walk past the sex worker stand in the Global Village and recognise a demure grey-haired woman who was one of a group of activists who'd met in Paris in November 1990 to establish what became the International Council of AIDS Service Organisations (ICASO). Ruth Morgan Thomas introduces me to a young American—tall, blonde, confident—who tells us he was born in the same month of that NGO meeting in Paris.

The opening of the Amsterdam Conference featured a clearly homoerotic performance by two dancers from the Nederlands Dance Theater, as well as appearances by the clearly gay grandson of film actor Omar Sharif and a speech by former Eurovision winner Conchita, who is both HIV positive and gender queer. I suspect the cumulative impact was to reinforce the views of both those who are pro-queer and those who suspect this is yet another version of Western decadence. Gay images are ubiquitous; I've seen the same styles in the streets of Tokyo and Mexico City as in Amsterdam and Sydney. Thai Air entertainment features the film *Love Simon* and the television series *Will and Grace*. But when we see teenagers overseas in baseball caps and designer sneakers we should not assume they understand these images as we do.

While the style of the Conference opening was gay, the rhetoric addressed the burden of infection among young women, particularly in Africa, where the highest rate of new infections occurs among women under nineteen years old. For most gay men in rich countries—with some striking exceptions, such as black men in the southern United States—the threat of HIV has become an essentially preventable and manageable one. For needle users and sexually active young people in other parts of the world—parts of Africa and the Middle East, the Philippines, the former Soviet Union—the possibilities of infection and the lack of treatments are very real. Both Papua New Guinea and Venezuela have seen interruptions to the supply of drugs that literally keep people alive.

The Conference reflected the unease born of a dying liberal internationalism. There was a moving session where activists from Venezuela, Hungary, the Philippines, Russia and Kenya talked of the shrinking space for civil society. But behind them lurked the spectre of Trump, whose enthusiasm for autocrats is undermining the already fragile international order. Trump was in Europe earlier in the month, insulting his allies at a NATO meeting, in particular Angela Merkel, undermining Theresa May's Brexit strategy and seemingly preferring the assurances of President Putin to his own intelligence services. The evening Trump met Putin in Helsinki I was in a hotel room in Berlin, transfixed by the telecast of his press conference and the disguised horror of American officials as Trump seemed to query the very idea of Russian interference in elections.

In some ways the presence of Trump hung over the whole Conference, even if he was rarely mentioned except in community protests at the decision to hold the next International AIDS Conference in San Francisco. Our perception of the United States has changed dramatically since President Obama welcomed the AIDS world to Washington in 2014, and there was genuine fear from many delegates at the global closing space for civil society. Trump is not responsible for the rise of authoritarian leaders like Orban in Hungary or Duterte in the Philippines but his embrace of them sends a powerful message. When

Trump was at the Brussels NATO summit last month he bumped knuckles with Turkish President Erdogan, no doubt seeing in him a common tough leader. Now they are locked in a bitter dispute, in which both are appealing to their nationalistic base. At one level this is two unpleasant autocrats playing tough guy. At another it is symbolic of the breakdown of the post-Cold War international order, with Turkey moving away from alliance with 'the West', and increasingly identifying with the new power centres of Eurasia.

Scariest is the way in which Trump's language is giving permission for more overt expressions of racism. Over the past few weeks there has been an upsurge in undeniably racist rhetoric from right-wing politicians and commentators in several countries who have been emboldened by Trump. Nations are turning inwards, rejecting refugees and migrants: the Australian device, of holding people in indefinite detention in overseas hell holes, is winning admirers in Italy and Austria. At home one hears increasing stories of racist rhetoric, exaggerated fears of African gangs and Muslim terrorists being propagated by politicians, including senior government ministers.

August 19: Melbourne

Back in the Forum Theatre, this time for the closing night party of the Melbourne International Film Festival. The gala screening was a documentary about last year's Coming Back Out Ball, a film that concentrated on twelve of the 'LGBTI' elders for whom Tristan Meecham organised the event. The underlying message of the film seemed to be the old gay liberation cry to come out; except today it has taken on a psychological rather than a political meaning, and 'coming out' means expressing an authentic self, that is assumed to be dormant, waiting for the right moment to declare itself.

'Coming out' is only possible when one's identity is not visible, which is why it rarely applies to racial identities, however complex they are in reality. I have the same choice when it comes to declaring that I am Jewish, and there have been times, especially in would-be 'progressive' circles, when it's seemed easier to come out as homosexual than as Jewish. But coming out is not only a personal journey, it also has political implications. There were early years living with Anthony when he accompanied me to university events in part to make the point that homosexual relations needed to be fully recognised.

Every generation needs to come out in its own way and coming out as trans* is far more demanding than coming out as homosexual, one reason why the concept of an 'LGBTIQ community' is so fraught. But the film appeals to something of a victim mentality, a narrative that ignores the reality that living openly as homosexual has been a lot easier for many people than the stories reflect. It was striking that only the long-lasting partnerships depicted are two heterosexual marriages, one between two people who conveniently both discovered their homosexual desires and separated amicably, the other a transwoman whose marriage has been stretched by her transition at the age of 60.

August 23: Melbourne

Juan Carlos is visiting from Ecuador and we're at *The Boy from Oz*, the musical built around the life of Australian singer-songwriter Peter Allen. Allen's life was almost contemporaneous with mine; we overlapped in New York in the early 1970s, when he was married to Liza Minelli and I was discovering the excitement of early gay liberation. Through my friend Dusty, who hung around the edges of Warhol's Factory, then based near Union Square, I may even have glimpsed the couple at a party. Minelli was then best known as the daughter of Judy Garland, who died on the eve of Stonewall, and the production mined the connection, giving Allen's life a political dimension that never existed. His song 'I Still Call Australia Home', centrepiece for many years of Qantas's advertising, was turned into a paean to multiculturalism, which seemed far removed from Allen's prosaic lyrics.

The show ends with Allen's most famous song, 'I go to Rio', and the audience react with appropriate enthusiasm. Juan Carlos is less impressed: both the rhythm and the references—'la Bamba', 'salsa fellow'—felt to him like crude stereotypes of Latin America, with little to do with Rio de Janeiro. Peter Allen died in 1992 from AIDS.

He became an Australian legend because he conquered New York and Hollywood, and the attempts to give a political dimension to the show—with dramatic outbreaks of rainbow and Aboriginal flags—feel fraudulent.

August 26: Sydney

We are having a family brunch in Sydney and my niece asks why do we have a new prime minister? It's a good question, the party coup two days ago that replaced him with Scott Morrison had even less reason behind it than the overthrow of either Rudd or Abbott. Since 2007 the prime ministership has changed six times.

Would Turnbull have survived had Trump not been elected? Trump's presidency has drip-fed the obsessions of the far right, both strengthening conspiracy theories which have bolstered right wing fringe parties but also emboldening the self-proclaimed conservatives in the Liberal Party and their mates in the media. Turnbull was right when he claimed he was overthrown by a cabal whose hatred for him outweighed any sensible evaluation of policy, but he also fell because he failed to grasp the initiative and confront the climate denialists and moral vigilantes head on, rather than just conceding ground to placate them. One can equally ask would John Howard have been re-elected in 2001 without the events of 9/11: the cataclysms of American politics help shape our views of the world. With Morrison we again have a Prime Minister who seems to disregard all evidence of climate change, and whose Pentecostal faith reflects a more American style of Protestantism than the gloomy Baptists and Methodists of my youth.

I knew Turnbull as an undergraduate at the University of Sydney, when he already had the self-confidence of a man destined for greatness. He was in one of my tutorials in American Politics, where it was not always obvious which of us was in charge. Over the years he seemed an admirable figure, a successful lawyer and merchant banker who stood for freedom of speech and then led the republican movement, ironically facing off against the man he would dethrone as Prime Minister, Tony Abbott. The last time I saw him was shortly after he lost the leadership in 2009 to Abbott. He was in a melancholy mood: "Maybe" he mused "there's no room for me any longer in the Liberal Party", but further reflection was interrupted when a more important guest joined us.

At that time most of us, even strong Labor supporters, believed he was a man of principle, who lost the Liberal leadership because of his commitment to responding to climate change. Over the past two years we've watched him hollow out, discarding one principle after another in a futile attempt to control the conservatives in his own ranks. If he'd had the guts to stand up for his original principles on climate policy he might well have stared down the unrest that unseated him.

Polls have consistently suggested that Foreign Minister Julie Bishop would be the most popular replacement were Turnbull to lose the leadership, and the lack of support for her within her own party has led her to move to the back benches. This has been taken as further evidence of the boys' culture within the conservative ranks, but my hunch is she is disliked as much for her style as her gender. The anti-intellectual suburbanites who make up much of the Parliamentary party would see in her the same pretentiousness they loathed in Turnbull and would be even less forgiving because she is a whip-smart woman.

September 6: Melbourne

I am writing this paragraph in the immediate aftermath of the decision of the Indian Supreme Court to finally strike down as unconstitutional the old colonial laws prohibiting sex "against the order of nature", usually understood to mean homosexuality. The consequences of this for other former British colonies are likely to be considerable, and the decision is clearly a major step towards global acknowledgement of queer rights.

I first visited India to attend an AIDS Conference in Delhi in 1992. Extraordinary efforts by my colleague John Dwyer, professor of medicine at UNSW, had ensured the beginnings of what would become a regional AIDS organisation (ASAP), and a series of regional conferences which took place every two years for the next several decades which would involve me in ways I hardly anticipated. The Conference took place in the Ashok Hotel, a sprawling remnant of colonial times, opposite Nehru Park in the diplomatic enclave of New Delhi. There was a swimming pool in the grounds, hardly used, and covered in dead leaves. When the organisers refused space for a meeting for gay men about thirty of us relocated across the road to the park, ironically already known for cruising, where several men who would become key figures in the Indian gay movement spoke to the small group of regional queers who gathered there. A couple of the men cruising the park hovered on the fringes, not sure if they wanted to join in.

It was on this trip that I began to know some of the people who would become leading figures in the regional response to the epidemic, and several of the first openly HIV-positive men in Asia. One of them from Singapore travelled with a suitcase of bottled water, a wise precaution as I discovered, belatedly, that the bottled water in our rooms came from the hotel's taps. I already knew some of the founders of Pink Triangle in Kuala Lumpur, the AIDS organisation that reached out to homosexual men, using as its name a reference that few Malaysians might have understood. During the 1990s there was a flourishing gay life in Kuala Lumpur, including the gay bar Blue Boy, and several saunas, including one with a rooftop terrace not far from the looming Petronas Towers, briefly the world's tallest buildings. Women, one lesbian told me, used a complex network of faxes to maintain social networks. Blue Boy was raided a month ago as part of what appears to be a concerted attack on queer Malaysians, with government statements about "mitigating the LGBT culture from spreading into our society."

I celebrate the Indian victory with a quiet drink with Lee Carnie in an extravagant mansion which fronts onto Wellington Parade, just next to a small row of kebab shops and 7-Elevens. The house was built in the 1850s with the profits from the gold rush; the current owners have stocked it with extravagant nineteenth century paintings, largely of women—buxom nudes, in parasols and hoop skirts, at work on engravings—and a remarkable collection of Ormolu clocks and porcelain figurines. Lee is one of the lawyers at the Human Rights Law Centre, and we're here tonight, perhaps fifty of us, to talk about the prospect of an Australian Charter of Rights. Julian Burnside, one of our most politically engaged lawyers, recounts the origins of the American Bill of Rights in the British civil wars of the seventeenth century; the Centre's Director Hugh de Kretser reminds us that Australia remains the only major Western democracy without such protection.

This is not a good moment for human rights. I attended lengthy discussions last week on Australian foreign policy, at which human rights were not mentioned. Since the Presidency of Jimmy Carter, the United States has seemed to care about human rights, however unevenly, and international institutions have developed to nudge countries towards greater awareness. Now with a President who seems unconcerned by the most flagrant atrocities, and seemingly prefers authoritarian regimes to democratic ones, the impetus is lost. In Europe the new chauvinism has spread from former Soviet bloc countries to Italy, and right-wing nationalist parties are growing in countries like Sweden and Germany.

Jonathan Symons thinks it's too early to sound the retreat; maybe there will be a turn back towards more respect for human rights once the current round of authoritarian governments collapse. As Barack Obama mused after Trump's election, history does not move in straight lines. "Sometimes it goes sideways, sometimes it goes backward."[35]

September 10–15: Melbourne

"There are not many Australian flags", comments Juan Carlos, who's lived in the United States. Which leads onto a discussion of terms like 'redneck', 'ocker' and 'bogan': "Rednecks!" he explains as we drive past one farm with two flags displayed on the gateposts.

I think it more urgent to change our flag than end the charade of monarchy; the reminder of British colonial status through the Union Jack is increasingly grating. For Juan Carlos it suggests we have yet to properly declare our independence, although the attachment to Britain

---

35 Quoted by David Remnick, 'It happened here', *New Yorker*, November 28 2016, p.54.

feels far less onerous than the instinctive desire of our politicians to align us with the United States, the need to feel we are sitting at the big table with access to Washington.

There is a depressing article by Maureen Dowd in the *New York Times*. Dowd is an influential columnist, vaguely liberal but with considerable antipathy towards the Clintons. She's in Australia and interviewing Scott Morrison, the new Prime Minister, a man who seems closer in spirit to Trump than most other democratically elected foreign leaders.[36] Morrison is a devout Pentecostal, one of the nine government members who skulked out of the House of Representatives rather than vote on the marriage bill.

I don't think Morrison shares many of Trump's personal characteristics; I understand the incentive to publicly support the President. But he also epitomises the shift within the Liberal Party towards a small-minded moralistic chauvinism, one that favours white male small-business men who see no contradiction between trumpeting Christian values and incarcerating families on Nauru. It's not accidental that some Liberal women MPs have been increasingly vocal about the culture of bullying and intimidation within their party. Pity they were all conspicuously silent about our treatment of asylum seekers offshore. Would this have happened without the Me Too movement? Probably not. Increasingly women feel able to articulate suppressed rage at what is regarded as acceptable behaviour by most men.

Looking back to the feminist energies of the 1970s it seems remarkable how slowly things have changed. The writer Anne Summers, whom I've known since she was a graduate student at Sydney University in the 1970s, has claimed that the gay movement has been more successful than the women's, and the current rebirth of angry feminism seems to support this. When Anne invited me to speak at the fortieth anniversary celebration of her book *Damned Whores and God's Police*, I was both flattered and a little apprehensive. On the first day of the conference the four of us who had been asked to comment on Summers' opening

---

36 Maureen Dowd, 'Trump finally makes a friend', *New York Times*, September 15 2018.

address filed on stage and I took an anxious look at the audience; perhaps four men in a sea of women of all ages, though like most such events skewed towards the elderly and the young. As it turned out I had no reason for concern; the audience was good-humoured and more interested in celebration than argument. As I wrote at the time:

> One of the striking events at the Damned Whores conference was a sex worker panel, at which five women sex workers presented the realities of their lives. I had expected fireworks, passionate assertions that their choices could not be as free as they claimed, demands for enactment of the Swedish model, which criminalises the buying, though not the selling, of sex. But the audience reacted with interest and muted sympathy; okay, I was on the side of the Damned Whores, but I would like to have heard at least a mutter from God's police. Unfortunately, lunch came too soon to allow for any discussion.

September 25–30: Melbourne

Carol and I muse, as we often do, about the impermanence of love. Four years ago I introduced Carol to a visiting author, which led to a tumultuous trans-Pacific affair that has precipitously ended. The same day that they met I also met someone who seemed, for a time, to be a potential partner. We've shared the pangs of both affairs, the recognition, as the performer Brodie Turner put it, that love is a combination of lust and anxiety. In neither case was the love unrequited, but it was not enough to keep us together. The discovery that one can feel the pangs of teenage heartbreak at any age is both frightening and reassuring. The confessions I share with Carol are not unlike those I used to have with my best friends back in New York over thirty years ago.

Is it inevitable that in any couple one will love more than the other? Or is it rather that the balance will shift over time? Before I wander off into advice to the lovelorn I am struck by the analogy to the relationship built over time between nations, which in Australia's case seems to follow a classically Freudian script, with Britain, the mother country, the United States the stern but forgiving father. Countries are not individuals, but at times our political leaders have spoken of the United States in terms far beyond those of strategic calculation: Harold Holt's "all the way with LBJ", John Howard's bromance with George W Bush; Julia Gillard's infatuation with Barack Obama. Maybe we should be grateful that in Donald Trump the United States has a leader whose transactional disregard for alliances based on shared values will force a greater degree of realism, may allow us to question the extent to which the American alliance should be a bedrock of Australian foreign policy.

Meanwhile the chaos around the White House mounts, even as Trump dominates the United Nations General Assembly with his strident defence of American patriotism. It is increasingly clear that there are many senior members of the Administration who both fear what Trump might do and how he might threaten their careers. Trump is clearly happiest when he is campaigning in middle America, where his oddest claims—"Kim Jong-un and I fell in love" he tells the crowd in Wheeling—draw rapturous applause.

The American media is obsessed with the allegations of sexual assault against Supreme Court nominee Brett Kavanagh, and the appearance before the Senate Judicial Committee of one of his accusers. This makes headline news here, with the *Australian* in an editorial that could have been dictated from the White House fulminating against the Democrats for trying to impose contentious policies on an unsuspecting electorate.[37] To their editorialists it seems fair game to revisit the misdeeds of Ted Kennedy and Bill Clinton but not to examine the evidence against Kavanagh. This week's edition of *The Economist* claims that the Me Too movement "could turn out to be the most powerful force for a fairer settlement between men and women since women's suffrage."[38] What became prominent as a howl of rage by women in

---

37   'The trials of Judge Kavanagh', Editorial, *Weekend Australian*, September 29–30 2018.
38   *Economist*, October 2 2018.

the elite worlds of entertainment has now spread far more widely, with employees at McDonald's and hotel housekeepers joining in the calls for protection against sexual harassment.[39]

A week later Kavanagh was confirmed, with only one Republican, Lisa Murkowski of Alaska, opposed. Trump has succeeded in one of his core promises, to change the balance of the Supreme Court for several decades.

October 4: Melbourne

Clare Wright noted that she knew more about Emily Pankhurst than she did about Australia's suffragettes, even though women won the vote far earlier here. She is speaking at the launch of her latest book, *You Daughters of Freedom*, an exuberant evening in a local Fitzroy pub. We're upstairs in a function room, decorated with flowers in the purple, white and green of the women's movement, and the book is extolled at some length by the new Labor MP Ged Kearney. She points to the impact Vida Goldstein had when she toured the United States to support votes for women, a reminder that Australia was once regarded by many Americans as a model of progress. My former colleague Marilyn Lake has also pointed to strong trans-Pacific links before and after Federation.[40]

But while there was considerable interest in Australia amongst progressives in the early part of last century, it's unlikely that Australia has much ongoing influence on American political debates. When the Keating government dropped the ban on homosexuals serving in the military in 1992 a minister's staffer rang me in great excitement and asked how this shift would impact on the United States. The decision went virtually unnoticed in Washington and several years later the Clinton Administration adopted the pusillanimous 'don't ask, don't tell' policy, not repealed until 2010. It's telling that when I typed 'Australia's influence on US' into Google the results all told me of American influence on us. Interestingly this misses the crucial

---

39   'After the Silence is Broken', *Time Magazine*, October 1 2018.
40   Marilyn Lake, *Progressive New World*, Harvard University Press, 2019.

influence of Rupert Murdoch who took his media empire to the United States and through FOX News helped create the angry tirades which propelled Trump into the White House.

Clare quotes writer Jeff Sparrow as saying that writing is "hard and hateful" and says we need moments to celebrate; the launch ends with a visiting American singer leading us in the Helen Reddy song: "I Am Woman". I think of Jeff's comment when I go home to discover that 120 books have showed up on the doorstep, with more to come. I am one of the judges for the Victorian Premier's non-fiction literary awards, and despite an entry-fee, publishers enter books with what seems a remarkable lack of discernment. It's very easy to winnow out most of the books on a first cull: first person misery stories, war histories, gardening books, academic volumes that are too specialist for the general reader all mount up in piles begging to be disposed. Much more difficult is the second round, which includes an extraordinary richness of discoveries. Reading through the books gives me a new appreciation of both archaeology and art history and of the sheer amount of interesting contemporary writing.

October 9: Melbourne

Back at the Wheeler Centre for a discussion about queer history, in a panel which oddly has no historian on it. But Daniel Marshall, our chair, pushes us to think about our own engagement with queer history, which means essentially telling stories. I define queer history as being ultimately about the desire to know there are other people out there like us, and regret the decline of reading, particularly of imaginative literature, among so many queer activists. If someone had the presence of mind to challenge me I'd have to acknowledge I have no proof for that assertion. But it is a generous audience, perhaps 200 in the long hall in the State Library, and several people come up afterwards saying they'd always wanted to meet me. I have never learnt the necessary grace with which to answer them, but I do thank one man who recalled a television interview from 1973 where I talked with football player Ron Barassi about masculinity. Barassi was already a football legend—the first player to be so named in Australian Football Hall of Fame—and surprisingly gentle and accepting of homosexuality.

Looking back at the tape of that program—in early 1970s black and white—I'm struck by how long our hair was, and at the naivety of some of the questions. The compere, Gerald Stone, a transplanted American, pressed us to talk about 'manliness', and Ron stressed how definitions were changing, so that now men could wear bangles and show affection to each other, though he drew back at my suggestions about the homoeroticism of contact sports. It's sad that more than forty years later there has still been no openly gay football player in the top ranks of Australian Rules football.

There is clearly interest in queer history, however we understand it, perhaps because unlike communities defined by ethnicity or religion we do not grow up learning at home, and must search it out, often hiding it from our biological families. I've just come from coffee with Tristan Meecham from the Coming Back Out Ball who tells me that he constantly receives calls from people terrified even today of coming out to their families and colleagues. Tristan shares with archivist Nick Henderson an extraordinary ability to speak to people many decades older than him, an empathy which I know I always lacked. When I ask Tristan what motivates him to spend so much energy working with much older people he seems slightly puzzled by the question.

As always, the discussion flirts in different ways with questions of identity and community, of whom we would include in the queer history month Daniel is proposing. I'm reminded that even people who are at ease with their sexuality don't always want that to be their primary identity. "I'm a Labor politician" one Parliamentarian said to me recently "Not always a gay politician." He's out, but also represents an electorate with a large number of conservative ethnic communities which voted no in the marriage survey.

October 20: Canberra/Sydney

In 1976 David Williamson wrote *Don's Party*, in which a group of friends gather together to watch election results on television. Tonight a group of us are gathered at the house of friends, but because their television is only accessible via Play Station we get interrupted coverage and intermittent sound—someone switches to ABC radio on their phone—as Independent Kerryn Phelps sweeps to victory in Malcolm Turnbull's former electorate of Wentworth, by most measures the richest in Australia. Most encouraging is that she won despite being outspent by the Liberals by five to one. Her win means the government no longer has a majority in the House of Representatives.

The by-election followed flailing efforts of the Morrison government to hold the support of their own base. A motion from One Nation Senator Pauline Hanson deploring attacks on "Western civilisation" with the line that "it is okay to be white" was supported by government Senators, until they were forced to retract and demand a second vote. Meanwhile in what seemed a desperate ploy for votes in Wentworth, which has a large Jewish population, the Prime Minister suddenly announced that Australia might move its Embassy in Israel to Jerusalem, following in the footsteps of the United States—and Guatemala. There was no sign that there had been any serious consideration of the implications of this announcement, and it led to an immediate angry response from Indonesia, a country of greater significance to Australia than Israel.

Phelps, one of the first leaders of the marriage equality movement, campaigned hard on the government's failures on climate change and inhumanity to asylum seekers. The latter is very much on my mind after last night, a dinner for Refugee Legal which drew several hundred people to the Fitzroy Town Hall. Refugee Legal, the largest provider of legal aid to asylum seekers and refugees in Australia, is headed by David Manne, who is exuberant, voluble, intelligent and deeply passionate. There's momentary drama as a woman at one of the tables faints; not surprisingly there is a surfeit of doctors in the hall. But we're here to listen to Gillian Triggs, former head of the Human Rights Commission. It's a mark of how badly we treat asylum seekers that few of us in the room have heard of Yongah Hill, a detention centre near Northam in Western Australia, holding 600 men who have fallen foul of our immigration system, and Gillian tells us stories of her visits to the Centre and the ongoing cruelties towards people who fall foul of our visa restrictions. Meanwhile Trump speaks of closing the Mexican border to stave off a group of desperate Central American refugees heading for the United States.

Like most of us in the room I want to believe that Australians are better, more generous, than our government. Despite increasing noise from the far right there are few signs that they are winning more than marginal support. The general mood is rather one of cynicism with all politicians, little enthusiasm for the nostrums of Trump-esque populism. Two days later, having a suspicious mole shaved off my back, my dermatologist talks to me of her disillusionment with politicians.

During the week newsreaders have been competing for superlatives to describe every move of the Duke and Duchess of Sussex—Harry and Meaghan—as they tour Australia, in what seems a replay of 1950s royalist hysteria. While the veneration for the Royals seems bizarre—Harry, after all, is only sixth in line to the throne—it has more to do with the inexhaustible appetite for celebrity than any allegiance to the monarchy. If the Australian Republican Movement's research is correct most Australians don't even realise the Queen is formally our head of state. In an era of authoritarian rulers this is not necessarily a depressing finding.

October 29: Melbourne

It's been a weekend of bad news: another mass shooting in the United States, this time at a synagogue in Pittsburgh. The President's response is to call for more guns and the death penalty. And on Sunday Jair Bolsonaro, a man whose rhetoric is a toxic mix of Trump and Duterte, was elected President of Brazil.

This dramatic lurch to the right is particularly upsetting because after the end of military dictatorship in 1985 Brazil became a global leader in social policies, especially in responses to HIV and to gay rights. I first visited Brazil in 1979 when I was the guest of the gay liberation newspaper *Lampiao da Esquina* and was briefly in both Sao Paulo and

Rio de Janeiro. In Rio I stayed in a small, fussily furnished apartment used by one of the *Lampiao* collective for meeting his tricks. He lived elsewhere with his mother. Inspired by the San Francisco journal *Gay Sunshine, Lampiao*—the name came from a famous bandit of the 1920s—brought together a group of prominent Brazilian leftist intellectuals but only lasted three years when fear of persecution led to its collapse. Looking back, I realise how oblivious I was to the pressures early gay activists faced in Brazil at that time, pressures which may resurface under the new President.

I made two further visits to Rio, both for meetings on sexuality research, where Brazil has played a leading role. Some of the most remarkable activists I've encountered come from Brazil, where the tradition of organic intellectuals, people able to straddle academic and political worlds, survives better than in the rich world. Like most tourists I was both enthralled and terrified by the crazy mix of beaches, hilltop favelas, acai bars, ostentatious wealth and grinding poverty, but I had several remarkable guides. On my last trip the extraordinary Sonia Correa, a leading feminist author and activist, drove me and a fellow Australian around the hills that straddle Rio. At one point she stopped the car, stripped, and took a roadside shower, without commentary, as if to demonstrate Brazilian ease with the body. On Ipanema Beach the equally redoubtable Cheryl Overs, a founder of the international sex worker movement and a former La Trobe student, marshalled a large group of near naked men gathered around her on the clearly gay section of the beach. With a group that included Cheryl and then head of UNAIDS, Peter Piot, there was a late-night drive to the northern outskirts to attend a huge samba school, an event that flowed in and out of the neighbourhood hall, loud, garish and sexy.

October 30: Melbourne

"Trump", said Bob Carr, "Is a genius without talent." He so liked the phrase he repeated it. Bob Carr, premier of New South Wales for ten years, was briefly Foreign Minister under Julia Gillard and

Kevin Rudd, since when he has become increasingly critical of the mainstream assumptions of Australian foreign policy. I'm sitting with him and Sally Warhaft on a panel at Wheeler, talking about next week's US mid-term elections. Carr is even gloomier than I about the state of American politics, and whether it makes sense any longer to think of the United States as a meaningful democracy. Which, we agree, raises questions about the constant assertion of the 'common values' used to justify the centrality of the American alliance in our foreign policy.

I've known Bob Carr for many years, in part because he shared my friendship with Gore Vidal. When I was writing about Vidal I visited Carr, then premier, and sat in his vast office overlooking Sydney Harbour while anxious flunkies tried to drag him away from long reminiscences about meeting Vidal and Noman Mailer. We've done two events together at Sydney's Gleebooks; our discussion about *Gore Vidal's America* prompted an ABC television program to put Vidal and Carr together in a car travelling around Los Angeles. Carr, no longer premier but still with Labor ambitions, looked somewhat embarrassed at Vidal's hyperbole about the failures of the American republic.

My fondest memory of Carr is of meeting him for coffee in the lobby of a Melbourne hotel, where he carefully exclaimed to the overly deferential waiter that he wanted a protein shake, complete with strawberries and a particular powder. The waiter turned away, then looked briefly at me, knowing that duty required him to take my order. "I'll have the same as Bob," I said.

Carr was one of those Labor politicians whose interest in the United States seemed to define their political worlds, so his disenchantment is significant. He thinks the chances of Trump's re-election are high, and we agree that the Democrats have no obvious candidate who can compete with his mastery of political manipulation. "The sort of politics I fought for", muses Carr, "are now in retreat", instancing the apparent withering away of mainstream democratic socialism and the rise of populist challenges from both left and right.

November 7: Melbourne

Two years ago, Donald Trump was elected. Today the Republicans have lost control of the House of Representatives and seven state governorships.

At one level this represents a major blow against Trump. As I write, the popular vote suggests the Democrats outpolled Republicans across the country by over 4 million votes, a better total than that won by Clinton two years ago. But the vagaries of the American system mean this doesn't translate into gains in the Senate, nor make it necessarily easier to defeat Trump in 2020.

When I pitched this book to my editor, I thought the mid-terms would mark a natural ending. But instead they are a weary continuation of the impasse between increasingly polarised forces within American society. As late results trickled in they underlined a swing away from Trump, even in reliable Republican strongholds in Oklahoma and Kansas. But there is no indication that this will have any effect on the President's behaviour, or his apparent capture of the Republican Party. There is a point in life where one's behavioural quirks are only likely to increase with adversity.

November 20: Melbourne

The American consul tells us a long story about observing elections in Kosovo. We are at the launch of *Academic Ambassadors* by my La Trobe colleagues Diane Kirkby and Alice Garner, a study of the Fulbright Scheme which fifty years ago had enabled me to go to the United States. The evening had been billed as a discussion about "finding a voice in a post-truth world", which seemed an invitation to talk about President Trump's debasement of political life. I am happy to have the opportunity to speak of my unrequited love for the United States, disappointed that the consul left before he could hear my comment that maybe Australians should act as observers of American elections, which often fall short of basic democratic procedures. He'd spoken enthusiastically of the almost 50 percent turnout at the recent midterm elections, not perhaps a wise boast when speaking in a country which has compulsory voting, and where over 80% responded to the voluntary postal vote on gay marriage. I would like to have asked him about claims of the North Carolina government deliberately distributing food benefit cards on the day of the 2016 elections to make it more difficult for poor people to vote.[41]

November 23: Melbourne

The campus of Deakin University downtown resembles a corporate office, complete with marble foyer, expansive glass panels and an alarming coffee machine. Outside a window cleaner, fluorescent in orange, clings to the building like a mountaineer. I'm speaking on a panel at *Queer Legacies, New Solidarities*, the annual homosexual histories conference, and we've been asked to think about our own histories and how we might forge solidarity with other struggles. I'm a little uneasy with the leftist rhetoric of the morning and discomforted when my attempt to suggest Australia did not have the same legacy of slavery as the United States is interpreted as downplaying the racism of Australian settlement.

But I'm also struck by law professor Di Otto's comments about the explosion of community organising in the 1970s, and declining grassroots participation as movements become successful and dependent on government and corporate funding. There's passion in the room which drew consciously on the histories of women's and gay liberation. Carole Ferrier, founding editor of the feminist journal *Hecate*, who was honoured the previous night by the Australian Women's and Gender Studies Association, takes us back to 1965, and the two women who chained themselves to the foot rail of a public bar in the Regatta Hotel Brisbane to protest the laws that made such bars male only spaces.

This is very different to the event I went to last week at Sydney University, a workshop on 'sexual revolutions' which brought together academics, primarily from Australia and the United States. In the discussions the idea of sexual revolution seemed somewhat anachronistic, the subject for nostalgic reflection rather than imminent participation.

---

41   Michael Lewis, *The Fifth Risk*, Allen Lane, 2018, p.100.

The spectre of reaction against sexual revolutions, however defined, seemed to dominate much of the discussion, not surprisingly in an era which is more conscious of sexual exploitation than sexual adventure. One participant suggested a return to Carole Vance's balance between "pleasure and danger", but I detected little enthusiasm for that.

In April 1985 I spoke at a Socialist Scholars Conference in New York entitled 'the left in crisis', a phrase which would be equally relevant today, even if a panel asking whether the Soviet Union "is historically progressive" seems embarrassingly anachronistic. I sat on a panel which asked: 'Is the Sexual Revolution Over', and in case the connection was not clear appeared the following day on an AIDS panel which included writers Richard Goldstein and Cindy Patton, whose *Sex and Germs* would be one of the first books to come out of the AIDS movement. Today the tone is very different: maybe this is what happens when movements become the stuff of academic research. At Sydney we are meeting in the aftermath of revelations of widespread sexual abuse of children, the Me Too movement and the emergence of a certain right-wing ideological misogyny, which combines justification for sexual assault with a strange puritanism, as in calls to abstain from masturbation from groups like the far right Proud Boys.[42]

Are we also more timid because of a spiralling identity politics which increasingly claims no-one can speak except from direct personal experience? My friends at Hares and Hyenas bookshop had recommended Rupert Thomson's novel, *Never Anyone But You*, based on the lives of a remarkable lesbian couple who were part of the Parisian avant-garde in the 1930s and lone resisters against the Nazi occupation of Jersey during World War II, where they narrowly avoided death by firing squad. But the most common response from their women customers was: 'Not if the story is written by a man'.

I've been thinking a lot about the limits of our experience as we've been meeting to determine the Premier's non-fiction awards, and what shapes our sense of 'excellence'. I didn't shortlist several books

---

42 Sarah Manavis, 'No Nut November: the insidious internet challenge encouraging men not to masturbate', *New Statesman* November 13 2018.

that my colleagues liked, and I wonder how much this was because I am the only male and considerably older than the others. All of us struggled to measure the books against objective criteria, but inevitably this was shaped by our own life experiences, so that what I thought was moving someone else saw as self-indulgent. Several times one of the judges would quote a line from a book that had disqualified it in their minds from winning; I didn't remember reading them. One of us wanted more personal disclosure in a historical narrative; some of us wanted less in a book about the justice system.

But we all agreed that on pure literary merit there was a clear winner, namely Behrouz Boochani's *No Friend But the Mountain*. Boochani is an Iranian Kurdish detainee on Manus, and his book was written in Farsi on a mobile phone and translated, itself a work of great art, by Omid Tofighian. I approached the book with some trepidation; I found it painful to read, striking in its empathy and the haunting imagery with which he captures the desolation of indefinite detention. Our decision led to some political manoeuvring, as technically Boochani was not eligible to be awarded the prize. To our relief the Premier agreed that given his status as a de facto prisoner of Australia an exception could be made.

November 29 – December 1: Canberra

From the visitors' gallery the most prominent feature of the House of Representatives is the gender balance. The government benches look like the graduates of a not very distinguished boys' school; the Labor Opposition is far more diverse, though whiter than the people they represent. What stands out are the four women crossbenchers, their clothes seemingly colour-coordinated, two of whom, Kerryn Phelps and Julia Banks, are there because of internal wars within the Liberal Party. (Phelps won the by-election last month; Banks defected from the Liberals a week ago). Rather like the large numbers of women elected in the Democrat victories in the American midterms they suggest a new stage in feminism, in part the impact of the MeToo movement on mainstream politics. The re-elected Victorian state government now has an equal number of female and male cabinet members: Trump has three out of fifteen.

Sadly, question time has become a farce, in which government and opposition MPs alternate rhetorical questions mass produced by the leader's office. When Kerryn Phelps asks a question of substance the Health Minister struggles to move beyond the pre-scripted lines about economic management. There is a moment of drama when Opposition Leader Bill Shorten uses a point of order to denounce the government in an impassioned speech, but this is theatre without an audience.

I've been in Parliament House since seven this morning to attend the annual World AIDS Day breakfast. We eat tired bacon and eggs as ministers and shadow ministers combine to talk up the ongoing bipartisan response to the epidemic, in a far more convivial spirit than would appear on the floor that afternoon. The Liberal MP at my table makes clear he won't discuss current politics; the three Labor women are more forthcoming. The breakfast ends promptly at nine, and there are a series of quick conversations with various MPs, some of them in the small café frequented by politicians, media and lobbyists. At one point the Prime Minister walks through, apparently in a great hurry, surrounded by a crowd of hangers-on. Upstairs in the Senate wing Pauline Hanson scurries by, looking rather like the rabbit in *Alice in Wonderland*.

I'm in Canberra to give a World AIDS talk at the National Gallery, in a large gallery flanked by extraordinary art works. I stand in front of a large ornamental wooden horse from the Nage people of Flores and talk about the long-term legacies of the epidemic, the fact that while it is now largely a manageable disease in countries like ours it remains a major challenge in many parts of the world for reasons of stigma, ignorance and lack of resources. As I speak I realise how much of my life has been shaped by this epidemic, which began before over half the people now alive were born. AIDS activism grew out of earlier gay activism, but without the celebratory cockiness of the early 1970s: it meant glamor and grief marched together as new structures were created and new friendships forged. AIDS has taken away many of the people who should be growing old with me, so that I have comparatively few gay male friends of my generation, and those I have are now themselves contemplating mortality.

Looking back on the past four decades the great shifts in queer life, at least in Western countries, are marked by HIV/AIDS; the marriage debate; the growth of the internet and the new assertion of trans* identities. We imagined none of these in the heady rush of early 1970s gay liberation, which should make us cautious about assuming we can foresee the next frontiers. Nor did we imagine the new respectability, summed up in the plans for a $37 million-dollar Pride Centre, largely government funded, which is planned for St. Kilda. It's a striking five-storey white building, all whirling curves and arches, that will house a variety of groups and activities, a symbol of Melbourne's claim to be a centre of queer life. I wish I could feel more enthusiasm for this project, but I wonder whether some of the money would not have been better spent on providing decent shelter to those kids made homeless because of their sexuality or gender.

December 6: Melbourne

Parliament rose today after obfuscation by the government prevented two major issues coming to a vote. Both attempts to protect queer students in schools and to facilitate medical transfers of asylum seekers from Nauru and Manus fell foul of a government which seemed oblivious to the messages of recent elections. Government Senators demanded toilet breaks and unnecessary amendments to stall measures being passed in time to go to the House of Representatives where the government feared losing crucial votes. The Prime Minister won the tactical battle but lost any claim to be a national unifier.

Meanwhile delegates are arriving in Katowice, Poland, a centre of coal production, for yet another international conference on climate change. Back home the Australian government has dropped any real attempts to control carbon emissions; the new President of Brazil denies climate change; Donald Trump has pulled out of the Paris agreement and refused to sign that part of the G20 statement dealing with global warming. The environmentalist Bill McKibben claims that almost ninety percent of Americans don't know there is a scientific consensus on global warming.[43] This ignorance is seemingly shared by a dominant rump within the government, if not by most Australians. This week thousands of school kids took to the streets to demonstrate against government inaction on climate change.

December 12: Melbourne

There are maybe a hundred people packed into the top floor of a city hotel for a Labor fundraiser featuring Penny Wong, who speaks eloquently of the need to elect a Labor government next year. In my lifetime Labor has only beaten an incumbent conservative government three times, but there is an air of anticipation in the room that next year will see another Labor victory, and that Victoria, where the state Labor government won a large majority last month, will be crucial. I still remember the thrill of the 1972 election, the 'It's Time' t-shirts and posters, the exuberance of the crowd at Randwick when Barry Prothero and I went to hear Whitlam speak in the campaign. Five days later we voted, and watched as Labor picked up seats, largely in suburban Sydney and Melbourne, some of them the same electorates that will be in play next year.

Today it is more difficult to believe in the redemptive power of the state, though Labor's current narrative has echoes of Whitlam's appeals for change and fairness. This week has seen riots in Paris against Macron's neo-liberal policies, the continuing failure of Theresa May to find an acceptable path to exiting the European Union, and the end of Angela Merkel's dominance of German politics. No Western government seems able to find a successful path to balancing demands for equity, recognition and sustainability; ours, like the current US Administration, seems to have given up the attempt.

Over thirty years ago, in the adrenalin rush after the collapse of the Soviet Union, Francis Fukuyama proclaimed "the end of history",

---

43   Bill McKibben, 'Life on a shrinking planet', *New Yorker*, November 26 2018.

essentially the triumph of Western liberal democracy. That claim becomes less convincing every year, more so since the election of Trump. As the year ends it feels as if Trump is finally coming undone, that the steady stream of revelations about his commercial dealings with Russia and the revolving door of Administration officials will create an environment in which newly energised Democrats might push for impeachment. But the gridlock that has become a feature of American politics is becoming the standard political mode of most Western democracies. The one thing I can be sure of is that the political landscape is unpredictable.

December 17: Melbourne

The news is full of new sexual scandals. Actor Geoffrey Rush, already suing a newspaper for allegations of improper conduct during a production of *King Lear*, has now been accused of sexual harassment by actress Yael Stone. And Nationals MP Andrew Broad has been exposed as using a website to meet "a younger woman" (described in the headlines as 'sugar baby') in Hong Kong. It's not clear whether he misused government funds for the trip, but as he was one of the most ardent defenders of traditional marriage in the equality debates last year his political downfall is assured.

I think of this as I dredge up reminiscences of the early 1970s for Kate Davison, who's writing a thesis on the Sydney psychiatrist Neil McConaghy, who used aversion therapy (i.e. electric shock treatment) to 'cure' homosexuals, even though he himself was behaviourally bisexual. In the intoxicating days of that period much behaviour that is today censored was defended as sexual liberation, as if the only possible response to mainstream wowserism was predatory sexism. Of course, there are differences: Rush is accused of harassment, Broad of hypocrisy, but their attitudes to women seem oddly similar, and the glee with which the media is reporting their stories is a sign of changing mores. Yet I feel unease at the way in which careers can be totally destroyed by allegations of behaviours that are offensive but not criminal.

December 21: Washington

The last adult has left the room. Defence Secretary Jim Mattis has resigned in protest at Trump's decision to withdraw all American troops from Syria. It is probably true that an American presence there is largely irrelevant to the larger tragedy unfolding, but even leftists will be uncomfortable with Trump's isolationism and apparent acceptance of Iranian and Russian influence in Syria. He is reported to be following up with major withdrawals from Afghanistan. This is an uncomfortable moment for those, like me, whose politics were shaped by opposition to the war in Vietnam. With a few exceptions we have opposed American military adventures overseas, and now a President whose values we detest seems bent on reducing them. But fewer people dying as a result of American pull-outs seems unlikely.

"America", claimed former Secretary of State Madeline Albright, "is the indispensable nation. We stand tall and we see further than other countries into the future." We can dispense with the hubris of her remarks without welcoming the partial retreat of Trump into bad tempered withdrawal from international cooperation, and his apparent penchant for attacking Western allies while embracing dictators. Meanwhile the United States seems headed for a possible government shutdown and stock markets, whose rise Trump has claimed as evidence of his success, are falling. He ends the year in a deadlock with Congress, and with increasing speculation that he will not survive a full term.

Over the past months I've read two speculative political novels: Matthew Glass's *Ultimatum* (2009) and Andrew Marr's *Head of State* (2014), both in some ways eerily prescient. In *Ultimatum* the threat of increasing global warming leads the American President into nuclear confrontation with China to force agreement on drastic reduction of global emissions. The plot becomes less and less plausible as the book winds on—and it winds on for 433 pages. But it points to the two major issues facing the world: climate change and the threat of real confrontation between the United States and China. Marr wrote his book before the disastrous British referendum on the European Union, which he foreshadows, and despite unbelievable body count and high-level conspiracies he captures the depth of division that Brexit reveals. I wonder how much political analysis written at the same time would feel as relevant. Social scientists are good at measuring what is, but no more able than novelists to imagine what will be.

As the year ends President Trump tweets enthusiastic support for the new right-wing President of Brazil, Jair Bolsonaro, whose inauguration is attended by Viktor Orban from Hungary and Benjamin Netanyahu from Israel. Senator Elizabeth Warren declares her candidacy for the presidency in 2020, and new Congresswoman Rashida Tlaib wants to "impeach the motherfucker".

2019

January 7–9: Hobart

Hobart is suddenly hip. There are cafes and Asian restaurants everywhere, and cranes dot the skyline. From the age of seven my family had lived here, an unlikely place for my European-born Jewish parents, who never really found a social world in a city that was almost entirely Anglo and socially conservative, despite a long series of state Labor governments. How would I describe Hobart to Americans, whose knowledge of geography is, at best, sketchy? Imagine a softer version of a port city in, perhaps, Maine or Oregon, but set on an island, and therefore linked to what we referred to as "the mainland" by boat and plane, a city that had never fulfilled its promise as the second British settlement in Australia, but was propped up by the apparatus of a state capital, although the population of the entire state is equivalent to a couple of local government areas in Sydney or Melbourne.

My parents moved from Hobart to Sydney in 1973, after my father retired. He died soon afterwards. I've been back a few times since, once to rekindle the memories I drew on in my only novel *The Comfort of Men*, which was based on the premise of a successful independence movement in Tasmania. The most gratifying comment for that book came from a literary agent in the United States who doubted American readers would be interested in the history of Tasmanian independence, unaware that the secession was fictional. The last trip I made with Anthony was a hasty drive around the island in 2012, where I got carsick on the spiralling descent into the scarred landscape around Queenstown, a brutal reminder of a gold and copper mining boom. I'm drawn back here in search of the person I was who left at the age of twenty-one to go to the United States, but I know few people and when I see a possibly familiar face on the street it is most likely the grandchild of someone with whom I went to school.

It's odd what one remembers. There's a two-storey white deco building on the rise above St. David's Park, where I went with my father to visit one of the lonely single Central European refugees who had somehow found refuge in Tasmania. My sister and I remember another refugee, Heidi, who opened one of the city's first coffee lounges, a fussy small café on Criterion Street. But when I drive past the house where we lived for much of my time at primary school it looks oddly unfamiliar, though its red-brick box shape and corrugated iron roof marks it instantly as part of Robin Boyd's 'Australian ugliness'. I went to school with the sons of most of Hobart's drapers and walking towards North Hobart I see the names of former department stores, now remembered in Palfreymans Arcade and the Jack Soundy Church Hall.

One day I drive to Richmond, one of the oldest colonial settlements in Tasmania. Jane Austen died in 1817 and the house Margaret and Henry Reynolds live in, two story red-brick Georgian, with its surprisingly small rooms, might have walked out of one of her novels though it was built a decade later. Margaret and Henry preceded me at the University of Tasmania, but I've come to know them over the ensuing decades. Since he published *The Other Side of the Frontier* in 1981 Henry's research on contact between settlers and Indigenous Australians has literally revolutionised our understanding of colonial history. He taught at James Cook University in Townsville for thirty years; Margaret became a Labor Senator for Queensland for sixteen years, and a minister in the Hawke government. They've retired to Richmond, to a house which belonged to a former Labor member of parliament. Gough Whitlam stayed here before he became Prime Minister, and there is a Whitlam Room overlooking the garden, complete with photographs of the former Prime Minister and other world leaders. We talk politics and the continuing need for a strong Labor Party linked to a trade union movement. Their daughter, Anna, was a stalwart Green until recently, when she ran and was elected as an Independent Lord Mayor of Hobart.

At Salamanca Place, once a seedy waterfront area now home to bars and cafes, I catch up with my former lecturer Peter Boyce, who encouraged me to look to American graduate schools, and is back in Hobart after serving as Vice-Chancellor of Murdoch University. Until he and the South African political scientist Ken Fryer arrived, the study of politics in Tasmania was little more than the conventional study of institutions. They showed me new possibilities, as when Ken introduced me to the writings of Hannah Arendt. Because of their encouragement I fell under the spell of the United States when I was twenty-one, and it's been a stormy if one-sided love affair ever since.

Postscript

February 2019: California

Back in Los Angeles: the government shut-down has ended, but the country seems increasingly socially and politically bifurcated. Chic restaurants are opening in the new glass shards of downtown, while there are more homeless prowling the streets, seemingly inhabitants of a parallel city like those in Mieville's *City and the City*. Los Angeles seems a futuristic re-run of how I saw New York in the 1970s. But even in a polarised United States, President Trump's declaration in his postponed State of the Union address that "this is the most extraordinary nation in all of history" could bring both Republicans and Democrats to their feet, chanting 'USA! USA!' Perhaps the most extraordinary moment in the speech was Trump's warnings against socialism, as if the Bolshevik hordes were about to lay siege to the Capitol.

    The weekend before Trump's address Juan Carlos and I visited the Joshua Tree National Park, two hundred kilometres east of Los Angles in the foothills of the Mojave Desert. It was wet and cold, and we decided to spend the evening at a famous live music bar in Pioneertown. The rain and wind were getting worse and driving up the dark winding road the car became bogged by a mixture of rocks and slush. Before we could figure out our options a black Cherokee jeep drove up and three men, dressed as highway rangers, leapt out and said they could tow us. Twenty minutes later, after we were bogged and towed out a second time, they drove off: on the back of their jeep was a sign saying: 'Trump is My President'.

    Sometimes the love is requited.

Index

Unfortunately Donald Trump hangs over this account of the past two years to the point that it seems unnecessary to index him.

Abbott, Tony 74, 115, 158, 172, 179, 190
ABC [Australian Broadcasting Corporation] 88, 179-80
Academic Ambassadors 204
Aciman, Andre 167
Adelaide 156-7
Advocate 16
After Homosexual 57, 76
Against Death 85
AIDS conferences:
   Amsterdam 1990: 40; 2018: 185-7
   Atlanta 1985: 84
   Bangkok 2004: 32
   Berlin 1993: 27
   Canberra 1990: 32
   Delhi 1992: 191-2
   Durban 2000: 32, 119
   Geneva 1998: 48
   Melbourne 2001: 31-2, 121; 2014: 48-9
   Vancouver 1996: 32, 48
   Vienna: 47
   Yokohama 1994: 32
AIDS In the Mind of America [AIDS and the New Puritanism] 82, 84
AIDS in the World 41
Albright, Madeleine 212
Allen, Peter 189
Alternate University 97
Alther, Lisa 157
Altman, Andrew 28-9, 71, 149, 215; mother of 28, 183
Altman, Assia 28-9, 147, 149; mother of 36, 94, 147
Altman, Vivien 123, 125, 216
Amar, Paul 9
Amateur House [Hobart] 117
Amelia 166
Amsterdam, Stephen 61

Andelson, Sheldon 81
Andrews, Penny 119-20
Angels in America 48-9, 114, 129, 185
Anglosphere, the 179
Another Country 77
Appadurai, Arjun 121
Archer, Robyn 89, 166
Arendt, Hannah 183, 217
Argonauts, The 88
Ariss, Robert 85
Arrival x
Ashok Hotel [Delhi] 192
Ateneo University 69-70
Atlanta 84, 158
Atomic Café, The 110
Aung San Suu Kyi xiii
Austen, Howard 24, 170
Australian, 196
Australian Lesbian and Gay Archives 74
Australian Research Centre for Sex, Health & Society [ARCSHS] 80
Ayoub, Phillip 164

Bachardy, Don 13
Bacon, Wendy 123-4, 136, 154
Bagehot, Walter 171
Balaclava Road [Melbourne] 147-8
Baldwin, James 12, 35, 76-7, 158
Ball, Jason 137
Ballarat 94
Bandt, Adam 130, 146, 165
Bandung Conference 88
Banks, Julia 207
Barassi, Ron 198-9
Barnard Women's Conference 7-8
Barracuda 99, 117
Barre-Sinousi, Francoise 47
Barrett, Loretta 82, 84
Batman [electorate] 130, 150-1, 159

Batrouney, Colin 129-30
Bell, Terry 85, 154
Bendigo 19, 60
Benn, Tony 139
Bent Street 2017 145
Berkowitz, Richard 17
Berlin 26-8, 182-3
Bernstein, Leonard 73
Bersani, Leo 182
Besnier, Niko 163
Better Together 133
Bhathal, Alex 150-1
Bhumipol, King 170
Bhutan, Queen of 31
Bilney, Gordon 121
Binet, Laurent 51
Biru, Ashenafi 171
Bishop, Julie 191
Black and White Men Together 77
Black Lives Matter 102
Black Panthers 73
Blair, Tony 123
Blasius, Mark 108
Blewett, Neal 83-4, 173
Blue Boy [Kuala Lumpur] 192
Blyton, Enid 36, 135, 145
Boba Guys 163
Bocahut, Laurent 63
Body Politic, The 6, 37
Bogarde, Dirk 37
Boisrouvray, Albina de 40
Bolsonaro, Jair 201, 209, 213
Bolton, John 160
Bonfil, Carlos 122
Boochani, Berouz 207
Book of Mormon, The 11
Boston, Kell 154
Bowtell, Bill 83
Box, Edgar 170
Boy From Oz, The 189
Boyce, Peter ix, 216-7
Boyd, Robin 215
Boys in the Band 87, 108
Bradford, David 176
Brady, Tiernan 88
Brain, Robert 83
Bram, Christopher 109
Brazil 171, 201-2

Brennan, Frank 61
Brett, Judith 70, 131, 156
Brighton [England] 30-1
Brim, Matt 35
Broad, Andrew 211
Brooker Avenue [Hobart] 135-6
Brooks, Philip 63
Brown, Bob 136, 168
Brown, Letitia 13
Burgmann, Meredith 152, 154
Burke, Simon 145
Burns, Lindy 180
Burnside, Julian 193
Bush, George W 74, 123, 196
Buttrose, Ita 173

Caddy, Anthea 27-8, 182
Calamity Jane 169
Califia, Pat 8
Call Me By Your Name 167
Callen, Michael 15, 17-8
Cameron, Edmund 119-20
CAMP 138
Campaign 46
Capp, Sally 177
Captain Matchbox Whoopee Band 166
Caracole 110
Carbery, Graham 57-8
Carden, Joan 104
Carey, Julienne 14
Carey, Peter x, 175-6
Carlotta 89
Carnie, Lee 192-3
Carr, Bob 202-3
Carter, Jimmy 193
Casita del Campo 10
Castlemaine 168-70
Castro [San Francisco] 2, 3, 163
Castro Theater 2
Charlton, Peter 14
Chase, Anthony 6, 163-4
Chauncey, Nan 36
Cheetham, Deborah 89
Christie, Agatha 34-5, 36, 76, 149
Christopher Street Day 184
Christopher Street Magazine 106
Circus of Books 5
City and the City 219

Index

City and the Pillar, The 23, 73
City Baths [Melbourne] 117
City of Night 3
City of the Plain 124
Cleaver, Eldridge 76
Clinton, Bill 197
Clinton, Hillary 1, 7, 31, 74
Cohn, Roy 49, 114
Colletaz, Paul-Gilbert 185
Collins, Wilkie 34
Columbia University 72, 75
Come Out 95, 98
Comfort of Men, The 215
Coming Back Out Ball, the 89-90, 188-9
Compton, Rachel 36
Conchita 186
Connell, Raewyn 21
Connolly, Gerry 89
Continental Baths 182
Conversation, The 131
Cook, Whitfield 175
Corbyn, Jeremy 31, 43, 72, 141
Cornell University ix, 183
Cornwall, Andrea 30, 162
Correa, Sonia 202
Court, Margaret 133
Crouch, Elizabeth 87
Crown, The 171
Cruikshank, Peggy 81
Cuaron, Alfonso 122
Cunningham, Sophie 65, 117

Damned Whores and God's Police 194
Danby, Michael 148
Darktown 158
Darling 73
Darwin 90
Dastyari, Sam 94-5
Daughters of Bilitis 75
Davidson, Jim 58
Davison, Kate 211
D'Cruz, Carolyn 2, 56-7, 66, 76, 195
Deakin, Alfred 70-1
Deakin University 205
Deal 33
Dean, Brett 157
Death and Life of Marsha P Johnston 65
Decter, Midge 96

Defying Gravity xii, xiii, 65
De Kretser, Hugh 193
Delaney, Samuel 24, 120
Delaney, Sheelagh 37
Denneny, Michael 106, 111-2
De Real, Andrew 69
Desir homosexual, le 183
Deutsche Eiche 181
Devil's Playground, The 145
Did You Meet any Malagas? 90
Dienstfrey, Harris 96-7
Dietrich, Marlene 29, 166
Different Light, A 9-10
Dirty Secrets 152
Dobrovic, Zvonomir 142-3
Don's Party 199
Doogue, Geraldine 179-80
Dorf, Julie 163
Double J [radio] 180
Dowd, Maureen 194
Downer, Alexander 121
Doyle, Robert 143, 177
Drake, David 143
Driggs, Adrian 108
Duberman, Martin 16, 98
Duncan, George 157
Dunera [ship] 54
Dunstan, Don 157
Duterte, Rodrigo 187
Dwyer, John 191

Eastern Ghouta 147
East West Street 147
Easy Way Out, The 61
Echols, Alice 7-8, 56
Ehrenreich, Barbara 111
Eldred-Grigg, Stevan 157
Elefant, der [Berlin] 29
Elliott, Sumner Locke 175
Ellison, Ralph 76
Emperor Concerto 67
End of the Homosexual? 45
Enigmatic Mr. Deakin 70
Entsch, Warren 115
Epstein, Joseph 96
Erdogan, Recep 188
European Conference on Politics and Gender 40-1

Eurovision Song Contest 75
Evans, Gareth 121
Everard Baths 18, 170
Exit International 61

Face in the Crowd, A 2
Faderman, Lillian 81
Fairyland 175
Falwell, Jerry 9
Family Law, The 44
Fassbinder, Rainer 181
Fell, Elizabeth 179
Female Eunuch, The 178
Ferguson, Laura 7
Fernando, Todd 71
Ferrier, Carole 205
FHAR 184
Fidelio 67
Fifty First State? 74-5
Fire Island 108-9, 114
Fisher, Peter 72
Fitzroy Street [St. Kilda] 139
Flanagan, Richard 129
Flying Dutchman 67
Forman, Milos 12
Forum Theatre [Melbourne] 91, 188
Foster, Andrew 14, 18
Foucault, Michel 50-1, 110, 129
Four Moons 19
Foyles Bookshop 36
France, David 15, 65
Frankowits, Andre 62, 182
Fraser, Malcolm 189
Freud, Sigmund 8, 28, 161
Friday, Barbara 135, 137
Frog Who Dared to Croak, The 110
Fryer, Ken 217
Fukuyama, Francis 210
Fullers Bookshop 136
Future is History, The 118

gai pied, le 51
Garcia, Adolph 95
Garland, Judy 189
Garner, Alice 204
Garner, Helen 63
Gay Activists Alliance 72, 96
Gay Community News 46

Gay Games 16-7
Gay Left 38
Gay Liberation Front 4, 95
Gay Men's Health Crisis 82, 114
Gay Sunshine 202
Gay's the Word 36
Gefter, Philip 112
George, Elizabeth 135
Gessen, Masha 44, 118-9, 144
Giles, Andrew 130-1
Gillard, Julia 74, 98, 99, 136, 155-6, 196
Ginsberg, Peter 82
Giovanni's Room 73, 76, 158
Glad Day Books 37
Glass, Matthew 212
Glee 71
Global AIDS Policy Coalition 40-1
Global Network of Sex Work Projects 185
Global Program on AIDS 6, 31
Global Sex 121-3
Golden House, The 134
Goldsmith, Andrea 35, 61-2, 66, 135, 157
Goldstein, Richard 82, 206
Goodman, Paul 95-6
Gordimer, Nadine 111
Gore Vidal's America 24-5, 203
Gorna, Robin 31-2
Gramsci, Antonio 104
Grattan, Michelle 132
Green Book, The 120
Greens, the 31, 118, 130, 136-7, 150-1, 165
Greenwich, Alex 153
Greer, Germaine 178-9
Griffith Review 55, 65
Grindr 100, 169
Growing Up Absurd 95
Gruen, Nicholas 54-5
Gruskin, Sofia 6-7, 163-4

Hagen, Daron 166
Hair 12
Hamburg 29-30
Hamilton 12, 167
Hamlet [opera] 157
Handmaid's Tale, The 60
Hanson, Pauline 208

Index

Hanson-Young, Sarah 100
Hares and Hyenas bookshop 145, 176, 20
Harlem 120
Harper's Magazine 96
Harvard University 6, 25, 118
Hassert, Reinhard 97, 127
Hay, Harry 9
Hayes, Bill 129
Head of State 212-3
Health and Human Rights 40
Hearts of Men, The 111
Hecate 205
Heckler, Margaret 84
Heide Gallery 56
Helms Bakery 164
Henderson, Nick 74, 90, 199
Hindley Street [Adelaide] 156
His Dark Materials 1
History of Popular Music in America 91-2
Hoad, Neville 57
Hobart 135, 149, 215-6
Hobsbawm, Eric 65
Hocquenghem, Guy 183-4
Hodge, Dino 90
Hodgman, Roger 49
Holas, Nic 91
Holleran, Andrew 109-10
Hollier, Nathan 176
Hollinghurst, Allan 158
Holt, Harold ix, 196
Homosexual: Oppression and Liberation 22, 55, 77, 96-8, 127
Homosexualization of America, The 81, 111-13, 185
Hong Kong 128
Hopper, Dennis 180
Horne, Donald 139
Horrocks, Lucinda 94
House of Cards 100, 171
How to Have Sex in an Epidemic 17
How to Vote Progressive in Australia 31
Howard, John 20, 140, 172, 178, 196
Howard University 13-14
Human Rights Campaign Fund 2, 16
Human Rights Law Centre 168
Hunter, Edward 11, 49, 135
Hunting Scenes from Bavaria 50
Hydro Electric Commission [Tasmania] 136

I Am Not Your Negro 76
Ibrahim, Anwar 122
Idier, Antoine 183-4
If Beale Street Could Talk 77
Ihimaera, Witi 157-8
Indian Supreme Court 191
Insert Self Here [ISH] 168-70
Institute for the Humanities (NYU) 109-10
International AIDS Society 32
International Council of AIDS Service Organisations 186
International Gay and Lesbian Human Rights Commission 163
Ireland, Doug 106, 108, 109, 184
Irving, Terry 124
Isakovic, Bruno 142
Isherwood, Christopher 12-14, 27, 29, 98-9, 149
Israel 148, 200

Jaensch, Terrence 168, 174
James, P D 11
Jayaseelan, Julian 32-3
Jewish Museum [Berlin] 26, 29
John, Elton 96
Johns, W E 36
Johnson, Lyndon ix
Johnson, Stanley 180
Jones, Alan 99
Jong, Erica 100
Jorgenson, Tina 180
Joshua Tree National Park 219
JOY 94.9 [radio station] 98, 102
Joyce, Barnaby 143, 145
Julius' [bar]108

Kahin, George 183
Kaleeba, Nordine 41
Kashish Film Festival 159-60
Kavanagh, Brett 196-7
Kazan, Elia 2
Kearney, Ged 151, 197
Keating, Paul 83, 164, 197
Kelly, Paul [singer] 168
Kelly, Paul [writer] 104
Kennedy, Jackie 84
Kim Jong Un 111, 174

King, Billie Jean 133
King, Wil 145
Kinky Boots 92-3
Kirby, Michael 21-2, 121
Kirkby, Diane 204
Kirner, Joan 32
Kiss of the Spider Woman 106
Knopfelmacher, Frank ix
Kramer, Larry 109
Kuala Lumpur 192
Kushner, Tony 49

La La Land 3
La Trobe University 2, 39, 45, 57, 69, 78, 119, 130,
  Bendigo campus 19-20
Labor Party 31, 118, 131-2, 137, 151, 203
Laird, The 141
Laird, John 82
Lake, Marilyn 197
Lampiao 201-2
Langer Family 117-8
Lascaris, Manoly 142
Law, Benjamin 44-5, 137
Lawrence, Carmen 22
Leahy, Gillian 179
Leavitt, David 109
Le Guin, Ursula 26
Leningrad 86-7
Les Miserables 12
Levine, Susan 106
Lewis, Brigitte 145
Leyonhjelm, David 100
Liberal Party 138, 191
Liberty Cinema [Mumbai] 159
Library bar [Manila] 69
Lindon, Mathieu 51, 129
Little Kings 168
Lively, Penelope xii, 27
Loaded [*Head On*] 140
London 36-9
London, Gene 9
Loop Bar [Melbourne] 102-3
Los Angeles 3-5,
Lost Europeans, The 29
Lovers 112
Lucas, Caroline 30-1
Lucia di Lammermoor 72

Ludwig of Bavaria 181
Lyons, Gilda 166

Mac, Taylor 91-3
McAuley, James 79
McCartney, Alastair 1
McConaghy, Neil 211
McKibben, Bill 219
McMaster, H R 160
Macquarie University 87
Macron, Emanuel 43, 210
Mad Dog Morgan 180
Magic Mountain, The 183
Mahathir, Marina 48, 69
Mahler, Alma and Gustav 28
Makow, Henry 114
Maltzahn, Kathleen 164-5
Mandela, Nelson 32, 119-20
Manila 68-70
Mann, Jonathan 6, 40, 41
Manne, David 200
Mantel, Hillary 4, 60-1
Manus Detention Centre 101-2, 104-5, 207, 209
Mapp and Lucia 34
Mapplethorpe, Robert 104
Marche, Guillaume 184
Mardi Gras, Gay and Lesbian [Sydney] 151-4, 178
Margolyes, Miriam 149
Maria Stuarda 67
Mario's Café 44, 74
Market Street [SF] 161
Marotta, Toby 36
Marr, Andrew 212
Marr, David 59, 154
Marriott, John 79
Marshall, Daniel 198
Mattachine Society 9
Matthews, Jill 157
Mattis, Jim 212
Matzneff, Gabriel 184
Maupin, Armistead 82, 129, 145, 157
Maurois, Andre 183
May, Theresa 43, 187, 219
Mayer, Henry 54-5
Mbeki, Thabo 119
Me Too movement xii, 144, 177, 206

Index

Mead, Margaret 101
Meanjin 70
Meecham, Tristan 89, 199
Melbourne 156-6
Melbourne City Council 177
Menzies, Robert ix, 58, 183
Mercurio, Paul 173
Merkel, Angela 187, 210
Merlis, Mark 95
Metropolitan Community Church 112
Mexico City 122
Midler, Bette 182
Midsomer Murders 135
Mieville, China 60-1, 65, 219
Mike and the Mechanics 39
Milk, Harvey 2
Miller, Tim 1
Millett, Kate 75-6
Minnelli, Liza 189
Mitcham, Matthew 116
Mitchell, Anne 135, 137
Mitchell, Douglas 121
Mitchell, Joni 107
Mitterand, Frédéric 50
Moldenhauer, Jearld 37
monarchies 171, 201
Mondale, Walter 16
Monkey Grip 63, 117
Monsivais, Carlos 122
Monteleone Hotel 109
Monthly [Magazine] 177
Moodie, Rob 31
Morali, Jacques 185
Morris, Meaghan 62-3, 85, 182
Morrison, Scott 190, 194, 200, 208
Mortimer, Rex 155
Moscone, George 2
Mosse, Richard 135
Mount Scopus College 148
Mr Gay Syria 159-60
Mullen, Thomas 158
Mumbai 159-60
Munich 181
Murdoch, Rupert 198
Murkowski, Lisa 197
Murphy, John 113
Murphy, Tommy 145
Museum of Love and Protest 153

My Own Private Oz 63
Myra Breckinridge 23, 142

Nabucco 167
Nash, Chris 123-4
Natale, Richard di 150
Nauru 101, 104, 194, 209
Nehru Park [Delhi] 192
Netanyahu, Benjamin 213
Never Anyone But You 206
New International Bookshop 164-5
New Orleans 109-10
New York City ix, 95-7, 106-9
New York Jacks 18
New York Native 106
New Yorker 100, 109
Nights in the Gardens of Spain 158
Nile, Fred 65, 156
Nitschke, Philip 61
No Friend But the Mountain 207
Norse Cove 2
Noumea 49-50

O

O'Brien, Maureen 176
O'Dwyer, kelly 137
O'Hara, Scott 173-4
O'Loughlin, Bill 172-3
O'Malley, Jeff 6, 40, 163-4
Obama, Barack x, 1, 7, 74, 187, 193, 196
Occidental College 1
Old Nick Company 37
Orban, Viktor 187, 213
Orlando [Florida] 112-3
Orlando 142
Orr, Sydney 79
Ortleb, Chuck 106
Oscar Wilde Bookshop 36
Other Side of the Frontier 216
Otto, Diane 205
Out for Australia 64
Out of Egypt 167
Outlook 155
Outrage Magazine 46
Overs, Cheryl 202
Oxfam 144
Oxford Street [Sydney] 128, 153-4
Oz Magazine 87

P

Palace, le 184
Palmer, Helen 155
Pandey, Rajyashree 39-40
Paper Ambassadors 139-40
Paris 43, 183-4
Paris Theatre Company 142
Parklands High shootings 146
Parliament House [Orlando] 112
Patkin, Aaron 29, 148
Patkin, Benzion 148
Patton, Cindy 206
Peck, Raul 76
Pendleton, Mark 57
Perfumed Sleeves and Tangled Hair 40
Perlman, Michael 84-5
Perry, Troy 112
Petulia 162
Phelps, Kerryn 200, 207-8
Philippines 68-70
Picano, Felice 109-19
Pingaud, Antoine 86
Pink Triangle [Malaysia] 33, 192
Piot, Peter 202
Pleasure and Danger 8, 206
POL Magazine 87
Policing Desire 34
Porter, Dorothy 34-5, 61
Praunheim, Rosa von 106
Premier's Literary Awards [Victoria] 198, 206-7
PrEP 18
Pride Centre [Melbourne] 139, 209
Pride March 139
Priscilla, Queen of the Desert xii, 92, 159
Prothero, Barry 51, 86, 210
Proud Boys 206
Puig, Manuel 106
Pullman, Philip 1
Push, the 62, 124, 179
Putin, Vladimir 187
Pybus, Cassandra 79

Q and A [ABC] 66, 99, 179-80
Queenstown [Tasmania] 215
Queer film festivals 50, 159-60
Queer Legacies, New Solidarities 295
Queer Wars 162
Queer Zagreb 143
Queers and Our Hidden Histories 138

R

Radcliffe, Russ 74
Radical Fairies 9
Ransome, Arthur 36
Reagan, Ronald 16, 81, 110, 112
Rebel Without a Cause 3
Rechy, John 3, 100
Red, Hot and Blue 48
Red ribbon [AIDS] 104-5
Reed, Lou 74, 166
Refugee Legal 200
Regatta Hotel (Brisbane) 205
Rehearsals for Change 22
Reuben, David 73
Revolutionary People's Constitutional Convention 73
Reynolds, Anna 216
Reynolds, Henry 216
Reynolds, Margaret 216
Rhodes, Ben x
Rice, Janet 20
Richmond [Tasmania] 216
Ricketson, James 107
Rieff, David 111
Rio de Janeiro 202
Rockhampton 115
Rocky Horror Show, The 53
Rodwell, Craig 36
Roxon, Lillian 96
Rubin, Gayle 8, 81
Rudd, Kevin 99, 156
Rush, Geoffrey 211
Rushdie, Salman 134
Russell, Leon 96
Russo, Vito 37, 73, 111

Sachs, Nelly 91
Sacks, Oliver 129
Safe Schools Project 45, 137
St. Marks Baths 181
Saints and Sinners 109
San Francisco 2, 127, 129, 161-3
Sanders, Bernie 43, 72, 141
Sands, Philippe 147
Santa Cruz 82

Index

Santa Monica Boulevard 2, 4-5
Scalmer, Sean 31
Scherer, Rene 184
Schultz, Julianne 65
Scruff 169
Secret and Divine Signs 169
Seddon, Tom 31
Sennett, Richard 109, 110-1
Seth, Sanjay 39-40
Seven Jewish Children 149
Sex and Germs 206
Sexual Politics 75
Sharman, Jim 12
Shaw, George Bernard 166
Shewey, Don 83
Shorten, Bill 98, 132, 208
Shriver, Lionel 61
Sicilian Vespers, The 181
Silverlake 9
Simon, Guy 145
Singh, Lisa 186
Single Man, A 12
Sippen, Joshua 15-16, 75-6, 82-3
Sisters in Crime 35
Sisters of Perpetual Indulgence 81
Slap, The 117
Smith, Anthony 1, 14-15, 24, 26, 32, 39, 47, 56, 80, 118, 128, 215
Socialist Forum 155
Socialist Review 8
Socialist Scholars Conference 206
Society for Individual Rights 127
Soho News 83, 109
Soldatow, Sasha 140
Sondheim, Stephen 12
Sonnabend, Joseph 15
Sontag, Susan 51, 96, 108, 110, 111
South Africa 118-9
Spacey, Kevin 99-100
Sparrow, Jeff 198
Steam 174
Stein, Jill 14
Stephens, David 14
Stephenson, Neal 179
Stone, Gerald 199
Stone, Yael 211
Stonewall riots 151
Strangers in Between 145

Strictly Ballroom 173
Summers, Anne 61, 194-5
swimming pools:
  Beaurepaire 117
  Collingwood 117
  Coburg 117
  Fitzroy 116-7, 166
Sydney 105, 107, 124, 127, 129
Sydney University *see* University of Sydney
Symons, Jonathan 7, 162, 193
Szubanski, Magda 168

Tales of the City 82
Talese, Gay 52
Tarantola, Daniel 41
Taste of Honey, A 37-8
Tatchell, Peter 38
Taylor, Elizabeth 48
Thais 66
They Found a Cave 36
Thomas, David 81
Thomas, Paul 136
Thomas, Ruth Morgan 186
Thomson, Rowland 145
Tinder 100, 169
Tlaib, Rashida 213
Todd, Peter 17
Tofighian, Omid 207
Toibin, Colm 32
Tonight Lola Blau 166
Torquay [England] 34-6
Totempole 23
Traviata, La 67
Triggs, Gillian 200
Tsiolkas, Christos 99, 140-2
Turnbull, Malcolm xiii, 43, 45, 70, 74, 145, 172, 190-1
Turner, Brodie 195
Turner, Ian 155
Twyborn Affair, The 142

Ultimatum 212
University of Adelaide 157
University of California, Santa Cruz 80-1
University of Central Queensland 115
University of Chicago 57, 121-2, 158
University of the Philippines 69

University of Southern California 5, 7
University of Sydney 21, 107, 124, 178, 190, 205
University of Tasmania ix, 37, 99

Vadasz, Danny 45-6
Valarezo Sanchez, Juan Carlos 163, 189, 193, 219
van Schilt, Stephanie 11
Vance, Carol 8, 206
Victim 37
Victorian AIDS Council 14, 129
Vidal, Gore 4, 12, 23-6, 51, 85, 132, 170, 203
Vienna 28
Vietnam War x, 71, 79, 154, 166-7, 178, 183
Village People 3, 185
Violet Quill 109
Viski, Vlad 177

Waddell, Thomas 16
Wallman, Sam 74, 140-1
Walsh, Richard 86-7
Warhaft, Sally 177-8, 203
Warren, Elizabeth 213
Warsame, Nur 104
Watney, Simon 33-4
Watson, Don x
Watson, Lex 127-8, 138, 178
Weeks, Jeffrey 38, 56
Well of Loneliness, The 73
Wentworth [electorate] 200
West Hollywood 4-5, 7, 163
West Side Story 10, 12
Wheeler Centre 48, 198
White Australia Policy 79
White, Edmund 106, 109-10, 129, 184
White, Patrick 51, 142
Whitlam, Gough 79, 132, 155, 180, 210, 216
Whitlam, Margaret 132
Wilenski, Peter 22, 121
Williams, Michael 15
Williams, Raymond 3
Wills, Sue 178
Wilson, Tim 115
Winterton, Jeanette 44

Witness to AIDS 119
Wodehouse, P G 36
Wolfe, Tom 73
Wong, Penny 88, 210
Wood, Sally 89
Working Papers in Sex, Science and Culture 85
World AIDS Day 208
Wotherspoon, Garry 124-5, 178
Woubi Cheri 63
Wright, Clare 197-8
writers' festivals:
　Adelaide 157-8
　Ballarat 94-5
　Bendigo 59-60
　Charleston 32
　Melbourne 118
　Perth 61
　Sydney 44

Yang, William 154
Yongah Hill detention centre 200

Zisin, Nevo 170
Zona Rosa (Mexico City) 122-3
zoos:
　Berlin 26
　Manila 68-9
　Paris 69
　Singapore 68

About the Author

Dennis Altman, a Professorial Fellow in Human Security at La Trobe University, has published thirteen books, most recently *The End of the Homosexual?* and (with Jon Symons) *Queer Wars*. In 2006 *The Bulletin* listed Dennis Altman as one of the 100 most influential Australians ever. He was appointed a Member of the Order of Australia in 2008.

CPSIA information can be obtained
at www.ICGtesting.com
Printed in the USA
JSHW011328090819
1060JS00001BA/1